"The consequence of tolerating 'small exceptions' to the truth is eventual and complete departure from the truth. Truth is not trendy. It is not our job to make truth easier and more attractive. A half-truth is a lie." Michael A. Youssef

Love, Apa

DUPED
AMERICA

DUPED
AMERICA

A FACTUAL FOOTNOTED AND FRIGHTENING ACCOUNT OF:

HOW DEMOCRATS AND THE MAINSTREAM MEDIA
HAVE DUPED THE AMERICAN PEOPLE
AND ARE HARMING OUR COUNTRY

RICHARD BERNSTEIN
A Lifelong Democrat's Disturbing Discoveries After 9/11

FORRESTER PUBLISHING COMPANY

Copyright © 2010 by Richard Bernstein

All rights reserved. No part of this publication may be reproduced or transmitted in any form or by any means, electronic or mechanical, including photocopy, recording, or any information storage and retrieval system now known or to be invented, without permission in writing from the publisher, except by a reviewer who wishes to quote brief passages in connection with a review written for inclusion in a magazine, newspaper, or broadcast.

Published in the United States by
Forrester Publishing Company
3840 West Hillsboro Boulevard, #174
Deerfield Beach, Florida 33442

ISBN 978-0-578-05124-6
Printed in the United States of America

Edited by Arnold Ahlert

I dedicate this book to my wife, without whom this book would never have been written. Her inspiration, guidance and research were invaluable; her love, patience and support kept me going. She has my thanks and my heart forever.

I also want to thank my editor for his tireless effort and tremendous contribution to the book.

To our four children and the next generation — stay informed, and be vigilant about safeguarding your freedoms and America's democracy.

CONTENTS

INTRODUCTION

"The trouble with the world is not that people know too little, but that they know so many things that aren't true." — attributed to Mark Twain

This quote certainly applied to me before 9/11. I was an ordinary American citizen who was thankful to be living in this great country. I did not take a huge interest in either politics or foreign affairs. Like many Americans, I read the local newspaper and watched the evening news. I thought this was enough to keep me informed about what was going on in our country and the world.

9/11 changed everything. I suddenly realized that the freedom, security and the way of life I had taken for granted was extremely fragile.

My wife's two children were in New York City at the time of the attacks. Her son was on the train going to work when the first tower was hit. We received his frantic call to turn on the television, and we watched in horror as the second jet slammed into the South Tower.

After this horrific attack on our country, my wife became obsessed with trying to learn everything she could about the perpetrators. (Remember, up until the day they carried out their heinous plan, virtually no one in America had even heard of al Qaeda.) She began buying books and ordering magazines. Because of a medical condition, my wife spends many hours of her day lying down; reading helps her to fill up those hours. She also started searching the Internet and collecting articles from a variety of domestic and foreign newspapers. She would print the interesting ones, and many days there would be a stack of them waiting for me to read when I came home from work.

We began reading, and reading and reading. We started re-educating ourselves about our country, our government and current world events. As the years flew by, our appetite for information grew steadily. Our reading and research continued with an almost alarming need for facts and the truth.

Much of this process was painful, because we learned many things that completely contradicted our prior beliefs. Let me explain.

1

We were both brought up in families who typically voted Democrat, so naturally we leaned that way as well. However, the more we learned the more we began to realize that we didn't identify with the Democrat Party and their policies.

This new knowledge made discussing politics with some family members extremely difficult. Sadly, we learned that people become so emotionally invested in their beliefs that they are unable or unwilling to change their views — even when the facts prove otherwise.

I would often argue with my sister and she would always say, "how come you know this stuff and nobody else does?" I began sending her articles to read and we were constantly engaged in long political discussions. She at least was open to hearing what I had to say.

My father, on the other hand, was a completely different story.

My father and I had always been extremely close. We spoke to each other often and usually about business, sports and family. I now wanted to share what I'd learned with him, but talking about politics was difficult. Although very alert for his advanced age, he was hard-of-hearing and a lifelong Democrat.

One particular conversation stays with me to this day. I remember telling him how upset I was that the Democrats in Congress had voted against drilling, even though gasoline prices were at an all-time high. He refused to believe it. "Ah, c'mon Rich" he groused, "why would they vote against drilling? They have wives and daughters that need to buy gas."

The next day I brought him an article showing him the vote. He just shook his head, not wanting to believe me. When he finally heard Democrats bash drilling on CNN, he was shocked and disappointed — but he still couldn't detach himself from the party that was letting us all down.

My journey continued — and my frustration grew. I discovered a troubling disconnect between what I was learning on my own and what I was being fed by my local newspaper and the mainstream media. I began cutting out articles from the newspapers and magazines I was reading and just saving them, in piles in a closet.

In retrospect, it had something to do with my increasing awareness of the incompetence, bias, misinformation — and outright lying — that had infected the media. In that respect, I'm not alone. Recent polls have shown that most Americans believe the media is slanted and that we are being fed a sub-standard form of journalism these days. But most people don't have the time or energy to spend ferreting out the truth. That's why Mark Twain's quote seems so relevant to me.

By the time the 2004 presidential elections rolled around, I was no longer a Democrat. I knew it was important for our country to re-elect George W. Bush, rather than John Kerry.

I also knew the race was a toss-up.

I was so anxious the night of the election that I was literally pacing the floor in my home, like an expectant father, waiting for the results to come in. When Bush won I was enormously relieved.

Fast forward four years. In 2008, my wife and I officially changed our party affiliation from Democrat to Republican, and voted for Mitt Romney in the primaries. We did our homework on him, were very impressed with his accomplishments and agreed with his positions on the issues. We thought he was, by far, the best candidate out there. His problem was that he was largely unknown to many Americans. We sent out e-mails to our friends and families trying to inform them about Mitt Romney. Unfortunately, our effort was too little and too late.

Staying true to my continuing quest for the truth, I also did extensive research on candidate Barack Hussein Obama — by my estimation, far more research than the mainstream media bothered to do.

As the 2008 election campaign wore on, it became increasingly evident to me that the mainstream media's lack of "curiosity" regarding Obama's past demonstrated an appalling abandonment of journalistic integrity. They were collectively indifferent to his relationships with radicals like racist reverend Jeremiah Wright, unrepentant domestic terrorist Bill Ayers, and childhood mentor Frank Marshall Davis, an avowed Communist.

They ignored his embrace of radical Saul Alinsky's community organizing methods, which included a stealth assault on America's capitalist system by pretending to embrace it at first, but eventually replacing it with socialism. And despite their vetting of every other candidate, the media apparently had no problem with the fact that Barack Obama's academic career at Columbia and Harvard, and his medical and passport records were kept completely secret before, during, and even after the presidential election.

In essence, America elected a man with a largely undocumented past, and the mainstream media went along with the program.

Needless to say, I was extremely worried about the 2008 elections. I found it hard to believe that this extremely liberal first-term Senator, with little work experience and no experience running anything, might be elected to the highest office in this country. I tried hard to inform my family and friends about my concerns, even as the mainstream media maintained an ongoing love affair with Obama.

My sister who had been listening and watching my transformation suggested that I should host a radio show so that I could share what I had learned. She had become impressed with all the valuable insights and information that I now had. Although I just laughed at her suggestion at first, I began to think about it. I discussed the idea with my wife — and told her I wouldn't do it without her. While I am what you might call, a "detail guy" who remembers all the facts and figures, she has an amazing ability to simplify things. I thought we would be more effective together. After much convincing on my part, and in spite of her health issues, she finally agreed.

With a radio show in mind, I began organizing and filing all the articles I had saved. I made some phone calls and purchased thirteen weeks of airtime on a local radio station. The "Nobody Knows Show" began airing every Sunday night from seven to eight. Although I had never done anything like this before, I found that I was able to express myself in a straight-forward, easy-to-understand way. The radio show was a great experience and I especially enjoyed talking to the people who called in.

Unfortunately, I was only able to host five shows before the 2008 election. My beloved father became ill and passed away at the age of 92.

At my father's funeral, my wife and I were shocked when a family member introduced us as "right wing radicals." Just because we no longer agreed with her, she had given us this new label.

In March 2009, while cleaning out some boxes, I found some financial aid books I had published back in the 1980s. I showed them to my wife and she looked at me and said, "Richard, this is it, this is why you have been cutting and saving articles for years.... you're going to write a book!"

And so it began.... I started writing the outline for this book while sitting at my kitchen table. From that day forward, I would spend all my free time working in the kitchen on my book. Eventually, my wife bought me a real desk and converted our third bedroom into an office.

After eight years of research, I had a pretty good idea what issues I wanted to cover. Even so, writing this book has been a gargantuan task. For those who may think this was written by some right-wing group, the Republican Party or someone with a staff of writers and researchers, you would be wrong. It has been painstakingly researched, footnoted and written by me — handwritten I might add. My wife would lie in bed with her laptop and help me with the research. No staff, just a few people trying to make a difference. My former secretary (of 26 years), now almost eighty years old, was willing to type the book for me.

By July 2009, I had already written 18 chapters. At that point I realized I needed an editor. Through the Internet my wife found me the perfect person. Arnold has helped me tremendously, as he is extremely bright and has a talent for organizing and editing. He is also what some might call a "political junkie" who not only reads what is going on but also writes his own political commentary.

Writing this book took its toll on me. I was not feeling well for several months but continued at the same relentless pace, day and night. Why, you might ask? I did it for our four children, our nieces, nephews, and cousins — for the grandchildren we may one day have. I feel America is at an historical crossroads. Will the next generation enjoy the prosperity this country has known, or will they be forced to endure a less prosperous future?

What I hope to accomplish with this book is to give you, the reader, a chance to learn, in a very short time, what has taken me many years. There is much to absorb, and I must warn you that, like me, you may become enlightened, then frightened — and then frustrated and angry.

I still believe there is hope for our great country, but only if American citizens are given the correct facts. I have tried very hard to do that for you. The web sites, newspapers, books and magazines I listed in the back of the book are just some of the resources I have used to determine where the truth lies. I recommend that my readers use the information I have given them, along with their own knowledge, belief, instincts and common sense when making decisions. I also recommend that the mainstream media be taken with a huge grain of salt, as they have all but forfeited their credibility as far as I am concerned.

In short, "we the people" are the best hope for the future of America.

And, unlike our Congress who voted on a huge stimulus bill without reading it, we ought to know all the facts before casting our votes. Corrupt politicians are counting on us to stay uninformed, but the American people are starting to awaken. We can no longer listen to the deceitful "sound bites" we hear repeated over and over and simply accept them as truth.

My hope is that this book will help bring some sanity back to Washington. It's going to take ordinary Americans like you and I being aware and staying informed…. so we are not "Duped Again."

PART I

CLEARING UP THE PAST

Chapter 1

THE DEMOCRATS ARE DANGEROUS WHEN IT COMES TO NATIONAL SECURITY

Before 9/11, I thought Democrats and Republicans were equally competent in protecting the citizens of this country. I was brought up in a time when Democrats, led by the likes of Harry Truman, John Kennedy and Lyndon Johnson, still believed evil had to be confronted.

After 9/11, I began to realize a new breed of Democrats, vastly different from their predecessors, had emerged. These were the children of the social revolution of the 1960s, who convinced themselves that evil should no longer be confronted. They naively believed America's enemies were not to be defeated, but rather appeased and accommodated through diplomacy and endless negotiation.

After doing the research for this chapter, I discovered, much to my disappointment, such naïveté has colored Democrat thinking since the early 1970s.

It has also colored my thinking. I no longer trust Democrats to keep America safe.

When it comes to national security, most Americans trust Republicans to do a better job than Democrats. Why? Senator Joe Lieberman, a former Democrat who split from the party over the issue, put it best:

"Democrats under Roosevelt, Truman and Kennedy forged and conducted a foreign policy that was principled, internationalist, strong and successful... It was a party that understood either the American people stood united with free nations and freedom fighters against the forces of totalitarianism, or that we would fall divided.... This worldview began to come apart in the late 1960s around the war in Vietnam. In its place, a very different view of the world took root in the Democratic Party. Rather than seeing the Cold War as an ideological contest between the free nations of the West and the repressive

9

regimes of the communist world, this rival political philosophy saw America as the aggressor – a morally bankrupt, imperialist power whose militarism and 'inordinate fear of communism' represented the real threat to world peace. It argued that the Soviets and their allies were our enemies not because they were inspired by a totalitarian ideology fundamentally hostile to our way of life, or because they nursed ambitions of global conquest. Rather the Soviets were our enemy because we had provoked them, because we threatened them, and because we failed to sit down and accord them the respect they deserved. In other words, the Cold War was mostly America's fault." [1]

The dramatic change in the Democrat Party's outlook — the shift from believing in a strong America willing to fight for democracy to a pacifist one willing to tolerate the evils of communism — began during the 1972 presidential campaign. Democrat candidate George McGovern broke with our post-World War II foreign policy consensus, which held that Communist aggression must be stopped and that American power was the protector of freedom. Until the McGovern campaign, both Democrats and Republicans were in agreement that American troops were in Vietnam to prevent the Communists from gaining a hold on the Southeast Asian Peninsula. Despite the war being started by John F. Kennedy and expanded by Lyndon Johnson, both fellow Democrats, McGovern campaigned on immediate and unilateral withdrawal — a clear change in the direction of the party. [2]

Republicans also wanted to end the Vietnam War, but wanted to do it honorably, by negotiating with the North Vietnamese on a truce that would prevent the takeover of the non-Communist South Vietnam by the Communist North.

American troops were eventually brought home from Vietnam in 1973 after a truce was successfully executed by the Nixon administration. But this did not satisfy the Democrat left. From 1973 through 1975, Congress steadily reduced aid to South Vietnam from a total of $2.8 billion to $300 million. As a result, the Communists from the North, whom many on the left viewed as "Liberators," toppled the South Vietnamese government. Communist regimes also took over Laos and Cambodia shortly thereafter. And two-and-a-half million Asian peasants were slaughtered after we left them defenseless. [3]

After Vietnam, any American promise of a prolonged commitment to any cause would be of little concern to our enemies or completely trusted by our allies.

In reality, Democrats' view of America as a "bankrupt imperialist" country was disgracefully played out as far back as 1971. Vietnam veteran John Kerry testified before Congress and charged his fellow soldiers, some three million Vietnam veterans, of being war criminals who " had personally raped, cut off ears, cut off heads, taped wires from portable telephones to human genitals and turned up the power, cut off limbs, blown up bodies, randomly shot at civilians, razed villages in a fashion reminiscent of Genghis Khan, shot cattle and dogs for fun, poisoned food stocks, and generally ravaged the countryside of South Vietnam...." [4]

What had Kerry personally witnessed? Nothing. His entire testimony was hearsay. [5]

Unfortunately, it was used by the North Vietnamese as a propaganda tool and a rationale to abuse American prisoners of war. And in an act that could be characterized as treason, Kerry, well before the signing of the truce in 1973, and just months after leaving the Navy, met in Paris with the Communist enemy we were fighting — representatives of the North Vietnamese government and a Communist group from South Vietnam — to "negotiate" a private diplomatic solution for American withdrawal. [6]

Kerry's subversive diplomacy was the beginning of unprecedented behavior by key Democrats: talking unilaterally to our enemies with complete disregard to existing U.S. foreign policy. Such behavior would be repeated by people like Jimmy Carter, Ted Kennedy, Nancy Pelosi and once again John Kerry.

It is important to note that many of today's liberal Democrats were anti-war Vietnam protestors, who became the heart and soul of the new Democrat Party. Many of them, including the Clintons, Ted Kennedy, John Kerry, Dennis Kucinich, and Howard Dean, eventually became the leaders of the party. [7]

In the final days of the Vietnam War, liberal elements of the Democrat Party also began systematically weakening our national defense. The Church Committee, led by Democrat Senator Frank Church, the Pike Committee, led by Democrat Congressman Otis Pike and the antiwar liberals "reformed" our intelligence agencies to the point where they became impotent. The CIA was gutted and intelligence capabilities were neutered for the next thirty years. [8] In addition, Frank Church led the committee in erecting a "wall" preventing FBI agents (domestic law enforcement) from communicating with their CIA counterparts (foreign intelligence investigations). [9]

Democrat President Jimmy Carter assumed office in 1977. Like many on the left, Carter believed America's enemies could be persuaded by pacifism. He thought the Communists were rational people who would respond to "positive inducements," if only we shed our "inordinate fear of Communism" long enough to offer them concessions. [10]

The reality was quite different. Communism was based on a totalitarian system of mass murder, torture, slave labor camps, and the elimination of human rights. It sought to eradicate religious faith, private property and basic political and civil freedoms. The Soviet Union was responsible for the state sanctioned deaths of more than 60 million people. It was a multi-national empire that enslaved not only the East European countries, but dozens of nations within its own borders.

Carter was unswayed by reality. Without consulting his military advisors, he withdrew U.S. missiles from South Korea, proposed removing all U.S. troops from the Korean peninsula and slashed the defense budget. [11] The Soviet Union's response to "positive inducements?" They captured Ethiopia, South Yemen, Angola, Cambodia, Mozambique, Grenada and Nicaragua. [12]

More disastrous, however, was Carter's withdrawal of support for our longtime strategic ally, the Shah of Iran. As the Islamic Revolution was gaining momentum, Carter encouraged the Shah to step aside and let Ayatollah Khomeini, a Muslim exile in Paris, lead Iran. [13] Carter didn't like the Shah's alleged mistreatment of imprisoned Soviet spies and he thought that Khomeini would be a fairer leader than the Shah because he was a religious man. [14] Other Democrats agreed with Carter. Senator Edward Kennedy (D-MA) went further, condemning the Shah's government as "one of the most oppressive regimes in history" and Carter's ambassador to Iran compared Ayatollah Khomeini to the Hindu pacifist Mahatma Gandhi, calling him a "20th century saint." [15]

The Democrats got it completely wrong. With U.S. support withdrawn, the Ayatollah returned to Iran and proclaimed it an Islamic nation. Just as the so-called Islamic Revolution began to take place in 1979, the Soviets invaded Afghanistan. The Afghan invasion attracted a young and charismatic warrior,

who raised money and recruited other Muslims to fight the anti-Soviet jihad.
[16]

His name was Osama bin Laden, and his group of anti-Soviet jihadists became al-Qaeda.

As *Investor's Business Daily* concluded, "Carter's glaring weakness in dealing with the Communists and Iran (led) directly to both the current terrorist nuclear threat of Iran and the birth of al-Qaida, a group of mass murderers that would never have been possible if the Soviet Union's Leonid Brezhnev had not been emboldened to invade Afghanistan after seeing an inept, appeasing American president, Carter." [17]

The liberals and Democrats weren't through weakening America's security apparatus. At the same time Carter was undermining the Shah, his CIA director, Stansfield Turner, eliminated 820 human intelligence positions from the CIA, forcing it to depend on foreign intelligence services for analyses. [18] Senator Kennedy and others helped pass the 1978 Foreign Intelligence Surveillance Act (FISA), which prevented the executive branch from wiretapping foreign enemies operating in the U.S. without first demonstrating to a special court "sufficient specific and articulable facts to indicate that the individual's activities are in preparation for sabotage or international terrorism." [19]

FISA was an unprecedented restriction on our ability to gather information. President Franklin Roosevelt had openly wiretapped Nazis and Communists operating in the U.S., which only made sense, and every successive President had the same inherent power. [20] FISA raised the standards so high that, for the *first* time in our history, we had to prove a person was preparing for a terrorist act without having the ability to first collect the evidence obtained from wiretappings or listening in to conversations between collaborators. This catch-22 made it virtually impossible to collect intelligence necessary to protect this country.

After 9/11, Kennedy and other Democrats in Congress blamed the FBI and CIA for the failure to "connect the dots." "There was no way to connect the dots when they weren't allowed to 'collect the dots.' " [21]

As Lt. Colonel Robert Patterson explains in his book, *Reckless Disregard,* the intelligence sabotage by the liberal Democrats in Congress in the 1970s "unmistakably culminated in the terror attacks of September 11, 2001." [22] When the FBI arrested the so-called 20th hijacker, Zacarias Moussaoui, on immigration charges in 2001 and wanted to search his computer, the wall created by the Democrats in the 1970s (and raised higher by Clinton's deputy attorney general, Jamie Gorelick in 1995) denied FBI agents the ability to do so twenty-six days before 9/11. [23]

Its contents would have disclosed the 9/11 plot and may have prevented the attacks. [24]

Carter's defeat and the election of Republican Ronald Reagan brought a new attitude to U.S. foreign policy. For the first time in many years, Americans were reminded that the Soviet Union was "an evil empire" and America was a "shining city on a hill." Reagan's motto was "peace through strength"— not through retreat, weakness and accommodation. He pushed the Communists out of Grenada and helped defeat them in Nicaragua, Ethiopia and Afghanistan. [25] He attacked Libya after Libyan terrorists bombed a Berlin discotheque, killing two and injuring fifty U.S. servicemen. [26]

In 1983, Reagan unveiled the beginning of the Strategic Defense Initiative (SDI) – a national missile defense system. Reagan took the position that the U.S. should defend the nation against nuclear attack rather than to base the nation's defense on mutually assured destruction. Reagan eventually passed funding for SDI despite the objections of Congressional Democrats. Kennedy speaking for other Democrats strongly denounced "the misleading red scare tactics and reckless Star Wars schemes of the president." [27]

Kennedy went even further. As anti-Communist expert Herb Romerstein reported in *Human Events,* Kennedy actively collaborated in 1983 with the KGB, (the Soviet intelligence apparatus) and Yuri Andropov, the General Secretary of the Soviet Communist Party, to convince the American public that Reagan was a militaristic madman. Kennedy even offered to help get Soviet propaganda on the major U.S. television networks to weaken Reagan's standing in our country. [28]

In 1985, newly elected Senator John Kerry (D-MA) also tried to undermine Republican president Ronald Reagan. Similar to what he did in Paris over a decade earlier regarding the Vietnam War, Kerry went to Nicaragua to negotiate a "cease-fire" with Nicaragua's Soviet-backed Communist government. His actions were clearly at odds with American policy and interests at the time, which was to back the counter-insurgency in an effort to keep the Soviets from gaining a foothold there. [29]

In other words, Democrat Senators Ted Kennedy and John Kerry both met with our Communist enemies in an attempt to undermine a Republican president and our country.

Fortunately, Reagan prevailed and the Soviet Union collapsed. Years later, a group of Russian generals were asked about the one key that led to the collapse. Their response was unanimous: "Star Wars." "Gorbachev feared it (our missile defense) would render the Soviets' nuclear missiles obsolete for an overwhelming first strike and they could not afford to build the hundreds more that would be needed or hope to match America's great technical ability." [30]

Despite America's success, Democrats continued to resist missile defense. In July 2002, Senate Armed Services Chairman Carl Levin (D-MI) led an effort to kill the missile defense program by removing key funding provisions without which the rest of the program would not function. [31] Levin was not successful, thanks to the Republicans.

Unfortunately in 2009, President Obama and the Democratically-controlled Congress picked up where Levin left off, ending almost all funding for the Airborne Laser program (ABL). [32] Despite these cuts, the ABL is the most effective defense program available to counter the threat of a missile attack. It is able to knock down a missile in its boost, or ascent stage, rather than in the more difficult descent stage. The Airborne Laser program is also an important tool for preventing an electromagnetic pulse attack (EMP) that could defeat us militarily by destroying America's electrical infrastructure.

During the Clinton administration, the Islamic threat against the West gathered momentum. In February 1993, terrorists bombed New York's World Trade Center the first time. In October 1993, two U.S. Black Hawk helicopters were shot down in Somalia, killing 18 Americans and wounding 73. Clinton, under pressure from a Democratic Congress, ordered the retreat and withdrawal of all U.S. forces. [33] In 1998, an emboldened Osama bin Laden told ABC's John Miller that he realized more than ever that the American soldiers are "paper tigers." [34]

In June 1996, Khobar Towers, which housed U.S. Air Force personnel in Saudi Arabia, was blown up, killing 19 U.S. servicemen and wounding 372. And in February 1998, bin Laden declared "war on America," making the murder of any American anywhere on earth the "individual duty" of every Muslim. In August 1998, al-Qaeda blew up U.S. embassies in Kenya and Tanzania, killing 200 and injuring 5,000. [35]

Even though terrorists were making it plain they were at war with the United States, Clinton apparently never believed it. He treated the burgeoning jihad as though each attack were an isolated incident committed by unrelated individuals. This so-called "law enforcement approach" to terror is still advocated by Democrats today.

President Clinton's belief in this law enforcement approach is one of the primary reasons Osama bin Laden is still at large. In March 1996, Sudan offered to extradite him to the United States. Clinton refused the offer because "he (bin Laden) had committed no crime against America so I did not bring him here because we had no basis on which to hold him, though we knew he wanted to commit crimes against America." [36] According to Michael Scheuer, a 22 year CIA veteran and head of the agency's bin Laden unit, Clinton had "at least eight to ten chances to capture or kill Osama bin Laden in 1998 and 1999. And the government on all occasions decided that the information was not good enough to act." [37]

James Woolsey, who served for two years as Clinton's CIA director, characterized Clinton's approach to terrorism as "PR-driven:" "Do something to show you're involved. Launch a few missiles in the desert, bop them on the head, arrest a few people. But just keep kicking the ball down the field." [38]

Clinton "bopped" them on the head just once. On August 20, 1998 Clinton ordered a strike on al-Qaeda for the first and only time in his presidency. But the administration gave up to 48 hours notice to certain people, including the chief of staff of Pakistan's army. It is strongly suspected that the Pakistan army warned bin Laden prior to the action, and as a result bin Laden and all of his associates were able to leave the area unharmed. [39]

How effective was our attack? We bombed an aspirin factory in Sudan. [40]

During his tenure, Clinton also drastically slashed defense spending, cutting

700,000 active duty military members and 293,000 reservists, a 40 percent reduction in total forces. He reduced the number of the Army divisions from eighteen to ten, the number of Air Force active duty fighter aircraft squadrons from twenty-four to twelve, and the number of ships from almost 600 to little more than 300. [41] As a result, the military that Clinton handed over to President Bush was the least combat ready since the Carter administration. Clinton also denied already planned and approved pay raises for the military, requiring 30,000 military families to turn to food stamps and 8,000 to rely on state-funded childcare assistance by 1999.[42]

Intelligence gathering was another target of Clinton's defense cuts. A year before 9/11, FBI chief Louis Freeh asked for 864 new counterterrorism agents. He was able to get only seven. [43] And Clinton's CIA director before George Tenet, John Deutsch, banned the CIA from recruiting informers who were "human rights violators" or had a violent past. [44] Unfortunately, these were the kinds of people who could infiltrate terror networks – people with shady pasts who could easily fit in with the groups from whom we were trying to obtain information. The CIA was forced to live with this restriction, furthering hampering our intelligence gathering.

Our intel efforts were also rendered ineffective in Iran and other Middle Eastern countries because none of the Iran desk chiefs could speak or read Persian, and none of the Near East Division chiefs knew Arabic, Persian, Turkish, or Pashto. Consequently, the CIA outsourced its translation of al-Qaeda transmissions to the Pakistani intelligence, whose agents routinely gave the information to al-Qaeda agents. [45] Clinton regarded intelligence-gathering, so crucial to our national security, as a relic of the Cold War. His CIA director, George Tenet implied as much in his memoir: "I found it odd that there was no job interview...no one asked me what I would do with the intelligence community should I get the job." [46]

Clinton also undermined the war on terror in other ways. He canceled two investigations into Islamic charities that funded terrorism, out of concern that they might offend Muslim religious sensitivities. He also waived sanctions against every foreign company that helped Iran build its nuclear program. [47] In 1993, his secretary of energy, Hazel O'Leary, declassified the largest amount of information on America's nuclear secrets in the history of the Department of Energy – to "level the playing field," as she put it, so that no country such as the U.S. would be allowed to gain decisive advantage over others. [48]

It is likely North Korea, Iran and Libya were able to increase their knowledge about how to build a nuclear bomb from the information the administration released. Was this the "playing field" Clinton's Energy Secretary wanted to level?

Another damaging move made by the Clinton administration with respect to national security involved the president's decision to allow the Loral Corporation to export advanced missile-technology to the Chinese, ignoring the Pentagon's warnings against it.

How did he do it? In 1996, President Clinton moved the oversight of satellite exports from the State and Defense Departments to the Commerce Department, allowing the Chinese Army to obtain "a vast array of advanced missile, satellite and space technology." [49]

Why did he do it? A possible explanation: From 1994 to 1998, Bernard Schwartz, who was the chairman of Loral Space and Communication Ltd., became the *single largest donor* to the Democrat Party by making contributions totaling about $1.5 million to various Democrat Party entities, including President Clinton's 1996 re-election campaign. [50]

In 2002, Loral reached a settlement with the State Department over charges it passed advanced military technology to the Chinese Army. They agreed to pay fines of $20 million, but did not admit nor deny wrongdoing. [51]

Draw your own conclusions, but the bottom line can't be ignored: whether by accident or design, the Chinese missile program was advanced to the point where, currently, they are able to destroy a space-based satellite – a feat they accomplished in January of 2007. The biggest impact to the U.S. of this transfer of technology is that it can be sold by Communist China to hostile or unstable regimes in Iran, North Korea or Pakistan to improve the accuracy of their intercontinental ballistic missiles – a huge threat to the U.S.

When Clinton did act militarily, he either focused on the wrong enemy or was ineffective. Without UN approval, he bombed the Balkans in an air war to support an al-Qaeda affiliate, the Kosovo Liberation Army, in its war against Orthodox Christian Serbia. In 1998, he sent UN Ambassador Bill Richardson to Afghanistan to impose an arms embargo on the friendly Northern Alliance, who ultimately helped us overthrow the Taliban in 2002.

In 1998, he bombed Iraq for its defiance of UN resolutions and the terms of the 1991 truce, but took no effective action to force Iraq to comply. [52]

The Clinton administration also did not respond when the warship, USS Cole, was bombed by al-Qaeda in October 2000, killing 17 U.S. sailors. In fact, Clinton's ambassador to Yemen stopped the FBI investigation at the scene. [53]

On December 31, 2000, right before leaving office, Clinton signed an agreement to join the International Criminal Court. Under that treaty, signed without the advice and consent of the United States Senate, U.S. servicemen could be brought before an international court at the request of a foreign enemy for actions carried out in wartime under the orders of their commanding officers. [54] If left in place, this treaty would have put our soldiers in Afghanistan, Iraq or anywhere else they might be deployed in the position of being prosecuted for war crimes by individuals or groups harboring anti-American sentiments — even if the allegations were unfounded. Thankfully, the Bush administration told the UN that they considered Clinton's signature void and wouldn't be a party to the treaty. [55]

Incredibly, the Clinton administration's final policy paper regarding national security — the document that provided the transition to the Bush administration — made no mention of al-Qaeda *anywhere* in its 45,000 words. [56] For Clinton and Democrats, the environment, domestic welfare programs and social liberalism were priorities, not national security.

Not only was the Clinton administration AWOL on the war on terror during its tenure, it tried to cover up its shortcomings after the fact. Before the 9/11 Commission hearings in 2003, Sandy Berger, Clinton's former National Security advisor, stole highly classified documents from the National Archives. Written by Clinton's counterterrorism czar, Richard Clarke, these documents were allegedly critical of the administration's handling of events leading up to 9/11. [57]

In 2005, Berger pled guilty to the theft of those classified documents, and received an extremely light sentence, considering the crime committed. More importantly, he never returned the stolen documents.

During the years of President George W. Bush, the Congressional Democrats continued to undermine our nation's fight against the newest threat to the U.S. — radical Islam. In a 2006 editorial, *Investor's Business Daily* elaborated on how the Democrats' national security record during the Bush administration was dangerous to America:

1) On missile defense of America — Democrats voted against it.
2) On the Patriot Act — Democrats voted against it.
3) On tapping terrorists' phone calls to the U.S. — Democrats voted against it.
4) On tracing terrorists' money flow between foreign banks — Democrats voted against it.
5) On building a border wall to control illegal immigration and stop dope-dealers, terrorists and criminals — Democrats voted against it.
6) On interrogating captured terrorists — 194 Democrats voted against it.
7) On telling the world (and our enemy) about a timetable for withdrawing from and deserting Iraq — this was the Democrats' retreat and defeat plan. [58]

Democrats were also willing to compromise national security for one of their favored special interest groups — the unions. They held up the creation of the Department of Homeland Security (DHS) insisting that airport inspectors be unionized, once again placing politics ahead of national security. [59] The attempt failed and a non-unionized DHS was approved, although 120 Democrats opposed it. [60]

In 2003, Senator Ted Kennedy (D-MA), Senator Russ Feingold (D-WI) and Congressman John Conyers (D-MI) worked to eliminate funding for what was at the time one of the most effective homeland security programs established after 9/11 – the National Security Entry-Exit Registration System (NSEERS), which required the fingerprinting and registration of foreign visitors from certain Muslim countries and state sponsors of terrorism entering the U.S. [61] Kennedy successfully slipped an amendment into the fiscal 2003 omnibus spending bill to defund NSEERS. Kennedy, Feingold and Conyers then wrote a joint letter calling the program "a second wave of roundups and detentions of Arab and Muslim males disguised as a perfunctory registration requirement." [62]

For Democrats, it was better not to offend Muslim sensitivities than to identify Muslim terrorists coming into our country — only two years after America endured the worst domestic attack in the history of the country.

During the Bush years, Congressional Democrats continued their politicization of national security. In April 2007, at the first Democrat presidential debate in South Carolina, former Senator John Edwards, along with Senator Joe Biden, Ohio Rep. Dennis Kucinich and former Alaska Senator Mike Gravel stated that they did not believe there was a global War on Terror. In a separate speech in May 2007, Edwards minimized the Bush administration's War on Terror, stating: "The War on Terror is a slogan designed only for politics, not a strategy to make American safe. It's a bumper sticker, not a plan." [63]

Aware that a U.S. victory in Iraq would enhance the chances of a Republican victory in the 2008 presidential election, Democrats refused to endorse the "surge" of 30,000 troops ordered into Iraq. Democrat Majority Leader Harry Reid, in a cowardly statement proclaimed: "… that this war is lost, that the surge is not accomplishing anything…" [64] Although we had American men and women in harm's way at the time, this was apparently irrelevant to the feckless Senator from Nevada. Apparently it was also irrelevant that Reid made his statement *long before all the troops had even arrived in Iraq.*

Reid was hardly alone among Democrats. When the U.S. Commander in Iraq, General David H. Petraeus, gave a positive progress report in September 2007 about how well the surge had been succeeding, then-Senator Hillary Clinton accused him of lying: "I think that the reports that you provide to us really require the willing suspension of disbelief." [65]

Instead of the surge policy, Democrats recommended a phased redeployment of our troops out of Iraq, willing to concede defeat — exactly as they had done in Vietnam three decades earlier.

The Democrats were wrong, and the surge eventually proved effective in stabilizing Iraq.

The primary job of the federal government is to keep its citizens safe. That means it is absolutely imperative to elevate the concerns of national security over partisan considerations.

Democrats have a long and tattered track record of getting those priorities exactly backwards.

Chapter 2

POLITICALLY CALCULATED AMNESIA

In this day and age, I am amazed that any politician thinks he can completely contradict himself, when virtually every public utterance can end up on a YouTube video or at the end of a Google search.

This chapter contains quote after quote by leading Democrats regarding the necessity of removing Saddam Hussein from power and the dire consequences of our failure to do so.

It also reveals the complete about-face major Democrats did when anti-war activist Howard Dean became the front-runner in the 2004 presidential primaries. It is extremely disturbing that Democrats were willing to turn against the Iraq War and divide our nation solely for political ambition.

The Iraq War produced many casualties. The Democrat Party's integrity was one of them.

It is often forgotten that George W. Bush did not invent the idea of deposing Saddam Hussein. In fact, removing Saddam had been a priority of Bill Clinton and his Democrat administration for years before Bush came on the scene. [1]

After all, it was Bill Clinton who introduced and signed into law the Iraq Liberation Act of 1998, which specifically called for regime change by force. The Act was passed on October 31, 1998 by a 360 – 38 vote in the House of Representatives and by unanimous consent in the Senate. [2]

At that time, Clinton was deeply concerned that Saddam Hussein's WMD programs, combined with his ties to international terrorists, posed a grave threat to the United States. [3] Clinton's statement on the night of December

16, 1998 when he announced a four day bombing campaign in Iraq revealed those concerns:

"Saddam Hussein must not be allowed to threaten his neighbors or the world with nuclear arms, poison gas or biological weapons... Other countries possess weapons of mass destruction and ballistic missiles. With Saddam there is one big difference: he has used them. Not once, but repeatedly... I have no doubt today that, left unchecked, Saddam Hussein will use these terrible weapons again." [4]

On that same evening, Vice President Al Gore went on CNN's *Larry King Show* and voiced a similar belief:

"You allow someone like Saddam Hussein to get nuclear weapons, ballistic missiles, chemical weapons, biological weapons. How many people is he going to kill with such weapons? ... We are not going to allow him to succeed." [5]

These statements remind us that when George Bush took office in 2001, the United States was already at war with Iraq. We had been at war with them for a decade since the first Gulf War ended in 1991. This was literally the case, because the end of the Gulf War was merely a cease-fire and not a formal surrender followed by a peace treaty. [6]

The Clinton air strikes failed to convince Saddam to end his WMD programs and open his regime to U.N. weapon inspectors. International trade sanctions also failed, as Saddam managed to evade them by manipulating the U.N. Oil-for-Food program. [7]

As a result, starting in 1999, the Clinton administration began to develop options to overthrow Saddam's regime, according to Ken Pollack, an official in Clinton's National Security Council. [8]   A plan for a land invasion of Iraq had been drawn up a few years earlier under the auspices of Colin Powell, then Chairman of the Joint Chiefs of Staff. [9] According to Pollack, although no one thought the American public would support such an invasion, it seemed to be the only option. [10] As it turned out, President Clinton lost interest in an armed invasion of Iraq, perhaps because he was already involved in a military campaign in Kosovo. In addition, wars are not popular and Clinton was always concerned about his popularity.

Like Clinton before him, President Bush initially decided to do nothing about Saddam and Iraq — until 9/11 occurred. Shortly thereafter, five people in the U.S. received fatal doses of anthrax in the mail from an undisclosed source. Since Saddam had the knowledge to produce anthrax, as well as having probable stockpiles of it, many leaders in this country, including Democrats, were very concerned that Saddam might give such biological weapons to a terrorist group like al-Qaeda. [11]

Just weeks before 9/11, a privately sponsored exercise had simulated a smallpox attack on the U.S., and the results indicated more than three million people would be infected within two months — and *one million* would die. [12]

Since the threat was real at that time, leading Democrats spoke as assertively as Republicans in calling for action against Saddam. From the Senate floor, October 10, 2002 — five months *prior* to the invasion of Iraq — several Democrat Senators voiced their concern:

Senator Charles Schumer (D-NY): "When I consider that Hussein could either use or give to terrorists weapons of mass destruction – biological, chemical or nuclear – and that he might just be mad enough to do it, I find, after careful research, the answer to my question: we cannot afford to leave him alone over the next five or even three years." [13]

Senator Hillary Clinton (D-NY): "It is clear, however, that if left unchecked, Saddam Hussein will continue to increase his capability to wage biological and chemical warfare, and will keep trying to develop nuclear weapons..." [14]

Senator John Rockefeller (D-WV): "Saddam's existing biological and chemical weapons capabilities pose real threats to America today, tomorrow.... He could make these weapons available to many terrorist groups, third parties, which have contact with his government. Those groups, in turn, could bring those weapons into the United States and unleash a devastating attack against our citizens. I fear that greatly." [15]

Senator Joseph Biden (D-DE): "Saddam is dangerous. The world would be a better place without him. But the reason he poses a growing danger to the United States and its allies is that he possesses chemical and biological weapons and is seeking nuclear weapons..." [16]

In the fall of 2002, mainstream Democrats were still on board with President Bush regarding the need to take action against Saddam, just as they were with President Clinton. More than half of Senate Democrats joined with Republicans in authorizing President Bush to use force against Saddam Hussein. The majority in Congress understood that the 17 U.N. resolutions against Saddam were totally ineffective, as he had defied them all. In the House of Representatives, 81 Democrats (out of 209) agreed. [17] Copies of the National Intelligence Estimate (NIE), on which the President's decision was based, were provided to every Senator. The NIE findings were confirmed by government intelligence agencies around the world, including those of France, Britain, Russia and Jordan. [18]

Three months after the war in Iraq began, a very sharp turn of events greatly divided this country. The Democrat National Committee released a television ad that focused on the legitimacy of the war. The ad accused President Bush of lying to the American people about the reasons for invading Iraq. It was based on a now discredited report from Joe Wilson debunking Saddam's interest in acquiring uranium from Niger. Wilson's disinformation campaign was orchestrated at the highest levels of the Democrat Party to persuade the electorate that the war was based on a lie.[19] The attacks against the Bush administration continued relentlessly, leading to the phrase coined by the left, "Bush lied, people died."

Between the invasion of Iraq in March 2003, which Democrats supported, and their attack on the legitimacy of the war three months later, nothing significant happened on the battlefield or took place in the Bush administration's war policy. [20]

So what *did* change? The internal politics of the Democrat Party.

In June 2003, Democrats were in the midst of a presidential primary campaign. Vermont governor Howard Dean, a veteran of the anti-Vietnam left and by then a vocal critic of the Iraq War, had gathered such momentum that he appeared to be the front runner for the Democrat presidential nomination. [21] On June 24/25, 2003, in the online primary vote of 317,000 voters held by MoveOn.org, Howard Dean received the highest number of votes, almost 44% of the total. His nearest competitor, Dennis Kucinich, amassed 24%. [22] Suddenly, prominent Democrats such as John Kerry and John Edwards, staunchly for the war until then, both did an about face in their respective quests for the nomination.

In other words, the leaders of the Democrat Party reversed their support for the war because their political ambitions, as opposed to the country's best interests, were more important to them. National unity in time of war was trumped by political ambition.

As time went on, many Democrats who originally supported the war began to claim they were "tricked, misled or lied to." These allegations, though, are simply not true. Democrat Senator John Edwards in an interview with *The New Yorker Magazine,* admitted he wasn't fooled by the Bush administration into supporting the war — and neither was any other Senator:

"I was convinced that Saddam had chemical and biological weapons and was doing everything in his power to get nuclear weapons. There was some disparity in the information I had about how far along he was in that process. I didn't rely on George Bush for that. And I personally think there's some dishonesty in suggesting that members of the United States Senate relied on George Bush for that information because I don't think it's true. It's great politics. But it's not the truth... I was on the Intelligence Committee so I got information from the intelligence community. And then I had a series of meetings with former Clinton administration people. And they were all saying the same thing. Everything I was hearing in the Intelligence Committee was the same thing I was hearing from these guys. And there was nary a dissenting voice..." [23]

In the middle of a war, Democrats unnecessarily divided this country into two camps – one supporting the President, the other relentlessly attacking him by claiming the reason for the war was a lie. These were the same politicians who spoke out unequivocally just months earlier about the threat posed from Saddam Hussein. What makes this period in history so disgraceful was that Democrats, pretending they were mislead about the motives for going to Iraq, were guilty of lying to the American people — *not* President Bush.

Honest mistakes are one thing — politically cynical calculations are quite another. A fundamental question American voters should ask themselves going forward: Can I trust a party that has lied to me about one of the most important issues of our time? As you will discover reading this book, this won't be the only important issue about which Democrats have duped the American people.

Chapter 3

LIES, SPIES AND YELLOWCAKE

Perhaps one of the greatest ironies of the Iraq War was that the slogan, "Bush lied, people died," was the biggest lie of all. It was so pervasive that it endures to this day, despite its complete rejection by two separate bipartisan investigations — investigations demanded by Democrats.

Honest people can argue about whether going into Iraq was the right thing to do. But these arguments should be fact-based. As this chapter demonstrates, the facts have been, and continue to be, distorted for partisan political gain.

In 2003, Congressional Democrats and the mainstream media collaborated in a relentless effort to convince Americans that the Bush administration manipulated intelligence about Saddam Hussein's weapons programs to justify an invasion of Iraq.

To this day, Democrats continue to assert this myth even though two separate bipartisan investigations have disproved their claim. In 2004, Democrats demanded an investigation; the result was a 610 page bipartisan report co-chaired by former Democrat Senator Chuck Robb and Republican Judge Laurence Silberman. The Robb-Silberman Report concluded that no political pressure had been put on intelligence officials by Vice President Cheney or the Bush administration to produce a desired result.[1] In 2004, a separate bipartisan Senate Intelligence Committee report also concluded there was *no evidence* that administration officials attempted to coerce, influence or pressure analysts to change their judgments related to Iraq's weapons of mass destruction capabilities. [2]

The effort by the media and Democrats to negatively influence public opinion about the Iraq War started *only* one month after we went to war.

Both *The New York Times* and *The Washington Post* ran articles (based on an anonymous government source) alleging that the Bush administration had lied to the country about Saddam Hussein's attempt to purchase significant quantities of uranium from Africa. [3] This was a key point in President Bush's 2003 State of the Union address just before the invasion of Iraq, when he said, "The British government has learned that Saddam Hussein recently sought significant quantities of uranium from Africa." [4]

The anonymous source turned out to be Joseph C. Wilson IV, a former U. S. ambassador to the African state of Gabon. Wilson said he was sent to Niger by Vice President Dick Cheney to determine whether Saddam Hussein sought to purchase yellowcake uranium, as the British intelligence had reported.[5] Yellowcake is a key ingredient for manufacturing a nuclear bomb.

Wilson insisted he found nothing during his trip supporting the British report. He also claimed to have seen the documents on which the intelligence was based, and to have recognized immediately that they were forged. Wilson said he told the Bush administration about all of this long before the 2003 State of the Union address. According to Wilson, the Bush administration ignored his report and lied to the American people because they didn't like what he had found. [6]

Although the Niger documents turned out to be forgeries, they had nothing to do with British (and U.S.) intelligence assessments about Saddam's efforts to buy uranium. The forged documents did not even emerge until after their intelligence assessments had already been made. [7] It is suspected that they were manufactured and planted by the French in an effort to sabotage the U.S. war effort. The French, as it turns out, were angry at the U.S. for disrupting their lucrative Oil-for-Food scam with Saddam. [8]

It is important to remember that prior to Joe Wilson's accusations the American public was firmly behind President Bush and the Iraq War. By the end of July 2003, an NBC News/Wall Street Journal tracking poll showed Bush with a 56 percent approval rating. A Pew Research Center poll found that 67 percent of those surveyed thought the United States had made the right decision to use military force against Iraq. [9]

The claim by Joe Wilson that President Bush had lied provided a way for Democrat presidential candidates like John Kerry and John Edwards, both of whom had previously supported the war, to reverse their stance and find common ground with the left-wing faction of the party who had vehemently opposed it. [10]

Yet despite his claims, nearly every one of Wilson's accusations was proven false.

An investigation by the bipartisan Senate Select Committee on Intelligence found that:

- Vice-President Dick Cheney's office not only had *no role* in sending Wilson to Niger, it had *never been told* about his mission or been briefed on his findings. They concluded that it was Wilson's own wife, Valerie Plame, a CIA weapons analyst, who recommended him for the job.

- Wilson *never* saw the documents he claimed were forgeries. The CIA had not even received the documents until eight months *after* Wilson's mission was completed and he was no longer employed by the government. This confirmed the fact that intelligence assessments about Saddam's weapons programs were not based on the forgeries. When the Senate Intelligence Committee asked Wilson how he could tell *The Washington Post* he knew the dates and names were wrong on documents he had never seen, Wilson admitted that he may have "misspoken."

- Contrary to what Wilson had claimed, *his own report* admitted that the Iraqi delegation had traveled to Niger and that the Niger prime minister believed the Iraqis were interested in purchasing uranium (lending more, not less, credibility to the British and CIA assessments). [11]

What's the most likely reason Joe Wilson was willing to distort the truth? Perhaps the fact he was a political activist (ignored by the mainstream media) who had contributed to Democrat candidates including Al Gore, Ted Kennedy, Charles Rangel and Barbara Mikulski had something to do with it. The media also did not tell the American public that in May 2003, prior to his accusations, Wilson had already taken a position as foreign affairs adviser to John Kerry's presidential campaign. [12]

Amazingly, despite the Senate Intelligence Committee's debunking of Joe Wilson's allegations, he had the audacity to write a book called *The Politics of Truth: Inside the Lies That Led to War and Betrayed My Wife's CIA Identity.* [13]

To counter Wilson's lies, the Bush White House decided to declassify portions of the October 2002 National Intelligence Estimate on Iraq's WMD programs, and instructed Vice President Dick Cheney's chief of staff I. Lewis ("Scooter") Libby to prepare a brief on the background on the Niger evidence. [14]

During the same period, covert CIA operative Valerie Plame who was Wilson's wife had her identity leaked in a column written by Robert Novak. Although a conservative writer, Novak, along with Wilson and Plame, was a critic of the Iraq war.

Disclosing the identity of a covert CIA operative is a federal crime. Novak identified his anonymous source as two administration officials. [15] The Bush-hating mainstream media ran stories speculating that Dick Cheney and/or Karl Rove were responsible for the leak. *Newsweek* and *Time* even ran cover stories. [16]

The leaker turned out to be Deputy Secretary of State Richard Armitage, who also opposed the war. Armitage, along with Novak, concealed this information while an investigation by a special prosecutor was ordered to determine the source of the leak. [17] That both Armitage and Novak were willing to remain silent during this investigation is a great illustration of the disgraceful depths to which the anti-war movement was willing to go to discredit the Bush administration.

Despite his guilt, Armitage was not charged for the crime of outing a CIA agent. On the other hand, Scooter Libby, who was also called to testify, was eventually indicted and convicted of perjury and obstruction of justice, *even though he was never charged with the underlying crime of outing a CIA agent.* [18] His allegedly contradictory statements were portrayed as a deliberate and malicious obstruction of justice, as opposed to the more likely possibility that he had a faulty memory.

Many people ask why Prosecutor Patrick Fitzgerald pursued his investigation of Libby even though he was never charged with the underlying crime of outing a covert CIA agent. According to Ken Timmerman, author of *Shadow*

Warriors, one reason had to do with the people involved. On the one side were Republicans Libby, Rove and Cheney; on the other were a pair of Clinton appointees. Before Fitzgerald was appointed, the investigation was headed by John Dion, a career federal prosecutor who was given a political appointment under Clinton. Assisting him was another Clinton appointee, Bruce Swartz, who was a contributor to Democrat Party candidates. Coincidently, at the same time they were pursuing Libby, these same Justice Department attorneys were heading the investigation into former (Clinton) National Security Advisor Sandy Berger for the theft of classified documents from the National Archives. [19]

Both men were convicted. Libby's sentence? 30 months in federal prison, a $250,000 fine, two years of supervised release and 400 hours of community service. [20] Berger's sentence? No prison time, a $50,000 fine, 100 hours of community service, and no security clearance for three years. [21]

Three years later, *The Washington Post,* a liberal newspaper which had earlier supported Joe Wilson's position, finally admitted that he had been lying. As their editorial stated "…it now appears that the person most responsible for the end of Ms. Plame's CIA career is Mr. Wilson. Mr. Wilson chose to go public with an explosive charge claiming – falsely, as it turns out – that he had debunked reports of Iraqi uranium-shopping in Niger …He diverted responsibility from himself and his false charges by claiming that President Bush's closest aides had engaged in an illegal conspiracy. It's unfortunate that so many people took him seriously." [22]

Even today, you will occasionally hear television commentators on networks such as the ultra-liberal MSNBC claim the allegations from Joe Wilson and his wife Valerie Plame were true.

Despite being proven innocent by two bipartisan investigations, the Bush administration remained under vicious attack by Democrats. Democrat Senate Minority Leader Harry Reid invoked a rarely used Senate provision and dramatically closed the Senate doors to discuss classified "national security" issues. Reid was disingenuous when he said:

"The Libby indictment provides a window into what this is really about: How the administration manufactured and manipulated intelligence in order to sell the war in Iraq, and attempted to destroy those who dared to challenge its actions. As a result of its improper conduct, a cloud now hangs over this administration." [23]

Also willfully ignoring the results of both investigations, Democrat Senator Dick Durbin seconded Reid's untruthful claims:

"Intelligence information was distorted, was misused, and we have seen as late as last week the length (to) which the administration has gone to try to silence and discredit their critics of the misuse of this intelligence information." [24]

This disturbing pattern of deception by Democrats and the left continued unabated. In an appearance in front of the House of Representatives on March 16, 2007, Valerie Plame went out of her way to dispute the conclusions of the Senate Intelligence Committee. She continued to insist she did not recommend her husband for the Niger trip.

On May 25, 2007, Plame was *proven to have lied*: the Senate Intelligence Committee released a copy of the e-mail from Plame to her boss, showing she had recommended her husband all along. [25]

The fact that most Americans believed the Bush administration lied about the intelligence leading up to the war is a stark reminder that the American people can be manipulated by a mainstream media and a Democrat Party who believe "a lie repeated often enough becomes the truth."

Chapter 4

SADDAM'S WMDs: FACT OR FICTION?

In my experience, I have found that people with a strong political agenda will often ignore facts that conflict with their beliefs.

Americans might be shocked to learn there were, in fact, weapons of mass destruction found in Iraq. Not only have Democrats and their media allies ignored this reality, they have also completely dismissed credible claims that WMD were also moved out of the country before the U.S. invasion.

This is another disturbing example of the poisonous atmosphere created in a deliberate effort to destroy the Bush presidency.

Congressional Democrats and the mainstream media have insisted that President Bush lied about the existence of Saddam Hussein's WMD programs and his nuclear ambitions. They have also falsely claimed that Saddam abandoned all of his weapon programs after his defeat in the 1991 Gulf War. Both of these assertions have been disproved by information discovered — but kept hidden — from the American people by the mainstream media.

After the invasion of Iraq, U.S. forces discovered a significant amount of evidence regarding the existence of WMD programs. In a report to the joint House and Senate intelligence committees, David Kay, former head of the Iraq Survey Group (ISG), emphasized the enormous scope of these programs. Kay concluded that the entire country had been a gigantic weapons plant and that there were over a hundred facilities engaged in various phases of the WMD effort. He said his team of investigators and intelligence analysts had found extensive evidence of chemical, biological and nuclear programs, and that Saddam's Iraqi Intelligence Service had been successful in keeping their most sensitive aspects hidden from international inspectors for years. [1]

The Duelfer Report, the CIA's 1500 page account of its intelligence mistakes in Iraq, noted that inspectors *did find WMD* – 53 chemical weapons to be exact. However, that number may have been a gross underestimation since technical experts only fully evaluated less than one-quarter of one percent of the 10,000 plus weapons caches throughout Iraq. The Duelfer Report also concluded that Saddam intended to "resume WMD production as soon as U.N. sanctions were lifted." [2]

An analysis of 600,000 documents found in Iraq, along with taped conversations between Hussein and his top advisors, revealed that Iraq was working on an advanced method of enriching uranium. They also revealed that Iraq was conspiring to deceive U.N. inspectors regarding weapons of mass destruction and that these weapons might be used against the U.S. [3]

That Saddam never abandoned his WMD programs after the 1991 Gulf War was confirmed by an April 1995 tape in which Saddam and several aides discussed the fact that U.N. inspectors had found traces of Iraq's biological weapons programs. On the tape, Hussein Kamel, Saddam's son-in-law, is heard gloating about fooling the inspectors:

"We did not reveal all that we have, not the type of weapons, not the volume of materials we imported, not the volume of the production we told them about, not the volume of use. None of this was correct." [4]

Other tapes reveal even more evidence. As late as 2000, Saddam was heard in his office talking with Iraqi scientists about his plans to build a nuclear device. At one point he discussed Iraq's plasma uranium program – something that was missed entirely by U.N. weapons inspectors looking for WMD in Iraq. [5] According to the Federation of American Scientists, the plasma separation process has been studied as a potentially more efficient uranium-enrichment technique that makes use of the advancing technologies in superconducting magnets and plasma physics. [6] This was particularly troubling since it indicated an *active, on-going* attempt by Saddam to build a nuclear bomb.

There is also evidence that Saddam's WMDs were moved out of Iraq and into Syria before the invasion. This was disclosed by Georges Sada, second-in-command in the Iraqi Air Force, and author of the book *Saddam's Secrets*. Sada detailed how the Iraqi dictator used trucks, commercial jets and ships to remove weapons from the country. The author explained that two Iraqi

Airways Boeing jets were converted to cargo planes and WMDs were moved to Syria in a total of 56 flights six weeks before the war. These flights were disguised as part of a relief effort to assist Syria after a dam collapse in 2002.
7

At an intelligence summit in February, 2006, former Deputy Undersecretary of Defense John Shaw confirmed Georges Sada's revelations:

"The short answer to the question of where the WMD Saddam bought from the Russians went was that they went to Syria and Lebanon. They were moved by Russian Spetsnaz (special ops) units... that were specifically sent to Iraq to move the weaponry and eradicate any evidence of its existence." 8

The Iraq Survey Group's David Kay also confirmed that unspecified materials had been moved to Syria shortly before the Iraq war. In an interview with the *London Telegraph* in January 2004, Kay stated, "We know from some of the interrogations of former Iraqi officials that a lot of material went to Syria before the war, including some components of Saddam's WMD program." Kay's successor as Iraq Survey Group head, Charles Duelfer, testified to a Senate Armed Services Committee in 2004 that "a lot of materials left Iraq and went to Syria." 9 In 2006, Israel's top general Moshe Yaalon stated that Iraq moved WMDs to Syria six weeks before Operation Iraqi Freedom began.
10

Many people wonder why the Bush administration ignored publicizing Russia's involvement in evacuating Saddam's WMD stockpiles. Retired Air Force Lt. General Thomas McIrney answered that question: "with Iran moving faster than anyone thought in its nuclear programs, the administration needed the Russians, the Chinese and the French, and was not interested in information that would make them look bad." McIrney also agreed there was "clear evidence" that Saddam had WMDs. 11

The mainstream media were not the only ones spreading the myth that President Bush lied to the American people. In 2003, Democrat Senator John Kerry demanded that President Bush apologize for misleading the nation. Contrast that with Kerry's words ten months earlier:

"We are in possession of what I think to be compelling evidence that Saddam Hussein has, and has had for a number of years, a developing capacity for the production and storage of weapons of mass destruction. Without question, we need to disarm Saddam Hussein. He is a brutal, murderous dictator, leading an oppressive regime. He presents a particularly grievous threat because he is so consistently prone to miscalculation. And now he has continued deceit and his consistent grasp for weapons of mass destruction. So the threat of Saddam Hussein with weapons of mass destruction is real." [12]

Perhaps the most compelling evidence of Saddam's WMD program was revealed in an *Associated Press* news release on July 5, 2008. According to that report, *550 metric tons* of yellowcake uranium — the seed material for high grade nuclear enrichment — were shipped to a Canadian uranium producer, Cameco Corp. in 2008 by the Iraqi government in a transaction worth "tens of millions of dollars." [13] American troops discovered the uranium in 2003 during the Iraqi invasion, but had to conceal this information and the uranium itself until they could figure out a safe way to ship it out of the country. Why? The Bush administration feared that the cache would fall into the hands of insurgents crossing into Iran, thereby aiding that country's nuclear ambitions.

As a result, the material was kept safe by U.S. and Iraqi forces in a 23,000 acre site surrounded by huge sand berms, until a plan to ship it out was finished. [14]

Such a significant find should have created a media firestorm. Instead, it was buried on a few websites and kept hidden from the American people. One can only speculate why. It is likely that Democrats and their media allies did not want to admit they were wrong about the Bush administration's motives for going to war. Democrats may also have been concerned that such a revelation would be extremely damaging to their party's chances in the November 2008 elections.

Americans might have felt differently about the war in Iraq had they been aware of the facts presented in this chapter. Denying the public critical information is as bad, if not worse, than lying to them.

Either way, the result is the same: Americans were duped.

Chapter 5

SADDAM'S REAL CONNECTIONS TO AL-QAEDA

Most Americans, including myself, had never heard of al-Qaeda before 9/11.

I'd be willing to bet that most Americans, even now, have no idea that Saddam Hussein and al-Qaeda had a connection prior to our invasion of Iraq.

Democrats have known all about this connection, but have chosen to remain silent.

I consider such silence appalling.

One of the chief claims made by Congressional Democrats who say they were "misled" about the Iraq war is that there was no al-Qaeda presence in Iraq. The real war, they say, was in Afghanistan.

This myth was debunked by many independent sources, including George Tenet, who was appointed by President Bill Clinton as Director of the CIA, and subsequently retained by President George W. Bush. In his book *At the Center of the Storm: My Years at the CIA,* he acknowledged the links between Saddam's regime and al-Qaeda — links that existed before the U.S. ever went to war in Iraq.

Tenet concluded that the Bush administration was correct in worrying that Iraq did have a relationship with al-Qaeda:

"The Intelligence told us that senior al-Qaeda leaders and the Iraqis had discussed safe haven in Iraq... up to two hundred al-Qaeda fighters began to relocate there in camps after the Afghan campaign began in the fall of 2001."
1

According to Tenet, former al-Qaeda leader, Abu Musab-al-Zarqawi supervised training camps in northern Iraq run by Ansar al-Islam before the Iraq invasion and engaged in production and training in the use of poisons such as cyanide. As a result of the CIA's tracking of those activities, we arrested nearly one hundred Zarqawi operatives in Western Europe planning to use poisons in operations. [2]

It wasn't just George Tenet who recognized Iraq's ties to al-Qaeda before the war. In 2007, *The Guardian* — a left-wing British newspaper — ran a story on the death of Abu Ayyub al-Masri, al-Qaeda's top operative in Iraq. They concluded that he likely entered Iraq in 2002, even before al-Zarqawi, and may have helped establish the first al-Qaeda cell in the Baghdad area. [3]

Investor's Business Daily also reported on al-Qaeda's ties to Saddam Hussein, citing the existence of a 1998 e-mail from Richard Clarke (Bill Clinton's national coordinator for counter-terrorism) to National Security Adviser Sandy Berger. The e-mail warned that if bin Laden were flushed from Afghanistan, he might just "boogie to Baghdad." [4]

And an ABC News report in 1999 revealed that Saddam offered bin Laden asylum, citing their "long relationship." [5]

Documents captured after the invasion of Iraq — *600,000 of them* — revealed that elite Iraqi military units trained 8,000 al-Qaeda terrorists, belonging to groups such as Algeria's GSPC, Palestinian Islamic Jihad, Ansar al-Islam and the Sudanese Liberation Army at camps in Iraq. [6]

A Pentagon study of those 600,000 captured documents also detailed Iraq's relationship with Abu Sayyaf, the al-Qaeda affiliate in the Philippines founded by Osama bin Laden's brother-in-law. *The Weekly Standard* pointed out that the Pentagon study did not mention the most significant element of those documents: *we learned that the Iraqi regime had been funding and equipping al-Qaeda in the Philippines.* [7]

Proof of Saddam's "long relationship" with al-Qaeda goes even further. Abdul Rahman Yasin, a member of the al-Qaeda cell that detonated the bomb at the World Trade Center in 1993, found safe haven in Iraq. Documents found in Iraq in 2006 revealed that Saddam provided Yasin with both a home and salary. [8]

Democrats would like Americans to believe the Bush administration was the only one that connected al-Qaeda to Iraq. This is simply not true. The Clinton administration also believed there were al-Qaeda ties to Iraq. The 1998 Clinton Justice Department indictment against bin Laden alleged that "al-Qaeda reached an understanding with the government of Iraq, that al-Qaeda would not work against the government and that on particular projects, specifically including weapons development, al-Qaeda would work cooperatively with the government of Iraq." [9]

Regrettably, the mainstream media and the Democrats kept this information hidden. They were more interested in convincing Americans that the Bush administration lied to the country about an Iraq-al-Qaeda connection. All evidence to the contrary — even captured documents from the fallen Iraqi regime itself — was ignored.

Once again, politics trumped the truth.

Chapter 6

EVERYONE THINKS REPUBLICANS CAUSED THE MORTGAGE CRISIS...

Americans wondering who was responsible for the mortgage crisis should ask themselves a question: is owning a home a privilege or a right?

Despite the meltdown in 2008, the seeds for the mortgage crisis were sown much earlier by a Democrat Party long convinced homeownership was an entitlement.

As this chapter shows, once that basic premise became conventional wisdom, it was all downhill from there.

If one listens to the mainstream media and many Democrats, the blame for the mortgage crisis rests with the Republicans and the Bush administration. They've convinced the public that Democrats had nothing whatsoever to do with our current financial woes.

Precisely the opposite is true: Democrats created the lax mortgage policies that precipitated the crisis while simultaneously stifling Republican efforts to prevent it.

The history of the crisis started with the Community Reinvestment Act (CRA), signed into law by Democrat President Jimmy Carter in 1977. The law was designed to foster homeownership in low-income communities by pushing banks to aggressively lend to low and moderate income people. At first, it was easy to comply with the CRA. Banks merely had to demonstrate that they did not discriminate in making loans in poor and black neighborhoods. [1]

When Democrat Bill Clinton became President in 1992, he broadened the Community Reinvestment Act in ways Congress had never intended. In 1995, rather than submit legislation that the Republican-led Congress was certain to reject, Clinton bypassed Congress entirely, ordering the Treasury Department to rewrite the CRA rules. [2]

As a result, banks were forced to fulfill loan "quotas" in low income neighborhoods. [3]

That wasn't the only problem. CRA also allowed community activist groups such as ACORN (Association of Community Organizations for Reform Now), for whom Barack Obama once worked in Chicago, and NACA (Neighborhood Assistance Corporation of America) to file complaints that could affect a bank's CRA rating. Failure to comply with CRA or a bad rating meant a bank might not be allowed to expand lending, add new branches or merge with other companies. Banks with poor CRA ratings were also hit with stiff fines. [4]

This rewrite of CRA gave activist groups like ACORN and NACA unprecedented power. Protests often held in bank lobbies or in front of the homes of bank officials, coupled with threats of litigation, allowed these groups to extort huge sums of money from financial institutions. [5] In response, financial institutions began allocating more funds to low-income, high risk borrowers.

Loans started being funded on the basis of race and often little else.[6] CRA became an excuse for lowering credit standards. Many Democrats have claimed that banks subject to the CRA represented few of the mortgages that led to our current problems. Not true. Nearly 4 in 10 subprime loans made between 2004 and 2007 were funded by CRA-covered banks such as Washington Mutual and Indy Mac. [7] Many other subprime lenders not covered by the Act were, in effect, beholden to CRA mandates because they were owned by banks that were subject to it. [8]

Since CRA only covered banks, the Clinton administration created a separate department at Housing and Urban Development to police "fair lending" policies at other institutions such as Countrywide and lending behemoths, Fannie Mae and Freddie Mac. [9]

The result? Countrywide made more loans to minorities than any other lender, and not surprisingly, was one of the first lenders overwhelmed by loan defaults. [10]

As groups like ACORN ran their intimidation campaigns against local banks, they eventually hit a roadblock. Banks told them they could afford to reduce their credit standards by only a little – since Fannie Mae and Freddie Mac refused to buy up these risky loans for resale on the secondary market. ACORN realized that unless Fannie and Freddie were willing to relax their credit standards as well, local banks wouldn't make enough loans to individuals with bad credit histories or with very little money for a down payment. [11]

Democrats such as Barney Frank (D-MA), Ted Kennedy (D-MA) and Maxine Waters (D-CA) allied with the Clinton administration to broaden the acceptability of these risky mortgage loans. When the Republicans attempted to restore fiscal sanity by paring back the CRA, they were stymied by Democrats — and by ACORN. [12]

In 1995, an unrestrained Clinton administration announced a comprehensive strategy to push homeownership in America to new heights – regardless of the compromise in credit standards that this would require. Fannie and Freddie were given massive subprime lending quotas, which would increase to about half of their total business by the end of the decade. [13]

Then came the single most catastrophic decision leading to the housing crisis: Clinton legalized the securitization of these mortgages, which allowed Fannie and Freddie to finance everything by buying loans from banks, then repackaging and securitizing them for resale on the open market. [14]

Thus began the meltdown. In 1997, Bear Stearns handled the first securitization of CRA loans — $385 million worth — all guaranteed by Freddie Mac. [15] Subsequently, a subprime market that had been a relatively modest part of the mortgage business with $35 billion in loans in 1994 soared to $1 trillion by 2008. [16]

Regrettably, this massive bundling of subprime mortgages wound up poisoning the entire mortgage industry.

Fannie and Freddie used their "affordable housing mission" to avoid restrictions on their accumulation of mortgage portfolios. They argued that if they were constrained, they wouldn't be able to adequately subsidize affordable housing. As a result, by 1997, Fannie was offering mortgages with a down payment of only 3 percent. By 2001, it was purchasing mortgages with "no down payment at all." [17]

By 2007, Fannie and Freddie were *required* by Housing and Urban Development to show that 55 percent of their mortgage purchases were to low and moderate income borrowers, and, within that goal, 38 percent of all purchases were to come from underserved areas (usually inner cities). [18] Meeting these goals almost certainly required them to purchase loans with low down payments and other deficiencies that would characterize them as subprime or Alt-A. [19]

The decline in lending standards was also facilitated by competition. Fannie and Freddie were now competing with private-label mortgage lenders such as investment and commercial banks to fulfill the affordable housing requirements imposed by Congress.

The inevitable result? Everyone was scraping the bottom of the mortgage barrel in search of new borrowers.

Once the looser lending standards were offered to low and middle income buyers, it was naïve to believe that they wouldn't lead to more relaxed standards for higher-income and prime borrowers as well. This spreading of looser standards to the prime market greatly increased the availability of credit for mortgages, and ultimately led to the bubble in housing prices. [20]

Unsurprisingly, Fannie Mae and Freddie Mac were huge campaign contributors to Congress, spending millions to ensure no reform would be implemented to restrict them. In all, 354 members of Congress received funds. The bulk of the money went to Democrats. [21] Between 1989 and 2008, the leading recipient of Fannie/Freddie campaign money was Connecticut Democrat Chris Dodd, the Senate Banking Committee Chairman, who collected more than $165,000. Dodd opposed restrictions on Fannie and Freddie and pushed hard for the continuance of subprime loans. In second place was then-Senator Barack Obama, who, in just three years in the U.S. Senate, took in $126,000. Third, was Massachusetts Democrat John Kerry, who received $110,000. [22]

Since the 1990s, Fannie Mae and Freddie Mac have been run by Democrats. From 1991 to 1998, Fannie Mae was led by James Johnson, a long-time aide to former Democrat Vice President Walter Mondale. Johnson made headlines in 2008 when Barack Obama picked him to chair his vice presidential selection committee. He had to resign in disgrace when it was revealed he had taken out at least five below-market real estate loans totaling more than $7 million from Countrywide Financial Corporation. [23]

Johnson's successor as head of Fannie Mae, Franklin Raines, had previously served as a budget director to President Bill Clinton. From 1995 to 2005, Raines pocketed nearly $100 million in compensation before leaving because of a scandal involving profit and loss reports manipulated to increase his annual bonuses. [24]

Another well-known Democrat, Jamie Gorelick, served as vice chair of Fannie from 1998 to 2003. Prior to that, she was Janet Reno's Deputy Attorney General during the Clinton years, when the Clinton Justice Department was aggressively compelling banks to make subprime loans to unworthy borrowers. [25] And Rahm Emanuel, current White House Chief of Staff, also served as a director at Freddie Mac. [26]

Most Americans are not aware that Fannie and Freddie, while lining the pockets of politicians, also funnels hundreds of millions of dollars to a host of leftist groups and causes promoting the Democrat agenda. [27] The grant-making arms of Fannie and Freddie – specifically the Fannie Mae Foundation and the Freddie Mac Foundation – gives tens of millions of dollars each year to predominantly left-wing organizations such as the American Civil Liberties Union; the NAACP and National Urban League; the left-wing financier the Tides Foundation; pro-illegal immigration groups like the Mexican American Legal Defense and Education Fund, and the National Council of La Raza; pro-Democrat community activist groups like ACORN; and former president Jimmy Carter's Carter Center. [28]

The Republicans were not oblivious to Fannie and Freddie's problems. Bush's 2001 budget called runaway subprime lending a "potential problem" and warned of "strong repercussions in financial markets." [29] In July 2003, Senators Chuck Hagel (R-NE), Elizabeth Dole (R-NC) and John Sununu (R-NH) introduced legislation to address regulation of them. The bill was blocked by the Democrats. [30] In September 2003 Bush's Treasury Secretary, John Snow, proposed what *The New York Times* called "the most significant regulatory overhaul (of Fannie and Freddie) in the housing finance industry since the savings and loan crisis a decade ago." [31]

Did the Democrats in Congress welcome reform? Here's how Barney Frank

(D-MA), the ranking Democrat on the Financial Services Committee, responded:

"I do not think we are facing any kind of a crisis. That is, in my view, the two government sponsored entities we are talking about here, Fannie Mae and Freddie Mac, are not in crisis.... I do not think at this point there is a problem with a threat to the Treasury.... I believe that we, as the Federal Government, have probably done too little rather than too much to push them to meet the goals of affordable housing and to set reasonable goals." [32]

In 2005, Republican Senators Hagel, Sununu, Dole, and later John McCain reintroduced legislation to once again address regulation of Fannie and Freddie. In essence, the bill would have required Fannie and Freddie to eliminate their investments in risky subprime loans.[33] According to Kevin Hassett, writing in *Bloomberg.com*, "if that bill had become law, then the world today would be different." [34]

But the legislation didn't become law for a single reason: Democrats opposed it on a party-line vote in the Senate Banking Committee, signaling that this would be a partisan issue. Republicans, tied in knots by the tight Democrat opposition, couldn't even get the Senate to vote on the bill. [35]

Had the bill passed in 2005, the mortgage meltdown would have been far less intense. In 2005, 2006 and 2007, approximately $1 trillion of these terrible mortgage loans were funded by Fannie and Freddie at a time when housing prices were at their highest. When housing prices fell dramatically, losses from those mortgages turned out to be tremendous.

Bottom line: if Fannie Mae and Freddie Mac weren't buying these subprime loans, the market for them would likely not have existed.

Rep. Artur Davis (D-AL) now admits Democrats were in error:

"Like a lot of my Democratic colleagues, I was too slow to appreciate the recklessness of Fannie and Freddie. I defended their efforts to encourage affordable home ownership when in retrospect I should have heeded the concerns raised by the regulator in 2004. Frankly, I wish my Democratic colleagues would admit when it comes to Fannie and Freddie, we were wrong." [36]

Democrats being "wrong" apparently had no effect on the mainstream media. In 2008, an inaccurate report from the *Associated Press* claimed that the mortgage meltdown was largely due to President Bush's failure to act in 2005. In an article entitled, "Bush administration ignored clear warnings," the AP claimed that the Bush administration backed off proposed crackdowns on no-money-down, interest-only mortgages years before the economy collapsed. The report went on to state that the Bush administration bowed to "aggressive lobbying" by banks and delayed doing anything for a year. This, said the AP, is "emblematic of a philosophy that trusted market forces and discounted the need for government intervention in the economy." [37]

Some Republicans were complicit in not preventing the mortgage crisis. But as *Investor's Business Daily* points out: Fannie and Freddie were created by Democrats, regulated by Democrats, largely run by Democrats and protected by Democrats. [38]

As demonstrated throughout this entire chapter, it was precisely "government intervention in the economy," via Fannie Mae and Freddie Mac, which was principally responsible for the subprime meltdown. All this vital information was kept from the American voter during the 2008 presidential election. In fact, it was shocking when candidate Obama told the American voters with a straight face that the Republicans caused the mortgage crisis, considering it was one of his key advisors who ran one of the agencies that made the crisis what it was.

What have the Democrats learned from the mortgage debacle for which they were largely responsible? Incredibly, as recently as June 2009, Barney Frank sent a letter to the heads of Fannie and Freddie urging them to *loosen* lending standards for condo buyers, claiming the new lending rules "may be too onerous." [39]

Owning a home has long been considered "the American dream." Gross fiscal irresponsibility, chiefly orchestrated by Democrats, has turned that dream into a nightmare for millions. Behind it all? The conviction that buying a home, historically considered a privilege, should be regarded as a right—regardless of the financial havoc it has wreaked on the nation.

Purchasing a home is a huge financial responsibility — which is precisely why the process of obtaining a mortgage ought to be relatively difficult.

Democrats, many of whom believe "social justice" trumps every other consideration — including fiscal sanity — turned that process on its head.

Chapter 7

REPUBLICAN DEREGULATION — OR DEMOCRAT DISINFORMATION?

Perhaps the most successful myth perpetrated during the 2008 election campaign was the notion that Republicans went on an eight year binge of massive financial deregulation that caused the economic crisis.

There is only a small problem with this story: it isn't true.

Some myths die harder than others. This is certainly one of them.

The media and Democrats blamed the housing bubble and ensuing financial crisis on "deregulation" by the Bush Administration. "Deregulation" is generally defined as the repeal or easing of particular rules. [1]

House Speaker Nancy Pelosi, for instance, stated in September 2008 that "the Bush Administration's eight long years of failed deregulation policies have resulted in our nation's largest bailout ever, leaving the American taxpayers on the hook potentially for billions of dollars." [2]   Similarly, in the second presidential debate, candidate Barack Obama claimed that "the biggest problem in this whole process was the deregulation of the financial system." [3]

Most viewers probably accepted this allegation, because Republicans are generally in favor of deregulation. There is one problem, however, with this claim: financial services were not deregulated during the Bush administration.

Although there has been significant deregulation in the U.S. economy during the last 30 years, virtually none of it has occurred in the financial sector. The only important legislation with any effect on financial risk-taking was the Federal Deposit Insurance Corporation Improvement Act (FDICIA) of 1991, which was passed during the first Bush administration after the collapse of the savings and loans. Rather than deregulate, FDICIA substantially *tightened* commercial bank and S&L regulations, including regulating a bank's capital levels when they decline below adequate levels. [4]

As for Republican deregulation, to which measures were Democrats referring exactly? Speaking for his party in 2008, Senate Majority Leader Harry Reid (D–NV) claimed that Republican Phil Gramm, co-sponsor of the Gramm–Leach–Bliley Act of 1999, "was responsible for deregulation in the financial services industries that paved the way for much of this crisis to occur." [5]

According to *Investor's Business Daily* this claim was incorrect: "Gramm-Leach-Bliley didn't make regulation go away. It modernized the rules to fit the realities of the financial markets (*author's note: by allowing banks and securities firms to be affiliated under the same holding company*). Washington doesn't always get the rules right, but in this case it did...Gramm-Leach-Bliley didn't take down the firewalls between deposit-based banking and investments. Banks (couldn't) play the stock market or trade credit default swaps with your savings account. Investment and banking operations (ran) under one corporate roof, but otherwise (stayed) separate...So why did banks and investment houses get into so much trouble?...They made mistakes that had nothing to do with the 1999 law." [6]

What were those mistakes? Investing in bad mortgages and in mortgage-backed securities, both of which they were allowed to do *prior* to the law's passage. More to the point, although the bill's key sponsors were indeed Republicans, the bill was supported by the Clinton administration and signed into law by the president.

In fact, Gramm-Leach-Bliley was likely to have *alleviated* rather than worsened the current financial crisis. [7] Charles W. Calomiris, professor at Columbia Business School and author of *U.S. Bank Deregulation in Historical Perspective* goes one step further: "Wasn't the ability for commercial and investment banks to merge (the result of Gramm-Leach-Bliley) a major stabilizer to the financial system this past year? Indeed, it allowed Bear Stearns and Merrill Lynch to be acquired by J. P. Morgan and Bank of America, and allowed Goldman Sachs and Morgan Stanley to convert to bank holding companies to help shore up their positions during the mid-September (2008) bear runs on their stocks." [8]

Was the Bush administration the deregulator Democrats claimed it to be? A 2008 report, *Regulatory Agency Spending Reaches New Height* from Washington University's Weidenbaum Center, put President Bush's regulatory activity in historical context. The report explained that when it came to spending on regulatory agencies, President Bush was almost in a class by himself, with an increase of almost 68% during his terms. In constant dollars, Bush regulatory budget increases greatly exceeded those of predecessors Clinton, Bush 41, Reagan, Carter, Nixon and Johnson.[9] And the *Competitive Enterprise Institute,* which tracks regulation across the entire federal government, reported that the Bush administration set an all-time record in 2004, when it published more than 75,000 pages of proposed and enacted rules in the Federal Register.[10]

A primary example of President Bush's regulatory activity was the Sarbanes-Oxley Act of 2002, which significantly *increased* disclosure requirements for public companies. Here's how the left-leaning *New York Times* described Sarbanes-Oxley on its front page, April 25, 2002:

"House and Senate negotiators agreed ... on a broad overhaul of corporate fraud, accounting and securities laws aimed at curbing the rampant abuses that have shaken Wall Street ... Some lawmakers called it the most sweeping securities legislation since the 1930s."

Democrats and the mainstream media have also referred to the Commodity Futures Modernization Act (CFMA) of 2000, and more specifically to its treatment of credit default swaps, as further evidence of Republican deregulation. This is disingenuous or an outright lie for one reason: credit default swaps were *already* exempted from regulation and all this bill did was clarify they weren't regulated by the Commodity Futures Trading Commission. [11] Furthermore, the bill was signed into law by Bill Clinton.

Question: how does something that was never regulated in the first place become deregulated?

What *are* credit default swaps? They are insurance policies covering losses on securities in the event of a default or bankruptcy. Financial institutions buy them to protect themselves. As it turns out, the market for credit default swaps *not tied* to the housing crisis has functioned normally. [12] Those markets never lost liquidity and their default rate, thus far, has been low. As *The Wall Street Journal* explained, the financial crisis was not caused by turmoil in the credit default swap market, but from soured mortgage loans. [13]

The Bush administration has also been blamed for "deregulating" Wall Street investment banks with a 2004 rule change known a Basel II. Rather than deregulation, however, Basel II was a regulatory leap for the Securities and Exchange Commission (SEC), which had traditionally focused on protecting individual investors. Under this new rule, the SEC would collect additional data from the parent companies of brokerages and require new monthly and quarterly reports. [14]

The rationale behind Basel II was to create a common set of global banking standards and a more intensive study of asset risks in order to yield a more efficient use of capital, and a more stable financial system. [15]

The United States was not the only country which adopted these standards. The world's central bankers also embraced Basel II largely to avoid crises such as the U.S. savings and loan disaster of the 1980s. [16]

Rather than deregulating them, Basel II required investment firms to provide a *more* detailed explanation of the risks they were undertaking. Fixed capital ratios, such as the ability to lend ten dollars for every dollar in assets (a 10-1 ratio), were replaced with mathematical models that crunched historical data to determine how risky an institution's assets were. [17] As opposed to the fixed-ratio method in which all assets were equally weighted, these mathematical models gave greater or lesser weight to certain assets—which in turn increased or decreased the amount of leverage an institution could employ in the lending process. Some assets were considered so safe that lending ratios as high as 30-1 were allowed.

Unfortunately, AAA-rated mortgage-backed securities were incorrectly considered to be some of the safest assets an institution could own—as safe as cash. This precipitated far too much leverage in the financial markets, which crashed when the housing market turned south. Thus, we now know that Basel II, though not the *cause* of the financial crisis, contributed to the *size* of it.

The Wall Street Journal put the SEC's actions in perspective: "As for SEC, if commissioners took on a massive burden in 2004 without realizing they had signed up to safeguard the world's financial system, then they overreached.

But they sure didn't 'deregulate'." [18]

And despite Democrat and media efforts to paint Basel II as an example of "Republican deregulation," it was unanimously approved by the SEC commissioners and Democrat Annette Nazareth, who ran the market regulation division at the time. [19]

Even though Democrats attempt to paint deregulation as a Republican-only policy, it has been a bipartisan undertaking since the late 1970s. The Carter administration deregulated airlines and certain financial sectors, like savings and loan institutions. The Reagan administration deregulated trucking, railroads and other industries. The Clinton administration deregulated foreign trade and the telecommunication industry.

If the Democrats were truly looking for the kind of deregulation at the heart of the financial crisis, the Clinton administration's decision to allow Fannie Mae and Freddie Mac to purchase and securitize subprime mortgages would be a great place to start. These measures ultimately made it possible for Fannie and Freddie to add *a trillion dollars in junk loans* to their balance sheets and sell securitized "assets" to investors around the world. We are now paying for the consequences.

Republican deregulation caused the financial crisis? Pure myth.

Chapter 8

EASY MONEY LEADS TO HARD TIMES

What is normal? With respect to interest rates, I discovered that finding the answer to that question was the key to understanding why the global financial crisis occurred.

This chapter reveals that countries whose interest rates were lowered below historical norms suffered severe housing booms and busts similar to those in the U.S.

Lower interest rates had a cascading effect: they led to a cheaper dollar, which in turn led to a sudden spike in oil prices and a subsequent slowdown in the world economy.

Economics is tough sledding for most readers. I hope this chapter will help them connect the economic dots.

The economic crisis in 2008 began with a sharp rise in U.S. housing prices between 2003 and 2005. This eventually led to a housing bubble which burst, causing financial destruction for both homeowners and financial institutions.

Without a housing boom, there would have been no bust. And while home prices escalated in the U.S., they also rose sharply in other countries as well. Why did other countries' home prices also rise dramatically around the same time? Before that question is answered, some background information is necessary.

The Organization for Economic Co-Operation and Development calculated that inflation-adjusted U.S. housing prices rose by 5.4 percent per year in the U.S. from 2000 to 2006 — in other words, 5.4 percent *in addition* to the general rate of inflation. [1] This is a national average, as housing prices increased substantially more in states such as California, Florida, Arizona and Nevada.

Yet that 5.4 percent U.S. figure pales in comparison with housing inflation in other countries during the same period: 6.7 percent in Canada and Sweden, 8.8 percent in Britain, 9.5 percent in France, 8.3 percent in Ireland, and 11.2 percent in Spain. [2] And non-inflation-adjusted annual housing price increases accelerated to reach around 30 percent in Poland, Bulgaria and Slovakia and over 25 percent in Russia. [3]

There were, however, certain countries where prices didn't rise much, such as Austria, Germany, Netherlands, Italy and Belgium. [4] Why did housing prices rise in some countries but not others? John Taylor, senior fellow at the Hoover Institute and the developer of the "Taylor Rule" for determining how central banks should adjust interest rates, explains why this occurred. According to Taylor, countries whose short-term interest rates were set lower than historical norms had the biggest booms. Conversely, countries with the smallest deviation in rates had the smallest housing booms, or none at all. [5] Chart I demonstrates this correlation:

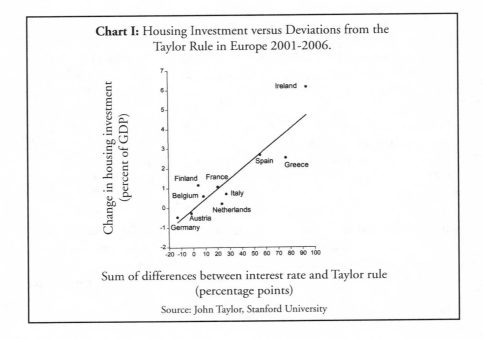

Chart I: Housing Investment versus Deviations from the Taylor Rule in Europe 2001-2006.

Change in housing investment (percent of GDP)

Sum of differences between interest rate and Taylor rule (percentage points)

Source: John Taylor, Stanford University

As one can see, Spain, the country with the largest deviation from the norm, had the biggest housing boom, while the country with the smallest deviation, Austria, had the smallest boom. [6] Thus, the above question can be answered with two words: easy money.

Foreign countries that mimicked prolonged rate cuts similar to the U.S. experienced the same housing boom and bust we did.

What were those prolonged rate cuts? The Federal Reserve reduced the federal funds rate from 6.5% in January 2001 to 1.75% by year-end, and then to 1% in 2003. It kept rates that low until June 2004. [7] This caused borrowing and lending to explode, particularly in real estate. Fannie Mae, Freddie Mac, mortgage-backed securities and credit derivatives were the conduits.

Current Treasury Secretary Timothy Geithner explained candidly on the *Charlie Rose Show* that the Federal Reserve played a critical role in the financial meltdown, admitting, "…monetary policy around the world was too loose too long. And that created this huge boom in asset prices, money chasing risk." [8]

The following chart illustrates what U.S. interest rates should have been had they remained within historical norms:

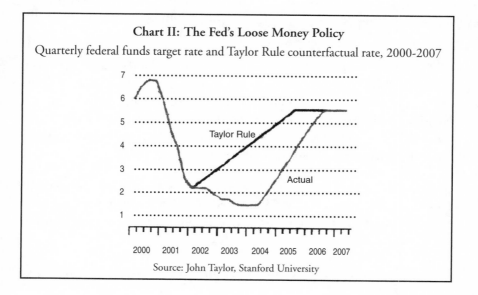

Chart II: The Fed's Loose Money Policy

Quarterly federal funds target rate and Taylor Rule counterfactual rate, 2000-2007

Source: John Taylor, Stanford University

America's housing boom was further magnified by lending policies designed to promote home ownership —100% financing, adjustable-rate and interest-only mortgages, and no income verification loans. Looser underwriting standards caused by intense pressure on lending institutions by politicians in Washington further amplified the boom by bringing more buyers into the housing market — many of whom were unqualified.

The inevitable decline in the U.S. housing market began in 2006, when home prices became unaffordable. What initially started as defaults on highly leveraged subprime mortgages spread to prime mortgages as well. As a result of steep price declines, many homeowners were "underwater on their loans:" the value of the home had become less than the amount of the outstanding mortgage(s).

This created a disincentive for many homeowners to continue to make payments. The lending institutions that made those loans ended up taking those properties back through foreclosure, and because housing prices had dropped significantly below the amount those institutions had lent out, they suffered gargantuan losses.

In response, financial institutions tightened lending standards. Beginning in August 2007, government actions worsened and prolonged the crisis: by focusing on a shortage of liquidity, rather than on the risky assets held by financial institutions, the government spent trillions of dollars trying to solve the wrong problem. [9]

By April 2008, the Federal Reserve had once again sharply lowered the federal funds rate from 5.25% to 2%. The most noticeable effect of those cuts was the steep depreciation of the dollar. The weakened dollar contributed to a large increase in oil prices, which doubled from about $70 per barrel in August 2007 to $147 in July 2008 (before eventually plummeting as expectations of a worldwide economic slowdown increased). [10]

In turn, the dramatic rise in oil prices caused a worldwide downturn in Gross Domestic Product and industrial production in 2008, which was less severe in the U.S. and Canada, and more severe in Europe, Scandinavia, Japan and the rest of Asia. [11]

Most of these countries had no significant exposure to the U.S. mortgage market and no abnormal incidence of bank failures. What they did have in common with the U.S was what ten of the eleven post-World War II U.S. recessions had in common: a vulnerability to sudden crude oil price increases. Around the world, the rising cost of oil reduced the profitability of producing and transporting goods. The drop in corporate earnings led to falling stock prices, which led to reduced household wealth and spending. And once the economies of our major trading partners started falling, the U.S. economy slowed even further as our exports fell sharply. [12]

Was all this the fault of Republicans? The Federal Reserve is a politically independent agency that was headed by Alan Greenspan for 18 years under four different administrations, both Democrat and Republican. Greenspan is primarily responsible for keeping interest rates too low for too long. Despite all the misconceptions promoted by Democrats and the media, Mr. Greenspan — not the Republican Party — deserves the lion's share of the blame for the economic meltdown of 2008.

Chapter 9

LESS TAXES, MORE REVENUE

In recent American history three presidents, Republicans Ronald Reagan and George W. Bush — and Democrat icon John Fitzgerald Kennedy — all lowered taxes in response to economic recessions.

In all three cases, more money flowed into federal coffers than expected, and all three recessions ended.

How many more times does the same idea have to work before today's Democrats get it?

Despite compelling evidence, Democrats continue to insist that raising taxes is the proper prescription for everything that ails America.

Are they right? Americans should ask themselves a commonsense question: are you better off having more of your own money in your own pocket — or sending it to Washington D.C.?

Many Americans have blindly accepted several myths about Republicans and the Bush administration — especially the one about giving tax cuts to the rich while cutting spending for the poor. The mainstream media also spread the myth that the budget deficits resulted chiefly from the "irresponsible" Bush tax cuts.

Neither of these claims, however, is supported by the facts.

If the critics were correct, when Bush's tax cuts took effect, the share of income taxes paid by the wealthiest Americans should have gone down. Reality, though, was very different. In 2000, before the cuts, the top 10% of earners paid 67.3% of all federal personal income taxes. In 2006, after the cuts, the top 10% of earners paid 70.8% of taxes, a significant increase.[1] Critics argue that this was true, but only because the top earners' share of income climbed so much. Treasury Department data contradict this claim: The top 10% received about 46% of the 2000 income and about 47.3% in 2006. [2]

In other words, their tax burden went *up,* not down, relative to their income.

Why do Republicans favor tax cuts? Because they benefit every income level by encouraging investment and job creation. When tax rates are lower, people have more incentive to work, save and invest, and less incentive to avoid or evade taxes. On the other hand, raising capital gain and dividend rates discourages investment, and raising income taxes may sometimes discourage work or the reporting of income.

Taxes do affect behavior.

Contrary to the myth that President Bush cut taxes only for the wealthy, the 2001 tax cut reduced taxes for *every* income-tax payer in the country. Bush reduced the bottom tax rate from 15% to 10% and increased the refundable child tax credit from $500 per child to $1,000 per child. Millions of lower income taxpayers were removed from the tax rolls, shifting the burden to those at the top, even *after* their taxes were cut. [3] By 2006, the bottom 50% of earners in this country paid only 3% of all income taxes, down from 3.9% they paid in 2000. [4]

Realty check: if one compares the taxes that taxpayers paid under Democrat Bill Clinton to the taxes paid after the Bush tax cuts were enacted, lower and middle-income borrowers at all income levels paid less taxes under Bush.[5] Yet, if you asked Americans, most of them believe Clinton was better for them tax-wise. Such is the power of the liberal mainstream media's ability to misinform the public.

Reality check #2: despite the myth that the poor received a smaller percentage of government spending, antipoverty spending increased by 39% under President Bush and reached a record 16.3% of all federal spending in 2004, up from 14.9% in 2000. [6]

Reality check #3: despite critics' contention that budget deficits under the Bush administration were caused by "irresponsible" tax cuts, *The Wall Street Journal* reveals the same old story: "the cause of the deficits was an explosion in federal spending." As a *result* of the tax cuts, federal tax revenues surged under Bush: in the four years after the 2003 tax cuts, tax receipts exploded by $785 billion. [7]

Historically — and quite surprisingly — tax revenues collected by the federal government have almost always come in at about 18% of Gross Domestic Product (GDP), regardless of the top tax rate. Table 1 shows that the top marginal income tax rate topped 90% during the 1950s and that revenues averaged 17.2% of GDP. In the 1990s, the top marginal income tax rate averaged just 36%, and tax revenues averaged 18.3% of GDP. And from 2000-2006, revenues were 18.1% of Gross Domestic Product. [8]

Table 1	**Regardless of Tax Rates, Revenues Remain Around 18 Percent of GDP**	
Decade	**Average Top Income Tax Rate**	**Average Tax Revenues as a Percentage of GDP**
1950s	90.5%	17.2%
1960s	80.3%	17.9%
1970s	70.2%	18.0%
1980s	48.4%	18.3%
1990s	36.7%	18.6%
2000-2006	37.3%	18.1%

Sources: Office of Management and Budget, *Historical Tables, Budget of the United States Government, Fiscal Year 2007* (Washington, D.C.: U.S. Government Printing Office, 2006), pp. 25-26, Table 1.3, at *www.whitehouse.gov/omb/budget/fy2007/pdf/hist.pdf* (January 16, 2007), and Internal Revenue Service, "U.S. Individual Income Tax: Personal Exemptions and Lowest and Highest Bracket Tax Rates, and Tax Base for Regular Tax, Tax Years 1913-2005," at *www.irs.gov/pub/irs-soi/histaba.pdf* (January 16, 2007).

The 2003 Bush tax cuts lowered income, capital gains and dividend tax rates. To illustrate how tax cuts grew the economy, Gross Domestic Product grew at an annual rate of just 1.7% in the six quarters before the 2003 Bush tax cuts. In the six quarters following the tax cuts, the growth rate was a robust 4.1%. While some growth was naturally occurring, the sudden and dramatic turnaround in the economy began at the exact moment these pro-growth policies were enacted. [9]

What Democrats and the left don't seem to understand is that the best way to increase federal tax revenues is to expand the economy. Pro-growth policies, such as low marginal tax rates, restrained federal spending, minimal regulation, and free trade help accomplish that. [10] Chart 2 illustrates this fact — as the economy grows, tax revenues grow with it. Conversely, we cannot increase tax revenues with policies that slow our economy, such as tax increases.

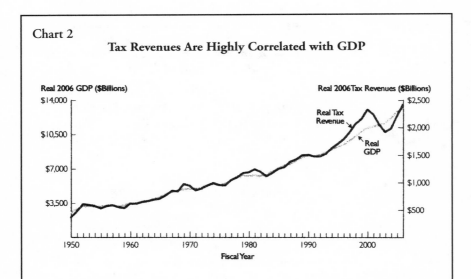

Chart 2

Tax Revenues Are Highly Correlated with GDP

Sources: Office of Management and Budget, *Historical Tables, Budget of the United States Government, Fiscal Year 2007* (Washington, D.C.: U.S. Government Printing Office, 2006), pp. 25-26, Table 1.3, at *www.whitehouse.gov/omb/budget/fy2007/pdf/hist.pdf*
(January 16, 2007), and Internal Revenue Service, "U.S. Individual Income Tax: Personal Exemptions and Lowest and Highest Bracket Tax Rates, and Tax Base for Regular Tax, Tax Years 1913-2005," at *www.irs.gov/pub/irs-soi/histaba.pdf* (January 16, 2007).

And yet, that's precisely what Democrats plan to do. Despite the rhetoric about cutting taxes for 95 percent of Americans, Obama and the Congressional Democrats may let the Bush tax cuts expire, which is equivalent to raising taxes. If that happens, the middle class, not just the upper class, will also be hit with massive tax increases, which will rise by *at least* $2.8 trillion between now and 2018. On average, 116 million taxpayers will see an increase of $1,800 in their annual tax bill. And 48 million married couples – the heart of the middle class Democrats say they want to help – will be hit with an average increase of $3,007. Even the elderly will take a big hit — $2,181 on average. And a single parent with two children making just $30,000 a year will have $1,600 added to his or her tax bill if the Bush tax cuts are allowed to expire. [11]

Regarding tax cuts, Democrats would be wise to emulate the policies of a former Democrat president who said the following:

"It is a paradoxical truth that tax rates are too high today and tax revenues are too low, and the soundest way to raise the revenues in the long run is to cut the rates now… The purpose of cutting taxes now is not to incur a budget deficit, but to achieve the more prosperous, *expanding economy* (italics mine) which can bring a budget surplus." [12]

The author of those words? John F. Kennedy, Democrat icon. He understood how an expanding economy benefits everyone, poor and rich, stating, "A rising tide lifts all boats." [13]

In conclusion, taxation is an extension of ideology. Democrats favor higher rates of taxation because they believe government is the best entity for allocating resources. Underlying this assertion is the Democrats' assumption that most Americans are incapable of running their own lives and should defer to the "superior" wisdom of the political ruling class.

Republicans favor lower tax rates because they believe individual Americans have a far better idea of what to do with their hard-earned money than the bureaucrats in Washington, D.C. They believe Americans with additional amounts of disposable income will spend and invest it, which grows the economy.

Taxation is also an extension of power. Democrats want more of it centralized in Washington, D.C. Republicans want it spread among individuals across the country. Democrats want to be the nation's arbiters of "fairness" and "social justice." Republicans believe fairness and social justice can be distorted beyond all recognition by elitist political ideology, so it is far better if such concepts are determined by millions of Americans free to act in their own self-interest.

Democrats want higher taxes to pursue their goals. Republicans want lower taxes so Americans can pursue their *own* goals. The contrast between the parties couldn't be sharper – which is something freedom-loving Americans should remember when they head to the polls in 2010.

Chapter 10

WHO'S THE PARTY OF WALL STREET AND BIG MONEY?

Like most Americans, I bought into the idea that Republicans were the "party of Wall Street and Big Business."

What I learned was surprisingly different.

I suspect most Americans would be shocked to learn that Democrats, who often refer to themselves as the "party of the people," are anything but.

The research I did putting this chapter together was a real eye-opener. The so-called party of the people received the bulk of campaign contributions from the country's largest corporations, banks and Wall Street firms.

As the saying goes "money talks." As I found out, it does most of its talking to Democrats.

When the economic crisis exploded in September 2008, most people were quick to point the finger at Wall Street for causing the problem. Both presidential candidates were among the first to publicly blame "greedy" Wall Street bankers for the turmoil.

For most voters that meant the Republicans caused the problem. For years, Democrats have benefited by denouncing Republicans as the "money-hungry party of Wall Street" pulling the puppet strings of the politicians in Washington. This perception was a major factor in helping Obama and Congressional Democrats win a majority of the elections in 2008.

It's a useful story for Democrats, but it's not true. It is actually Democrats themselves who get most of Wall Street's political donations.

And it wasn't just Wall Street that poured money into the Democrats' coffers. 19 of the top 20 corporate donors in the 2008 national elections leaned Democrat. Of the top 100, only 10 leaned Republican. [1]

Here is a breakdown of the largest donors in the financial sector and the percentage of money they gave to Democrats in the 2008 election cycle: [2]

- Goldman Sachs   74% (versus 23% to Republicans)
- Citigroup   61% (versus 33%)
- J P Morgan Chase + Co. 54% (versus 36%)
- Morgan Stanley   53% (versus 43%)
- Bank of America   46% (versus 35%)

So why has Wall Street and Big Money tilted towards the Democrats? Despite their free market rhetoric, bankers and big business don't really want free markets. They prefer expansive government intervention in the form of regulations and protectionism that make it difficult for smaller businesses to compete. Democrats are more than willing to accommodate them with their policies.

An example is the 2009 cap and trade bill, rejected by all but eight Republicans, but passed by the Democratically-controlled House of Representatives. There's billions of dollars to be made in auctioning off permits to emit carbon dioxide, and to manage a so-called "carbon offset" market. This is one of the primary reasons General Electric, a huge Democrat donor, and its employees spent $20 million lobbying Washington to pass the cap and trade measure and why Goldman Sachs, another huge Democrat donor, is heavily invested in the "carbon offset" market. [3] If passed, this bill will benefit big business and government at the expense of the American people.

There's also a cultural issue. Most of the Wall Street players are not social conservatives, and feel more of an affinity toward the more socially liberal Democrat Party.

It is likely Democrat voters themselves don't realize their party has become the party of Wall Street and big business elitists. They probably have no idea that nearly 75 percent of all hedge fund and buyout-firm donations went to Democrat presidential candidate Obama, or that, in 2007, Senator Charles Schumer (D-NY), who sat on the Senate finance and banking committees, fought on behalf of hedge funds to oppose a controversial tax-code change. [4] The proposed bill, which Schumer was able to defeat, would have closed a loophole that allows billionaire hedge fund managers to pay a much smaller share of their income in taxes than many middle-income Americans. [5]

The White House has also rolled out the welcome mat for big business elitists. After Obama was elected president, he appointed Rahm Emanuel as his Chief of Staff. Emanuel was a former investment banker at Wasserstein Perella. Another of the president's key economic advisors is Robert Rubin, treasury secretary for the Clinton administration, former chairman of Goldman Sachs — and the man chiefly responsible for bringing Citigroup to the brink of insolvency. And let's not forget Jeffrey Immelt, CEO of General Electric, who was awarded a seat on Obama's economic advisory board. [6]

This unholy relationship between the Democrat Party and big business also extended to insurance giant AIG, which received $180 billion in taxpayer-founded bailouts. Unsurprisingly, the three largest recipients of donations from AIG employees were Democrats Chris Dodd at $280,238, Charles Schumer at $111,875 and Barack Obama at $107,332. [7] In addition it was Chris Dodd who added the provision to the $787 billion stimulus bill that allowed AIG employees to collect $450 million in bonuses agreed to before the passage of the bill. After public outrage, Dodd was questioned and at first denied knowing about *his own amendment*. [8]

If Dodd were a Republican, I'm certain the media would have gone after him like rabid dogs.

No discussion of the relationship between the Democrat Party and big business can be complete without mentioning Fannie Mae and Freddie Mac, whose close relationships with Democrat politicians such as Barney Frank and Chris Dodd allowed them to avoid restrictions on their risky lending practices. (Author's note: see chapter six for more details)

Still, Republicans remain the party of Wall Street and big business in the public's mind. This carefully crafted misconception by the mainstream media and Democrats was most likely the deciding factor of the 2008 presidential and congressional elections. Perhaps if more voters had been aware of reality, the election may have turned out differently.

Don't bet on the media or Democrats ever altering this enduring misconception. Being cast as the party of the people is a huge advantage in any election. Americans should remember this in 2010, when Democrats are once again campaigning as the "party of main street America."

Democrats are the party of "Main Street?" The party of Wall Street is more like it.

Chapter 11

CODDLING CLINTON

Bill Clinton presided over a great economy. I use the word "presided" because much of the credit for that economy should go to Republicans who pushed conservative polices after they became the majority party in Congress in 1994.

Ironically, the reason Republicans became a majority was due to the public's growing disenchantment with Clinton's liberal tendencies — pork-barrel spending, increased taxes and the attempt to nationalize health care.

Does this sound familiar?

If you asked Americans about the Bill Clinton years, most will say that he *created* a great economy. While it is true that Clinton *presided* over a prosperous economy, this was largely due to conservative policies pushed by the Republicans and the favorable economic environment he inherited.

When Clinton was elected in 1992, he immediately did what Democrats like to do – he pushed for a large tax increase in general, a huge tax on energy to drive down electricity usage, and an enormous increase in pork-barrel spending, including an attempt to have the federal government take over the entire health care system (commonly referred to as HillaryCare).[1]

Before he was able to push through his liberal agenda, Clinton was stopped by the Republican minorities in both the House and Senate. Although he was able to pass a hefty tax hike, Congressional Republicans were able to significantly scale it back. They also vetoed his pork-barrel stimulus package and killed his broad-based energy tax as well.[2] HillaryCare, a project worked on largely in secret, was exposed by Congressional Republicans as an enormously complex and expensive endeavor, and as a result, it collapsed under steady opposition.

Had Clinton been successful in nationalizing health care, there would have been a huge increase in government spending along with enormous tax increases to pay for it. Even without the passage of HillaryCare, the deficit as a percentage of Gross Domestic Product in 1993 was higher than any compiled by the highly-criticized Bush administration. * [3]

Shortly before the November 1994 mid-term elections, House GOP Whip Newt Gingrich and more than 300 House Republican candidates united to create a "Contract with America." This conservative alternative to the Clinton administration's liberal policies offered to provide American families major tax relief, cut taxes substantially for investors, make wholesale changes in the welfare system and balance the budget. [4]

Unhappy with the Clinton economy, Americans embraced this new direction. Not only did Republicans capture control of the Senate, but they also won a majority of seats in the House of Representatives for the first time in forty years. [5]

As usual, the media's reaction was biased. *ABC News* anchor Peter Jennings claimed the American people had a "temper tantrum," comparing voters to a "two-year old," with stomping feet," "rolling eyes" and "screaming." [6] Translation: voting for Republicans was irrational behavior.

A panicked Bill Clinton brought in political advisor Dick Morris to save his presidency. As described in his book, *Behind the Oval Office,* Morris instructed Clinton to "work to eliminate the deficit, require work for welfare, cut taxes and reduce the federal bureaucracy." [7]

Clinton embraced Morris' advice, commonly referred to as "triangulation," to govern more conservatively.   As a result, Clinton adopted many of the proposals in the Republican's "Contract with America." In August 1997, he signed into law a bipartisan balanced budget measure that not only restrained spending, but also included several important Republican tax-relief items. These items included a middle class tax cut, a nearly 30% cut in capital gains tax rates, a decrease in estate taxes, repeal of the alternative minimum tax on

* The federal deficit reached 3.9% of Gross Domestic Product at the end of 1993. The worst deficit under George W. Bush was in 2004 at 3.6% of GDP.

small businesses, and a new retirement savings account known as the Roth IRA.[8]

Just as important, the Republican Congress didn't impose or even threaten to impose the kind of dangerous domestic spending and regulatory programs that would harm the economy. "What proved critical," says former Congressional Budget Office Director June O' Neal, "was the absence of legislation that meddled with the economy or that had major long-run spending consequences on the budget." [9]

It wasn't just the conservative policies pushed by Republicans that helped curb Clinton's initial liberal impulses and allowed the economy to prosper during his presidency. Clinton also inherited a favorable environment as a result of two prior Republican administrations. The policies of the Reagan administration – ending the Cold War, deregulation, free trade, and falling inflation set the stage. They were reinforced by the policies of the first Bush administration – successfully quelling the threat to global peace from Iraq in the 1991 Gulf War and also placing a cap on government spending growth with the 1990 budget agreement ("pay-as-you-go rule"). These factors contributed far more to the emergence of a prosperous era than did Clintonomics. [10]

And Clinton didn't inherit a recession, as many mistakenly believe. The mild recession preceding Clinton ended in early 1991 and the recovery had already begun before he took office.[11] GDP growth showed that the U.S. economy was clearly expanding starting in March 1991. During the year ending in the second quarter of 1992 (before Clinton was elected) the economy expanded at a respectable 3 percent annual rate.[12]

Many on the left falsely claim that the 1993 tax increases by Clinton helped restore growth to the economy and deserve credit for the eventual budget surpluses. This idea is contradicted by Clinton Administration budget documents. In early 1995, nearly 18 months *after* enactment of the 1993 tax increase, the Clinton Administration's Office of Management and Budget projected budget deficits of more than $200 billion for the next 10 years. [13]

In other words, the economy grew in spite of, not because of, the Clinton tax hikes. [14]

The economy took off in 1995 when then-Federal Reserve Chairman Alan

Greenspan lowered interest rates. At the same time, Clinton was the beneficiary of a technological revolution and its resulting prosperity. The Pentium chip was released in March 1993 and Microsoft's Windows program followed in August 1995. These innovations made the Internet boom possible. [15]

Clinton did nothing specific to cause this boom. Microsoft, Oracle, Apple and the rest of the real companies that emerged during this technological revolution were products of the free market. In fact, the most significant action taken by the Clinton administration during the technological revolution was its anti-trust case against Microsoft. [16]

Clinton was also fortunate that the booming stock market of the 1990s, especially in the technology sector, created an explosion in capital gains revenue for the government. This event, along with globalization changes that were proceeding before Clinton took office, also created the favorable economic environment over which Clinton presided.

Clinton also benefited from the fact that Ronald Reagan defeated the Soviet Union and ended the Cold War, which allowed him to substantially reduce military spending. This economic benefit, or "peace dividend," proved crucial in generating the surpluses the Democrats keep reminding us about. According to a *Washington Post* article by John Shalikashvili, Chairman of the Joint Chiefs under Clinton and Clinton Defense Secretary William J. Perry, "This 'peace dividend,' amounting to about $100 billion a year, has been a major contributor to the balanced budget that our economy now enjoys." [17]

Unfortunately, Clinton went too far cutting defense spending. In 1990, defense spending represented almost 30 percent of the total annual federal budget. By 2000, his last year in office, it had been chopped to 15 percent. [18] He left us with a weakened military. So where did the money go? The so-called peace dividend precipitated "the greatest era of federal social spending in our history, bigger than Franklin Roosevelt's New Deal in the 1930s and Lyndon Johnson's Great Society in the 1960s, in terms of real dollars ..." [19]

There was also a downside to the aforementioned tech revolution — the dot-com bubble. The dot-com bubble was created by people promoting the idea that any company associated with "cutting-edge" technology would invariably turn a profit. The Clinton administration was the beneficiary of this colossal misperception, collecting billions of dollars in capital gains revenue generated by the technological feeding frenzy, aka "irrational exuberance" on Wall Street. Extra tax revenue also came from sales by real companies with real products to thousands of those short-lived tech companies.

When reality caught up with perception, the dot-com boom ended in a stock market bust in 2000, resulting in an official recession in March 2001, a few months after George Bush took office. [20]

Thus, it was Bush who actually inherited a recession, not Clinton, as the media had everyone falsely believing.

Perhaps the biggest myth perpetrated by the mainstream media is the claim that President Clinton not only balanced the budget, but left the Bush administration with a surplus. This claim is used as an argument to contrast the fiscal irresponsibility of the Bush administration by comparison.

It is true the Bush administration was not fiscally responsible. But most Americans are not aware that Bush had to make spending concessions to Democrats to fund the War on Terror. In other words, he had to agree to numerous wasteful spending programs that Democrats wanted in order to finance the war appropriation bills.

It is generally asserted that Clinton had a budget surplus in fiscal years 1998, 1999 and 2000. However the facts don't support that claim.

Here is the national debt at the end of each year of Clinton budgets:

Fiscal Year	Year Ending	National Debt	Deficit
FY1993	09/30/1993	$4.411488 trillion	
FY1994	09/30/1994	$4.692749 trillion	$281.26 billion
FY1995	09/30/1995	$4.973982 trillion	$281.23 billion
FY1996	09/30/1996	$5.224810 trillion	$250.83 billion
FY1997	09/30/1997	$5.413146 trillion	$188.34 billion
FY1998	09/30/1998	$5.526193 trillion	$113.05 billion
FY1999	09/30/1999	$5.656270 trillion	$130.08 billion
FY2000	09/29/2000	$5.674178 trillion	$17.91 billion
FY2001	09/28/2001	$5.807463 trillion	$133.29 billion
Source: Treasury Direct.gov/NP/BPDLogin?application=np)[22]			

As you can see, during Clinton's presidency the national debt never went down, nor was President Bush left with a surplus that he subsequently turned into a deficit. The growing deficits started in the fiscal year (FY) of the last Clinton budget (FY 2001 of $133.29 billion), not in the first year of the Bush administration.

Although President Bush took office in January 2001 and his first budget took effect October 1, 2001 for the year ending September 30, 2002 (FY 2002), the $133.29 billion deficit in the year ending September 2001 was Clinton's. Even though $38 billion of that deficit was the result of Bush refunds to taxpayers in 2001 and not part of Clinton's last budget, Clinton's last budget still produced a deficit of $95.29 billion.

So why does the mainstream media claim Clinton left Bush with a surplus?

Apparently they, like most Americans, don't understand that the national debt is made up of public debt and intergovernmental holdings. The public debt is held by the public, and includes investments in Treasury bills, savings bonds, and other instruments the public can purchase from the government. Intergovernmental holdings, on the other hand, are when the government borrows money from itself – mostly borrowing from Social Security. [21]

The Social Security Administration is legally required to take any surpluses and buy U.S. government securities, such as treasury bills, e.g. In theory, these surplus funds are supposed to be set aside to pay for the benefits of future retirees. In political-speak, they are supposed to have been put into a "lock box."

In reality, Clinton used these surpluses to pay down *public* debt in order to make it appear that the government was running a surplus during his administration. In layman's terms, this amounts to robbing Peter to pay Paul. Therefore, while the *public* debt went down in each of Clinton's last four years, *intergovernmental holdings* went up by a far greater amount. As a result, the total *national* debt (public debt plus intergovernmental holdings combined) went up. Therein lies the discrepancy.

The following table illustrates the makeup of the national debt and the alleged surplus for the last few years of the Clinton administration:

Fiscal Year	End Date	Claimed Surplus	Public Debt	Inter-gov Holdings	Total National Debt
FY1997	09/30/1997		$3.789667T	$1.623478T	$5.413146T
FY1998	09/30/1998	$69.2B	$3.733864T	$1.792328T	$5.526193T
			⬇ $55.8B	⬆ $168.9B	⬆ $113B
FY1999	09/30/1999	$122.7B	$3.636104T	$2.020166T	$5.656270T
			⬇ $97.8B	⬆ $227.8B	⬆ $130.1B
FY2000	09/29/2000	$230.0B	$3.405303T	$2.268874T	$5.674178T
			⬇ $230.8B	⬆ $248.7B	⬆ $17.9B
FY2001	09/28/2001		$3.339310T	$2.468153T	$5.807463T
			⬇ $66.0B	⬆ $199.3B	⬆ $133.3B
Source: Treasury Direct.gov/NP/BPDLogin?application=np)[23]					

Thus, the claim made by Democrats and the media that Clinton paid down the national debt is plain wrong. As you can see from the Treasury Department's historical record, the national debt under Clinton rose by about 32% over his 8 years, from $4.4 trillion in FY 1993 to $5.8 trillion in FY 2001.

Lastly, no accurate assessment of Clinton's economic policies can be made without acknowledging his administration's critical role in mortgage lending policies that led to the current economic crisis. The fact that he has escaped blame for this is a testament to the distortion advanced by the media and Democrats.

Chapter 12

BASHING BUSH

To hear Democrats and the mainstream media tell it, George W. Bush was the "worst president in history."

I have conflicting emotions regarding the 43rd president, but I believe this characterization is way over the top. Such judgments are better left to future historians, who will decide how his failures measured up against his successes.

I am not blind to George W. Bush's many shortcomings, as this chapter will reveal. But Americans should never forget that, after 9/11, we did not endure another domestic terrorist attack for the rest of his term in office.

That may be somewhat inconsequential for a lot of Americans — perhaps even more so as that tragedy diminishes with the passing of time.

Not me. With a wife who had two children in New York City on September 11, 2001, the fact that he kept us safe is something for which I remain eternally grateful.

Much of the feelings of the American left and the Democrat Party toward George W. Bush's eight years in office can be summed up by long-time White House correspondent, Helen Thomas. She referred to George Bush "as the worst president in American history." [1] Such assessments are better left to historians. As it stands today, George Bush's legacy is one of both success and failure on the domestic and foreign fronts.

It is fairly obvious to most Americans that most, if not all, of George Bush's foreign policy was framed by the 9/11 attacks. Despite his aversion to nation-building, which he espoused during his first presidential campaign, George Bush considered the invasion of both Afghanistan and Iraq part of a crucial strategy designed to defeat international terrorism.

Right after 9/11, Osama bin Laden was the darling of the Arab street, viewed as the most successful Muslim warrior in centuries. The Saudi royal family paid him protection money, and individual princes donated to the jihadist cause. Recruits flocked to al-Qaeda because it seemed like a winning organization. [2]

The invasion of Iraq changed everything. Our presence in that country led al-Qaeda fighters to flock there, but when they started butchering their fellow Muslims, the Sunnis switched to the American side in the war. This "great awakening" of Sunni Muslims along with the Bush administration's troop surge dealt al-Qaeda a stunning defeat both militarily and psychologically. They suffered thousands of losses in Iraq, including many of their most senior commanders. Today, al-Qaeda is not welcome in a single Arab country. The Saudi royal family not only stopped funding them, but cracked down hard on them within their country. [3]

Most importantly, no one of importance in the Arab world sees them as a winner anymore. [4]

The war in Iraq led to other successful consequences in the Middle East. Syria was forced out of Lebanon for the first time in decades, allowing democratic politics to flourish. Pakistan closed down the A. Q. Khan nuclear proliferation ring, and Libya gave up its quest for nuclear weapons because its leader Moammar Gadhafi feared suffering the same fate as Saddam Hussein.

George Bush also gets credit for backing out of an agreement by Bill Clinton to join the International Criminal Court, which would have placed our soldiers deployed in Iraq, Afghanistan or anywhere in the world in the vulnerable position of being criminally sued for war crimes by individuals or groups harboring anti-American sentiments — even if those allegations were completely unfounded. [5]

Like every president who prosecuted every war throughout the course of American history, Bush made his share of mistakes along the way. He stayed with Defense Secretary Donald Rumsfeld's "war on the cheap" strategy too long before changing tactics. He failed to let American soldiers in Iraq pursue terrorists across the borders into Syria and Iran. His failure to properly articulate to the American people that the war on terror was both global and religious allowed Democrats to convince the public that the "real fight" was only against al-Qaeda terrorists in Afghanistan.

President Bush also failed to respond to the vicious attacks from Democrats and the media about how he allegedly manipulated the intelligence and lied to the American people regarding Iraqi WMDs. Those attacks were proven to be lies by two bipartisan investigations, but most Americans never heard about those reports. Bush should have explained the results of those investigations to the American people. His silence was incorrectly interpreted by many as an admission that the politically motivated lies spread by the American left were true.

Bush also should have prosecuted government officials and/or members of the elite media who leaked classified information about top secret programs designed to keep America safe. *The Washington Post* ran a story about the CIA's "secret prisons" while *The New York Times* published one about the highly classified National Security Agency program to intercept the communications of suspected terrorists. *The New York Times* also exposed the secret S.W.I.F.T. program that traced the flow of money among suspected terrorists and their supporters. [6]

On the other hand, Bush's unwillingness to accept defeat in Iraq, despite negative public opinion, proved he was a steadfast leader. He understood that Americans could not be seen to lose in Iraq without it being exposed as the "paper tiger" Osama bin Laden once called us.

President Bush also changed the way America handled Islamic terrorism. Under Bill Clinton, it was treated as a criminal activity, to be solved mainly by the efforts of policemen, prosecutors, judges and juries. Under Bush, it was rightly described and prosecuted as a war. (Under President Obama, we are reverting to the law enforcement approach, and his administration has taken it even further, giving Miranda rights to terrorists captured on the battlefield).

On the broader international front, George Bush received unjustified criticism for damaging America's image abroad. The Democrats characterized this as "cowboy diplomacy." A careful analysis of our alliances proves otherwise. American relationships with Western European governments were in good shape when Bush left office, as evidenced by our good standing with leaders such as Brown (England), Sarkozy (France), Merkel (Germany) and Berlusconi

(Italy). Our relationships were also excellent with Denmark, Holland, and the leaders of Eastern Europe, most specifically Ukraine and Georgia. The only European countries with which American relations were strained were Spain and Russia. This was due in large part to the socialist mindset of Spain's current Prime Minister Zapatero, and the confrontational mindset of Russia's Vladimar Putin. [7]

America's image in Africa is quite good because of President Bush's aid programs for AIDS and malaria, which saved over 1.1 million lives according to a study by two Stanford University doctors. [8]

In Asia, our relations with India were never better than under Bush, who instituted a bilateral civilian nuclear agreement in 2008. America also maintained good relations with Japan, South Korea and China simultaneously. [9]

In Latin America, the U.S. enjoyed especially warm relationships with Mexico, Columbia and Brazil when Bush was president. As in Europe, the Latin America countries with whom our relations were strained, specifically Venezuela (Chavez), Bolivia (Morales) and Nicaragua (Ortega), were also due to the socialist, anti-democratic tendencies of those leaders. [10]

Regarding the Middle East, Bush maintained strong relations with Israel, Turkey, Saudi Arabia, Jordan and Egypt, while making Iraq an ally – which directly led to Libya no longer being a threat. [11]

Lastly, our relations with two of American's traditional allies, Canada and Australia, were also good. [12]

So was criticism of Bush's international relationships justified? Like every president, he made mistakes when dealing with other countries. At times he could have used more finesse. But for Democrats to assert that our alliances needed to be totally restored is utter nonsense. Foreign policy is not based on popularity but on America's best interests. George Bush himself explained the difference:

"You can get short-term popularity in the Middle East if you want, by blaming all problems on Israel. That'll make you popular. You can be popular in certain salons of Europe if you say, 'Okay, we'll join the International Criminal

Court.' I could have been popular if I said, 'Oh, Kyoto is the way to deal with the environmental problem.' That would have made me liked. It would have made me wrong, however. And ultimately, you earn people's respect by articulating a set of principles and standing by them." [13]

Like his foreign policy, Bush's domestic policy was a series of pluses and minuses. When Bush took office in January 2001, he inherited major problems he didn't cause such as a recession that officially began in March of that year, a dot-com-led stock market collapse that wiped out $8 trillion in national wealth, and an attack on 9/11 that sank the economy even further. His tax cuts in 2003, especially cuts in capital gains and dividends designed to spur business incentives, were extremely effective in turning the economy around, leading to impressive growth. The jobless rate fell to 4.4% in October 2006, and real wages began to grow, despite rising food and energy prices. [14] The Gross Domestic Product grew from $9.7 trillion when Bush took office in 2001 to $14.3 trillion when he left in 2008. [15]

President Bush also dramatically strengthened port security and inspections of cargo aboard passenger aircraft. Information on nearly 100% of all containerized cargo is now carefully screened by the Department of Homeland Security before it is loaded onto vessels destined for the United States. Higher risk shipments are physically inspected for terrorist weapons either at the foreign port or upon arrival into the U.S. Advanced technologies such as large-scale X-ray and gamma ray machines as well as radiation detection devices are being deployed to identify warning signs of chemical, biological or radiological attacks. [16] In 2007, the Bush administration also passed legislation which mandated a phased-in approach that will screen 100% of the cargo carried on passenger aircraft by 2010. [17]

On a minus side, the passage of the Medicare Prescription Drug Act in 2003 (Medicare Part D) was fiscally irresponsible, creating trillions of dollars in unfunded liabilities. Bush also signed a farm bill in 2002 that pushed annual farm spending to double the levels of the 1990s and a 2005 highway bill that was the most expensive ever. [18] He also signed the McCain-Feingold bill into law, which restricted free speech by banning advertising that identified a federal candidate within 30 days of a primary election or 60 days of a general election.

As for George W. Bush's ostensible role in the housing crisis and the subsequent multi-billion dollar bailout, consider the following quote from Paul Krugman, a Nobel Prize-winning columnist for *The New York Times* — and one of Bush's harshest critics. In a June 7, 2009 editorial, Krugman admitted that even if Al Gore were president, "there would have been a huge housing bubble, and a financial crisis when the bubble burst."

It is also worth remembering that Bush sounded the alarm about the irresponsible lending practices of Fannie Mae and Freddie Mac on several occasions going back as far as 2001, long before the meltdown of either occurred—a reality conspicuously ignored by the mainstream media.

Another reality conspicuously ignored by the mainstream media: President Bush was an honorable man. Bush made it a priority to ensure the transition from his administration to Obama's went smoothly. On the other hand, when Bush took office in 2001, the outgoing Clinton administration removed the letter "W" from dozens of computer keyboards, obscene words were scrawled on walls and other despicable acts were committed. [19] Most Americans were also probably not aware of the $190,000 worth of sofas, china, flatware, rugs and other items taken from the White House by the Clintons when they left office. [20] (After the Clintons were criticized, they returned or paid for over $100,000 of those items.)

In conclusion, was Bush, as many Democrats contend, the worst president in history? Much of the condemnation of President Bush was driven by the enormous hatred of his personality and leadership style, rather than an objective assessment of his accomplishments.[21] Much of this hatred was fueled by a biased mainstream media, as well as Democrat politicians who, just as in the days of Reagan, were driven to destroy a Republican presidency, regardless of the truth.

Whatever genuine historians' verdict of the Bush years might be, it will likely be very different from what we are hearing today. Consider Harry Truman, who because of the unpopularity of the Korean War, left office in 1952 with the lowest approval rating (22%) of any president in history. [22] Yet today, he is viewed favorably by most Americans. Also consider the treatment of Ronald Reagan, who during his presidency, was criticized by the press for being "incompetent" and a "militaristic madman, out of touch with reality." When he passed away, even the left leaning mainstream media had nothing but praise for Ronald Reagan and his presidency.

Historical hindsight will invariably put things into perspective. A government's most important function is to protect its citizens. After September 11, 2001, few people believed there wouldn't be additional domestic terrorist attacks over the next seven years. Perhaps President Bush's greatest achievement will be that he kept America safe from any further attacks, despite our enemies' determined efforts.

Chapter 13

BAMBOOZLING BLACK AMERICA

As a former Democrat, I found the information contained in this chapter to be some of the most surprising discoveries I made writing this book.

Like far too many of my fellow citizens, I grew up believing that Democrats had ALWAYS been the champions of black America — and that Republicans were either uncaring at best, or overt racists at worst.

History demonstrates such an assessment is a complete fraud.

It's time to set the record straight. Black America deserves to know the truth — especially about their "friends" in the Democrat Party.

Most Americans would be shocked to discover Martin Luther King Jr. was a Republican. After all, the myth perpetuated by Democrats and the mainstream media is that it has always been Democrats, not Republicans, who have stood up for the blacks in America.

The reason Dr. King was a Republican is simple: Republicans, not Democrats, have consistently fought for freedom and civil rights for blacks since their founding in 1854 —*as the anti-slavery party.*

In fact, American history reveals how Democrats wanted to keep blacks in slavery. They passed Black Codes, Jim Crow laws, and other discriminatory pieces of legislation denying blacks their rights as citizens. Democrats also founded the Ku Klux Klan in 1866 and opposed the passage of every civil rights law, beginning in the 1860s and continuing through the 1950s and 1960s. [1]

Furthermore, it was the Republicans who fought to free blacks from slavery by amending the Constitution to grant blacks their freedom (13ᵗʰ Amendment), citizenship (14ᵗʰ Amendment) and the right to vote (15ᵗʰ Amendment), often against intense Democrat opposition. [2] For example in 1865, Congressional Republicans unanimously backed the 13ᵗʰ Amendment, which made slavery unconstitutional. Among Democrats, 78 percent of House members and 63 percent of senators voted "no." In 1866, 94 percent of Republican senators and 96 percent of GOP House members approved the 14ᵗʰ Amendment, guaranteeing all Americans equal protection of the law. Incredibly, *every* Congressional Democrat voted no. [3]

Republicans were also champions of civil rights legislation, including the Civil Rights Act of 1866 and the Reconstruction Act of 1867. These bills provided protection from legislation initiated by Southern Democrats and established a new government system in the South that would be fair to blacks.[4]

Republican President Dwight Eisenhower pushed to pass the Civil Rights Act of 1957 and sent troops to Arkansas to enforce the Supreme Court's landmark Brown vs. the Board of Education school desegregation ruling. [5] Democrats' reaction? Resistance by State Governor Orval Faubus and the signing of a "Southern Manifesto," a document denouncing the Court's ruling, by Congressional Democrats. Eisenhower also signed the GOP's 1960 Civil Rights Act — after it survived a five day filibuster by 18 Senate Democrats.[6]

Another myth which has gained traction is that Democrat icon, President John F. Kennedy, was a staunch proponent of civil rights. Yet Kennedy voted against the 1957 Civil Rights Act while he was a Senator, along with Democrat Senator Al Gore Sr. President Kennedy also opposed the 1963 march on Washington by Dr. King that was organized by A. Phillip Randolph, a black Republican. [7] JFK, in collaboration with his brother, Attorney General Robert Kennedy, also had Dr. King wiretapped and investigated by the FBI. This was a disgraceful attempt to prove that King was associated with the Communist Party. [8]

Few Americans know that it was Republicans who established the NAACP and that Republican President Richard Nixon's 1969 "Philadelphia Plan" set up the nation's first goals and timetables for affirmative action. Nixon did this to counter the harm caused to black Americans by Democrat President Woodrow Wilson, who kicked them out of federal government jobs in 1912.
9

Even fewer black Americans know that it was Republicans who founded and financed all the earliest black schools and colleges in the U.S., even as Democrats opposed their every effort with "brutal force." [10]

The 1964 Civil Rights Act has been heralded by the left as an example of how Democrats, not Republicans, have been the party which has championed civil rights for blacks. However, the facts reveal a different story. Although Democrat President Lyndon Johnson signed this bill into law on July 2, 1964, it was only after former Ku Klux Klansman Senator Robert Byrd's 14 hour filibuster along with the votes of 22 other Senate Democrats failed to stop the measure. Illinois Republican Everett Dirksen finally rallied enough Senators to invoke cloture, stop the filibuster and allow the bill's passage. [11] More Republicans voted for this law than Democrats, as 82 percent of Republicans supported it, versus only 66 percent of Democrats. [12]

Tellingly, there is rarely any mention anywhere in the media of the Republican role in the passage of the Civil Rights Act.

Many historians cite the opposition to the bill by Republican Senator Barry Goldwater, the Republican nominee for president that year, as a reason black Americans have migrated to the Democrat Party. It is true Goldwater opposed the bill. However, his opposition had nothing to do with race. He had supported the 1957 and 1960 Civil Rights Acts and called for integrating Arizona's National Guard — two years before Democrat President Truman desegregated the military. [13] And when Goldwater was a city councilman in Phoenix, he became a founding member of the Arizona NAACP, and he remained a proud member until his death. [14]

So why did Goldwater oppose the bill? He was fearful that two of the sections contained in it, regarding housing and public accommodation, unlawfully expanded the role of the federal government. He was a true libertarian. [15]

In 2008, Dr. King's niece, Dr. Alveda C. King, wrote an article affirming that her grandfather, Dr. Martin Luther King Sr., or "Daddy King," and her uncle Dr. Martin Luther King Jr., were Republicans. But her explanation for the migration of black Americans to the Democrat Party is different from those of the historians:

"Moved by Mrs. King's gratitude for Senator Kennedy's intervention, Daddy

King was very grateful to Senator (John) Kennedy for his assistance in rescuing Dr. King, Jr. from a life threatening jail encounter. This experience led to a black exodus from the Republican Party. Thus, this one simple act of gratitude caused black America to quickly forget that the Republican Party was birthed in America as the antislavery party to end the scourge of slavery and combat the terror of racism and segregation. They quickly forgot that the Democratic Party was the party of the Ku Klux Klan."[16]

How ironic, since it was the Kennedy administration, as mentioned previously, who tried to undermine Dr. King by attempting to prove he was associated with the Communist Party.

The Republican Party is also the party of numerous "firsts" regarding black Americans. Some notable examples:

- Republican presidents Gerald Ford in 1975 and Ronald Reagan in 1982 promoted Daniel James and Roscoe Robinson, to become, respectively, the Air Force's and Army's first black four star generals.

- On November 2, 1983, President Reagan designated Dr. Martin Luther King Jr.'s birthday as a national holiday, the first such honor for a black American.

- President Reagan named Colin Powell America's first black National Security Adviser while Republican President George W. Bush appointed him as our first black Secretary of State.

- President George W. Bush also named Condoleezza Rice America's first black female National Security Council Chief, then our second (consecutive) black Secretary of State. [17]

Another part of the continuing negative narrative regarding Republicans' relations with minorities is that they spend less on anti-poverty programs than Democrats. They don't. Under George W. Bush, anti-poverty spending increased by 39 percent, [18] and reached a record 16.3 percent of all federal spending in 2004, up from 14.9 percent in 2000. [19]

Not only have the actions of Democrats over the past 150 years overwhelmingly demonstrated a lack of support for the civil rights of black

Americans, some of their words have been just as damning. Angry with Dr. King's protest against the Vietnam War, Democrat President Lyndon Johnson in 1967 referred to Dr. King as "that Nigger preacher." And in reference to Dr. King leaving Memphis, Tennessee after riots broke out in March 1968 where a teenager was killed, Democrat Senator Robert Byrd referred to Dr. King as a "trouble-maker who starts trouble, but runs like a coward after trouble is ignited." [20]

That was the same Robert Byrd (a former KKK member) whom Democrat Senator Chris Dodd praised as someone who would have been "a great Senator for any moment," including the Civil War.[21] Imagine the backlash if a Republican had said that.

Today a common misconception is that the Democrat Party is more interested than Republicans in helping black Americans. Democrats point to Lyndon Johnson's establishment of the "Great Society" welfare program as a shining moment in race relations.

In reality, the "Great Society" wasn't so great. It undermined the two-parent family with welfare incentives, and encouraged the societal acceptability of single-parent households along with their dependence on government handouts.

As part of those handouts, monthly welfare checks to single mothers were increased with each additional birth. Forty-six years later, the statistics are damning: in 1963, the out-of-wedlock birthrate in the black community was 23.6% [22] By 2009, it had risen to 71.6%. [23]

In the mid 1990s, realizing the welfare system was out of control, Republicans introduced welfare reform. The bill was designed to end dependence on government benefits by promoting job preparation, work and marriage.

What was Democrat President Bill Clinton's response? He vetoed the bill twice before finally relenting under pressure from the Republican-controlled Congress, signing it into law in 1996. [24] In 2004, *The New York Times* called welfare reform "one of the acclaimed successes of the past decade." [25] The number of Americans on welfare dropped from 12.2 million in 1996 to 4.5 million in 2006.[26]

Leading Democrats were opposed to the bill, with Senator Ted Kennedy (D-MA) calling it "legislative child abuse," Senator Chris Dodd (D-CT) denouncing it as "unconscionable," and Senator Frank Lautenberg (D-NJ) declaring that welfare reform would force poor children to take up "begging for money, food and even…engaging in prostitution." [27]

Democrats not only opposed Clinton's welfare reform, but also fought the passage of George W. Bush's Marriage and Healthy Families Fatherhood Initiative in 2005, which sought to increase the number of healthy marriages to reduce dependence on social services. [28]

Why do Republicans put such an emphasis on a stable two-parent household, aka the nuclear family? "According to the Index of Leading Cultural Indicators, children from single-parent families account for 63 percent of all youth suicides, 70 percent of all teenage pregnancies, 71 percent of all adolescent chemical/substance abuse, 80 percent of all prison inmates and 90 percent of all homeless and runaway children." [29] Also, the connection between family breakdown and poverty has been well established.

Nevertheless, the "dependency model" of the Democrat Party continues to be promoted. The 2009 Stimulus Bill passed by the Democrats created financial incentives for states to *increase* the number of people on welfare, reversing the successful welfare reform of the mid 1990s. [30]

Although Democrats would vehemently deny it, it seems they are determined to maintain the status quo of substandard education in black communities as well. For example, they have consistently opposed school choice opportunity scholarships (vouchers) that would help black children get out of failing schools.

Why? Because Democrats care more about the teachers unions than doing what's best for our children.

That "affection" between the Democrat Party and the teacher unions is reciprocal. According to the non-partisan Center for Responsive Politics, between 1990 and 2008, the National Education Association — the largest teachers union in the country — contributed 93 percent of its massive campaign donations to the Democrat Party. [31]

Today's black Americans have been duped into believing the myth that the Democrat Party has been the one historically working in their best interests. In reality, Democrat policies from the Great Society onward have convinced black Americans they are victims. This Democratically-fostered mentality has contributed greatly to keeping much of black America mired in poverty, single parenthood and dependency on the government. Democrats define this government dependency as "compassion" and there lies the difference between that political party and Republicans: Democrats are more interested in keeping blacks *on* government programs — thereby securing their votes — while Republicans are more interested in getting people *off* government programs via job training and educational freedom.

Black Americans might want to learn who *really* looked out for their interests in the past — and who's looking out for their interests in the present. The choice is stark: black Americans can stay with the Democrat Party, which has given them 40 years of dependency, or move toward the Republican Party, which promotes individual responsibility, freedom and prosperity.

PART II

UNDERSTANDING THE PRESENT

Chapter 14

ANATOMY OF A SCAM:
THE SCIENCE, POLITICS AND MONEY BEHIND
GLOBAL WARMING

Is there a more "inconvenient truth" than the REAL story behind the global warming campaign?

I can't think of another agenda which contains a more deadly combination of skewered science, partisan political ideology and financial corruption — all designed to benefit the "true believers" — than this one.

And who are those true believers? The same people they've always been: elitists with an appetite for power, using whatever vehicle they need to acquire it.

Toward that end, they have attached themselves to "saving the planet" even if it means ruining the economies of the world.

After doing the research for this chapter, I have come to one very uncomfortable conclusion: the global warming agenda is the biggest scam in the history of the world.

And while a few Republicans are caught up in the hysteria, liberal Democrats are totally on board.

The United Nations, environmental groups, the media, and most of the Democrat Party have promoted the idea that global warming is "settled science" and the greatest threat in modern times.

The reason this issue is so significant is that the Democrat Party has been rushing to implement a scheme known as "cap and trade" for controlling carbon dioxide (CO_2) emissions. If enacted, it would greatly harm our economy and job market.

First, the science. This issue used to be referred to as "global warming" but is now called "climate change." Why? Perhaps it's because global temperatures have actually *decreased* since 1998. As more and more scientists and climatologists began speaking out about the decline in temperatures, the global warming alarmists responded — by simply changing the name of their "crisis."

The fact that world temperatures have declined since 1998 is undisputed and has been confirmed by many scientists and organizations. The United Nations World Meteorological Organization reported that global temperatures have not risen since 1998.[1]   A study released in January 2009 by two professors in the Department of Mathematical Sciences at the University of Wisconsin-Milwaukee showed that "the Earth has been cooling since 2001, and projected that due to 'global variation,' the climate would continue to cool for the next 20 to 30 years." [2]   Imperial College London astrophysicist and long-range forecaster Piers Corbyn wrote British members of Parliament on October 28, 2008: "According to official data in every year since 1998, world temperatures have been colder than that year, yet CO_2 has been rising rapidly." [3]

Even President Obama's own internal study on climate science written on March 16, 2009 by Alan Carlin, senior operations research analyst at the EPA's National Center for Environmental Economics, confirmed this fact. Referencing compiled works and analyses from published scientists, Carlin noted that global temperatures have declined from 1998 until 2009, with a particularly rapid decline in 2007 – 2008. [4]

Furthermore, Carlin's analysis acknowledged the decline in temperatures — even though CO_2 levels have increased. This fact alone punches a serious hole in global warming theory, which contends that a continued rise in CO_2 emissions will raise temperatures.

Bottom line: if global warming theorists were correct, temperatures should have increased, not decreased during that period.

Carlin's report was so damaging that the Obama administration suppressed the study and forbid him from having "any direct communication" with anyone outside his office. [5]   Apparently, the Obama administration's campaign promise to be "transparent" and "elevate science over politics" rang hollow. Not only did the Obama administration suppress the report, but so did almost all of the mainstream media, except conservative publications such as *The Wall Street Journal* and *Investor's Business Daily*. Unbelievably, there wasn't one television news report on this story. [6]

Why was the report kept under wraps? So it would not influence the vote on the cap-and-trade bill passed in June 2009 by the House of Representatives. The Democrats once again placed political ideology above the truth, just as they have done with nuclear energy, wind, solar, and other important energy issues we are facing today.

Despite Democrats' ideological rigidness, even some of their own realize the fallacy of global warming. Dr. Martin Hertzberg, a physical chemist and retired Navy meteorologist, wrote about it in September 26, 2008's *USA Today:*

"As a scientist and life-long liberal Democrat, I find the constant regurgitation of the anecdotal, fear-mongering clap-trap about human-caused global warming to be a disservice to science. From the El Niño year of 1998 until January 2007, the average temperature of the Earth's atmosphere near its surface decreased some O.25 C (O.45 F). From January 2007 until the spring of 2008, it dropped a whopping O.75 C (1.35 F)." [7]

In fact, the Earth's temperature has always fluctuated between cooling and warming periods. In 2006, the National Academy of Sciences reaffirmed the existence of a Medieval Warm Period from about 900 AD to 1300 AD as well as the Little Ice Age from about 1500 AD to 1850 AD. Both of these periods occurred long before the invention of the SUV or human industrial activity could have possibly affected the Earth's climate. Many scientists believe the Earth was warmer during the Medieval Warm Period, when the Vikings actually grew crops in Greenland. [8] Today Greenland is under permafrost.

Global warming alarmists have failed to explain these anomalies. They also can't explain why temperatures cooled from 1940 to 1975 while CO^2 emissions were rising sharply. [9]

The media has been equally alarmist, which is ironic considering their historic track record. A 1975 issue of *Newsweek* contained an article titled "The Cooling World," predicting a fundamental cooling of the Earth that will "reduce agricultural productivity for the rest of the century." [10] *The New*

York Times reported in the same year that "a major cooling of the climate" was "widely considered inevitable" because it was "well established" that the Northern Hemisphere's climate "has been getting cooler since about 1950." [11] Other publications anticipated "a full-blown" 10,000 year ice age involving extensive Northern Hemisphere glaciations (*Science News*, March 1, 1975 and *Science* magazine December 10, 1976). [12] Although *The New York Times* believed in global warming in 1952, they hyped global cooling in the 1970s. [13]

Time magazine first warned of a coming ice age in the 1920s before reversing to warning about global warming in the 1930s before switching yet again to promoting the 1970s coming ice age. [14]

Flip-flopping has not been the only problem with media reports. Most of them today are unabashedly tilted toward global warming propaganda. For example, on February 19, 2006, CBS News' *60 Minutes* produced a segment on the North Pole that was completely one-sided, alleging rapid and unprecedented melting at the polar cap. [15] *60 Minutes* failed to inform its viewers of a 2005 study by a scientist named Ola Johannessen and his colleagues that revealed the interior of Greenland is gaining ice and mass, and that according to scientists, the Arctic was warmer in the 1930s than today. [16] The correspondent of that misleading segment, Scott Pelley, told the CBS News website that he justified excluding scientists skeptical of global warming alarmism from his segment because he considered skeptics to be the equivalent of "Holocaust deniers." [17]

Also, global warming proponents rarely ever mention the ice levels in the Antarctica. Why? Perhaps John Christy of the U.N.'s Intergovernmental Panel on Climate Change and now a global warming skeptic has the answer. His response to a question posed by CNN anchor Miles O'Brien in 2007:

"...we don't see the catastrophic changes that are being promoted all over the place. For example, I suppose CNN did not announce two weeks ago when the Antarctica sea ice extent reached its all-time maximum..." [18]

In April 2006, *Time* magazine devoted an issue to global warming alarmism entitled "Be Worried, Be Very Worried." The report cited partisan left-wing environmental groups – with a vested financial interest in hyping alarmism – without making any effort to balance the report with interviews of skeptical scientists. [19]

There were plenty of skeptics with whom *Time* could have consulted. There are 31,000 scientists who signed a petition organized by the Oregon Institute of Science and Medicine (OISM) saying global warming is probably natural and is not a crisis. [20] According to the OISM's board, "there is no convincing scientific evidence that human release of carbon dioxide, methane, or other greenhouse gases is causing, or will in the foreseeable future cause, catastrophic heating of the Earth's atmosphere and disruption of the Earth's climate." The OISM further pointed out that increases in carbon dioxide emissions have produced many beneficial effects, including increased plant growth rates. [21]

They could have also consulted with the nearly 100 scientists listed in Cato Institute ads that were run in magazines and newspapers in 2009. The Cato scientists maintained that the case for alarm regarding climate change is grossly overstated, that surface temperature changes over the past century have been episodic and modest, and that computer models forecasting rapid temperature change fail to explain why there has been no new global warming for over a decade. [22]

The ads were a response to President-elect Barack Obama's false statement on November 19, 2008, where he said that "the science (on climate change) is beyond dispute and the facts are clear." [23]

Other mainstream media omissions include the results from the National Snow and Ice Data Center which found that Arctic sea ice *expanded* 13.2% in 2008, or a Texas-sized 270,000 square miles. [24] The University of Illinois Arctic Climate Research Center disclosed that global sea ice levels now equal those of 1979, and that the increase in global sea ice since September 2008 has been the fastest since that year. [25] Josefino Comiso, a senior research scientist with the Cryospheric Sciences Branch of NASA's Goddard Space Flight Center reported that recent satellite images show that the allegedly endangered polar ice cap has recovered to near normal coverage levels. [26]

So who's pushing the man-made global warming agenda? The chief proponent has been the Intergovernmental Panel on Climate Change (IPCC), an organization established by the United Nations in 1988. The IPCC periodically releases reports on many topics related to climate change.

Unfortunately, the IPCC has always been a political, rather than scientific, entity. Its leading scientists reflect the positions of their respective governments, or seek to induce their governments to adopt the IPCC position. [27] Most importantly, a small group of "activists" write the all important Summary for Policymakers for each published report. [28] Their agenda is to justify control over the emission of greenhouse gases, especially carbon dioxide. Consequently, their reports have focused solely on evidence that might point toward human–induced climate change. [29]

While we often hear about the thousands of scientists on whose work the Assessment reports are based, the vast majority of these scientists *have no direct influence* on the conclusions reached by the IPCC. [30] Instead, those reports are produced by the aforementioned group of activists, and the Summaries are revised and agreed to on a line-by-line basis by representatives of member governments of the U.N. [31]

The results? Reports not grounded in science, but rather the "politics and money" of global warming.

Tellingly, the IPCC's key personnel and lead authors are appointed by their respective governments. Almost all the scientists involved are supported by government contracts, which pay not only for their research, but also for their IPCC activities. [32] This conflict of interest directly affects the results they churn out.

As a result, IPCC reports are marred by errors and misstatements, ignore scientific data available but inconsistent with the authors' pre-conceived conclusions, and have been contradicted by subsequent research. [33]

The fact that the IPCC is pre-programmed to produce reports to support the hypotheses of man-made warming and the control of greenhouse gases is undeniable. For example, the first IPCC Summary in 1990 completely ignored satellite data, since they showed no warming. [34] Regarding the second IPCC report in 1995, the lead author B. D. Santor, changed the report significantly without the approval of the scientists who first drafted it to convey the impression of a human influence for global warming. Not only was the report altered, but a key graph was also manipulated to suggest a human influence.[35] Such behavior upset Dr. Freidrich Seitz, President emeritus of Rockefeller University, and the former President of the National Academy of Sciences:

"I have never witnessed a more disturbing corruption of the peer-review process than the events that led to this IPCC report. Nearly all the changes worked to remove hints of the skepticism with which many scientists regard global warming claims." [36]

Undaunted, the IPCC's 2001 report continued the deception, falsely claiming the twentieth century showed "unusual warming" based on the so-called and now discredited "hockey stick graph." This graph purported to show that temperatures in the Northern hemisphere remained relatively stable over 900 years, then spiked upward in the twentieth century, presumably because of human activity. [37]   In his movie *An Inconvenient Truth*,   Al Gore used the hockey stick to convince viewers that the twentieth century was the warmest century in the last 1000 years. "Conveniently" omitted? The Medieval Warm Period and the Little Ice Age. [38]

In 2006, Congress commissioned a review by the National Academy of Sciences to examine the hockey stick evidence. That report refuted the hockey stick theory and confirmed the existence of the Medieval Warm Period and the Little Ice Age. [39] The reality of those cycles shows that the twentieth century is in no way unusual and that warming periods of greater magnitude have occurred in the past — before automobiles and coal plants. The report also refuted the argument made by global warming proponents, including Al Gore, that the 1990s was the hottest decade in a millennium, citing "substantial uncertainties." [40]

In fact, the year 1934 has emerged as the warmest of the twentieth century and the 1930s the warmest decade. [41] That discovery was made in 2007 when scientists realized that there was a decline in a number of temperature measuring stations worldwide, especially in Siberia after the fall of the U.S.S.R., which had skewed the temperature readings misleadingly upward. [42]

For obvious reasons, the fourth and most recent IPCC report, produced in 2007, no longer emphasized the hockey stick analysis. But it completely ignored the available evidence *against* a human contribution to current warming and the significant research of the past few years on the effects of solar activity on the climate. [43]

Here's what Alan Carlin, senior operations research analyst at the EPA's National Center for Environmental Economics, concluded about the 2007

IPCC report on climate change: [44]

- The "Fourth Assessment" report relies on outdated research that ignores the latest scientific findings.

- Satellite data after 1998 show a decline in real temperatures (which some think will continue until about 2030) which is inconsistent with the theory that man-made greenhouse gas and CO_2 emissions cause temperature to warm.

- Lack of warming in the upper troposphere (the region of the atmosphere up to 15 kilometers in altitude which has now shown a slight cooling with altitude [45]) that contradicts the IPCC hypothesis that there should be a warming, or "fingerprint" in the atmosphere caused by increased greenhouse gas emissions.

- The idea that warming temperatures cause Greenland to rapidly shed its ice has been greatly diminished by new results indicating little evidence of that.

- A 2009 report by Scafetta and Wilson suggests the IPCC used faulty solar data in dismissing the direct effect of the sun on global temperatures. Their report suggests that solar variability could account for up to 68% of the increase in Earth's global temperatures. There appears to be a strong association between solar sunspots and global temperature fluctuations, perhaps through its influence on cloud formation.

- The IPCC models do not take into account the most important ocean oscillations (El Niño, La Niña) which clearly do affect temperatures.

- The IPCC measurement of temperature increases since the 1970s relies heavily on faulty data that has been influenced by rapid urbanization and the heat island effect – asphalt, buildings, air conditioning units and other parts of urban life cause warming of urban areas and have nothing to do with greenhouse gases. (The IPCC report refers only to Earth surface temperatures and ignores the more reliable data collected from satellites and balloons that contradict their data).

Perhaps the greatest miscarriage of science in the global warming hoax is its near total dependence on worst-case scenarios conjured up by computer models. Models do not represent reality, yet the IPCC and Al Gore persist in treating them as if they do. These climate models have never been validated by actual observations. [46] They are only as accurate as the data and assumptions that are used.

Computer models, for example, are what the IPCC and Al Gore have used to hype rising sea levels. Their ultimate apocalyptic scenario is that the ice cap over the North Pole – which is not land but is simply ice that is floating in the Arctic Ocean – is melting and will cause the world sea levels to rise, flooding hundreds of cities on the coasts. Al Gore's movie showed computer graphics of cities such as Shanghai and San Francisco being half under water from sea rises of 20 feet.

Even Al Gore's ally, the IPCC, refutes this over the top scenario. In their most recent report (2007), their *worst-case scenario* is a 59cm (23.2 inches) rise in sea levels—from the date of the report until the year 2100. This averages out to one quarter-of-an-inch per year for the next ninety-three years. Yet even more telling is the fact that each successive IPCC report forecast a smaller sea level rise than the previous one. Their best-case scenario? 18cm (7 inches), which exactly equals the rate of sea level rises in recent centuries. [47]

How preposterous is Al Gore's hypothesis? A simple experiment demonstrates its falseness. Fill a glass to the top with water and ice cubes and let the ice cubes melt completely. If Al Gore's science were correct, the melted water would overflow the confines of the glass. However, as you will observe, the water level will be exactly the same as when you started. You'll get the picture — even if Al Gore doesn't.

And even though it should also be obvious, but apparently is not, melting glaciers and disappearing Arctic sea ice are entirely irrelevant with regard to determining the *causes* of warming. *Any* significant warming, whether man-made or natural will melt ice. The alarmists are simply confusing the "consequences" of warming with the "causes" – a common logical error. [48]

For example, most Himalayan glaciers are melting, but they have been retreating "since the earliest recordings began around the middle of the nineteenth century," according to a report from India's ministry of environment and forests. [49] This, of course, was prior to the days of automobiles and coal plants. And undersea volcanic activity has melted some areas of the Arctic ice cap. [50] As a result, this naturally-caused melting of ice in some Arctic areas, especially Greenland, has opened up the prospect of using the newly navigable seaways to explore the Arctic's rich energy reserves. [51]

Al Gore has also mixed up cause and effect regarding temperature increases and CO_2 levels. As Gore correctly points out, over the past half million years, the Antarctic ice core records show a correlation between temperature and CO_2. What he neglects to mention is that these records consistently show that temperatures rose some 800 years *before* CO_2 levels increased, not afterward. [52]

And high CO_2 levels in the atmosphere don't necessarily correlate with warmer temperatures. About 440 million years ago, when CO_2 levels are estimated to have been over 10 times today's, the Earth was in the depths of the coldest temperatures in the last half billion years. [53] High CO_2 levels have also coincided with warm periods at other times. Even in the past century, the correlation between CO_2 and global warming is poor, since significant cooling took place between 1940 and 1975 while human- produced CO_2 emissions were rapidly increasing. [54]

How scientifically accurate was *An Inconvenient Truth?* In 2008, a High Court judge in Great Britain ruled that the "apocalyptic vision" presented in the film is politically motivated and thus not impartial scientific analyses of climate change. While ruling that Gore's movie is a "political" film, he also cited nine important scientific errors in it. Although the judge did not ban the film from British schools, he ruled "it can only be shown with guidance notes to prevent political indoctrination." [55]

The movie was perhaps the slickest science propaganda film of all time — and the mainstream media's bias was never more apparent. The *Associated Press* ran an article on June 27, 2006 by Seth Borenstein that boldly declared "Scientists give two thumbs up to Gore's movie" — five of them — despite the AP having contacted *more than 100 scientists*. The fact that more than 80% of the scientists contacted by the AP had not even seen the movie, or that many scientists have harshly criticized its science, did not prevent the AP from promoting his alarmism. [56]

Even more remarkable, however, is how many people have taken Al Gore seriously, despite the fact that he *has no scientific credentials whatsoever*. Tellingly, despite numerous challenges, Gore has refused to debate the issue of global warming with any credible scientist who is a skeptic.

This is not surprising. Al Gore's academic performance was dismal, particularly in science. His high school performance on the college based achievement tests in physics (488 out of 800 "terrible," according to St. Alban's retired teacher John Davis in *The Washington Post)* and chemistry (519 out of 800 "He didn't do too well in chemistry," Mr. Davis also observed) suggested Gore would have trouble with science for the rest of his life. His grades at Harvard bear this out. As a sophomore, Mr. Gore earned a "D" in Natural Sciences 6 and as a senior a "C+" in Natural Sciences 118. To reiterate, Al Gore has only a B.A. in government - and no science degrees whatsoever. [57]

Just as amazing as Al Gore's lack of credentials is the idea that carbon dioxide could possibly be labeled a dangerous pollutant. How can it be considered "poison" when plants need it to survive? Higher levels of CO^2 in the air enable plants to grow bigger, produce more branches and leaves, expand their root systems and produce more flowers and fruit. [58]

Carbon dioxide is odorless, colorless and benign. It is literally the substance we exhale with every breath.

And carbon dioxide makes up only a tiny part of the Earth's atmosphere. How tiny? The chart below illustrates this along with mankind's tinier contribution to the overall percentage.

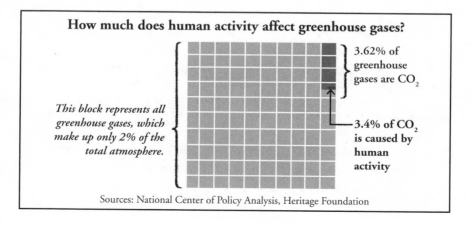

How much does human activity affect greenhouse gases?

3.62% of greenhouse gases are CO_2

This block represents all greenhouse gases, which make up only 2% of the total atmosphere.

3.4% of CO_2 is caused by human activity

Sources: National Center of Policy Analysis, Heritage Foundation

Along with dubious scientific claims, global warming proponents also resort to distortion. Even though carbon dioxide is harmless and *colorless*, they consistently show photos of *dark smoke* coming out of factories, in a *deliberate* attempt to confuse carbon dioxide with genuine pollutants such as sulfur dioxide, carbonic and nitric oxides, benzpyrene, soot, heavy metals and other toxic substances responsible for causing cancer and mutations. These *genuine* pollutants are the greatest environmental challenge to governments and the public, and international agreements should seek to reduce *their* emissions. The public should also be made aware of the fact that monitoring of such substances in the atmosphere is easy. [59]

Ironically, the so-called anti-environment president, George W. Bush, proposed the first-ever regulation of pollutant emissions, something ostensibly pro-environmental president, Bill Clinton talked about but never did. Bush introduced the "Clear Skies Initiative," a set of regulations aimed to reduce sulfur dioxide emissions by a projected 73 percent, mercury by 69 percent and nitrogen oxides by 67 percent. [60]

Despite the fearmongering, empirical evidence strongly suggests that the main cause of warming and cooling, from decade to decade, derives from solar activity's modulation of cosmic rays. This modulation affects cloud formation in the atmosphere.[61]

Cloud formation has much to do with shielding us from the sun's warmth.

So if the hysteria about man-made global warming has little to do with science, what is it really about?

Politics and money.

In the political arena, insisting that global warming is a problem caused by humans provides an excuse for massive increases in government power and taxation at every level, and drives the United Nation's dream of becoming a world government.

A case in point is the United Nations' 1997 Kyoto Protocol, an international environmental treaty ratified by 184 countries, the purpose of which was to reduce greenhouse gas emissions.

As French president, Jacques Chirac stated in the opening remarks to the Sixth Conference of Parties to Kyoto in 2000:

"Kyoto is the first component of an authentic global governance." [62]

The global warming scam is the perfect vehicle for a United Nations looking to extract money from developed nations. Why? The wealthier a nation, the more CO_2 it produces. "To atone for its sins," it must pay non-producing or under-producing nations billions of dollars as "penance."

A headline from an *Associated Press* article in 2007 confirmed this exact point: "U.N.: Poorest Countries Most Vulnerable to Climate Change Need Help from Rich." The report said that rich nations will need to contribute $86 billion per year by 2015, half of which would go for "climate-proofing" developing nations' infrastructure, while the other half would help the poor cope with climate-related risks. [63]

Given the U.N.'s track record, it is likely most of this money would be skimmed off by the bureaucrats and dictators that run the U.N. If the Oil-for-Food scandal is any indication, perhaps that's their real agenda.

A similar scenario is taking place in this country. The Democratically-controlled House of Representatives passed so-called cap and trade legislation in June 2009, which could give activists, courts, and bureaucrats control over virtually every aspect of our lives. The bill would enable them to confiscate hard-earned taxpayer dollars, and convert them to payoffs for activists and companies that get on the man-made global warming bandwagon.

All but eight Republicans in the House of Representatives voted against cap and trade. This issue demonstrates there *is* a difference between the two political parties, and why we can't keep voting for Democrats who are willing to pass harmful regulation based on faulty and inaccurate science.

Which brings us to the money – and the amount of money spent on global warming is staggering. Since 1989, the U.S. government has spent over $79 billion on funding related to climate change, including science and technology research, administration, education campaigns, foreign aid and tax breaks.[64] Further, spending in the U.S. alone has jumped to over $7 billion per annum, and tax concessions add to this.[65]

Private enterprise is also grabbing its piece of the global warming pie. General Electric stands to make billions as one of the key players in the carbon offset market. As a result, GE, which owns television networks NBC and MSNBC, has played on global warming fears in the past few years by running documentaries and specials hyping it. Al Gore has a partnership in the venture capital firm, Kleiner Perkins Caulfield and Byers, which has invested over $1.2 billion in private start-up and expanding "green growth" companies. [66] A firm Gore chairs, Generation Investment Management, created a $683 million fund in 2008 to invest in public "green" companies. [67]

Further, Al Gore's venture capital firm has invested $6 million in a software company that helps track greenhouse gas emissions and stands to make billions of dollars from cap and trade regulation. [68] His non-profit organization, Alliance for Climate Protection, has been running a $300 million, three-year advertising campaign to raise awareness about global warming, with frequent television commercials hammering away his message. In just eight years, Al Gore's net worth has reportedly increased from around $1 million when he left office in 2001, to approximately $100 million today, thanks to the global warming frenzy he helped create. [69]

Global warming is also a staple of modern university budgets. For example, the University of California is preparing to spend $500 million to create a think tank to analyze the subject. [70]

Such spending creates enormous momentum and a powerful set of vested interests. Understanding this dynamic is important to understanding why the science is corrupted. Ask yourself this question: would this enormous amount of money keep flowing to scientists if they concluded tomorrow that global warming is no longer a threat or problem? It is imperative to the many scientists who receive federal grants and foundation money that the hysteria continues.

After all, their jobs depend on it.

The other side of the debate? Skeptics have been so poorly funded that research has become a community service project for unpaid volunteers with expert skills and a passionate interest. [71]

Fortunately, these volunteers have succeeded in exposing serious scientific errors. Two researchers, Steve McIntyre and Ross McKitrick, exposed major flaws in the hockey stick graph   used by Al Gore and the IPCC to promote their theories. [72] That graph had falsely wiped out centuries of recorded history demonstrating temperatures in prior centuries have fluctuated between warm and cool periods.

Likewise, Anthony Watts, a former television meteorologist, self-funded a project to quality-check 1,221 ground weather stations around the country used by NASA to measure the "official" average annual temperature of the United States. [73]

What Watts and his volunteers found was shocking. 89% of all stations they checked thus far have failed to meet the National Weather Service's own siting requirements. [74] Recording stations were found to have been placed next to outlets of air conditioning units, above asphalt in car parks, on scorching hot concrete roof-tops, and near heated buildings. [75] The National Oceanic and Atmospheric Administration, the agency that installs the sensors, has done a horrendous job, considering they receive around $4 billion annually in funding. [76] One should seriously question whether this is negligent or *deliberate.*

Meanwhile, global warming alarmists have attacked Exxon-Mobil Corp for paying a grand total of $23 million to skeptics – a small fraction of what the U.S. government spends to keep the global warming industry alive. [77]

In conclusion, it has become apparent that genuine science cannot withstand the corrupting influence of politics and money. On the political side, global warming is the perfect vehicle for the United Nation's dream of becoming a global governing body with the power of international taxation. On the money side, global elitists and their comrades are poised to make hundreds of billions of dollars.

But let's play devil's advocate. Even if the Earth were warming, as the global warming alarmists falsely tell us, so what? Does anyone seriously believe the Earth has been the same temperature throughout the ages? Testifying before the U.S. Senate, Al Gore said "if your baby has a fever, you go to the doctor." But here's the big deception in that statement: Humans have a normal body temperature of 98.6 degrees, whereas the Earth has never had a normal temperature, since we know it has experienced fluctuating temperatures throughout its history.

Perhaps the entire global warming charade is best summed up by Vaclav Klaus, the President of the Czech Republic:

"Global warming is a false myth and every serious person and scientist says so… IPCC is not a scientific institution: it's a political body, a sort of non-government organization of green flavor. It's neither a forum of neutral scientists nor a balanced group of scientists. These people are politicized scientists who arrive there with a one-sided opinion and a one-sided assignment."[78]

Or if you prefer brevity, consider this statement from John Coleman, founder of *The Weather Channel:* "Global warming is the greatest scam in history." [79]

I couldn't have said it any better.

(Editor's Note: After this chapter was written, the scandal known as Climategate, a series of e-mails from scientists at the University of East Anglia, "brazenly discussing the destruction and hiding of data that did not support global warming-claims," erupted.

Readers could be forgiven if they are unaware of this, as major news organizations refused to report anything about this scandal for over two weeks. Even now, global warming advocates are dismissing it as insignificant; despite the fact the University of East Anglia was one of the primary sources for IPCC's reports. Requests to review the original data on which East Anglia drew its conclusions went unfulfilled for one alarming reason: the data has allegedly been destroyed.

Draw your own conclusions.)

Chapter 15

AN ENERGY POLICY — FOR *LESS* ENERGY

Despite the anti-environmentalist label attached to those on the right by the mainstream media and Democrats, conservatives like me are very much in favor of maintaining a clean country. Unlike most Democrats, however, I don't believe it's necessary to sacrifice America's economic future to do so.

Democrats' energy policy is a mixture of unrealistic hopes for "renewable" energy sources, coupled with a dogmatic resistance to nuclear power.

Even worse, they are stifling the production of domestic resources such as coal, oil and natural gas, America's most abundant — and most reliable — energy sources. Sources which could provide jobs and help insulate us from the whims of our enemies.

No doubt everyone would like to live in a world where clean, renewable energy sources are all we need. But wishing for something doesn't make it so.

Bottom line: moving towards a renewable energy future is a noble goal. But at the present time, it remains just that — a goal.

A sensible balance can be found between future hopes and present-day realities.

Too bad Democrats appear determined not to look for it.

President Obama and Democrats have offered Americans a false choice between promoting renewable energy and relying on oil. "We can remain the world's leading importer of oil, or we can become the world's leading exporter of clean energy," Obama said when visiting a wind turbine factory in Iowa in April 2009. [1]

The President was being disingenuous at best. The two options are mostly disconnected. Wind and solar mainly produce electricity. Most of our oil is used for transportation (cars, truck and planes) and only about 1.5 percent generates electricity. [2] Therefore, expanding wind and solar energy sources won't displace much oil.

Oil, gas, coal and nuclear power currently account for 91 percent of our nation's electricity. [3] As a result, they will be relied on overwhelmingly to meet the nation's energy needs for at least several decades. For perspective sake, wind and solar power currently generate less than 1 percent of U.S. electricity. [4] Thus, even *tripling* their contribution to our energy infrastructure would barely make a dent in our energy needs.

Despite this reality, Democrats are adopting stifling policies that will reduce the amount of energy we produce. They have proposed removing all tax incentives to produce oil and gas, passed a 13 percent excise tax on all energy derived from the Gulf of Mexico, and increased the corporate tax by 3 percent on all companies that produce or process oil and gas. [5] These tax policies are likely to create three bad trends: increased gasoline prices, higher electricity prices, and an America more dependant than ever on foreign oil. [6]

Taxing oil production is only the beginning of the Democrats' new energy-killing policies. In early 2009, Obama's Interior Secretary Ken Salazar cancelled 77 oil and gas leases that had been issued in Utah. He halted plans to lease the oil shale region in five states, even though a Shell Oil study concluded that 1 to 2 trillion barrels of recoverable oil there. He also justified the listing of the "yellow-billed loon" as an endangered species, even though it could limit the development of a huge, oil-rich region off Alaska's west coast. [7] In addition, Democrats decided not to issue leases for gas well drilling on the Roan Plateau in Colorado, and have shown little interest in developing the "Chukchi" region off north Alaska. [8]

Many Americans would be surprised to learn the United States has huge oil and natural gas resources. The Outer Continental Shelf may contain 86 billion barrels of oil. [9] In May 2009, *Science* magazine reported that the U.S. Geological Survey believes the Chukchi waters off Alaska hold 1.6 trillion cubic feet of undiscovered gas, or 30% of the world's supply, and 83 billion barrels of undiscovered oil. [10] The U.S. Geological Survey estimates the Bakken Formation in North Dakota and Montana may hold 3.65 billion barrels of oil, as well as upwards of 2 trillion barrels of oil shale concentrated in Colorado. If only 800 billion barrels were recoverable, that would be *triple* Saudi Arabia's proven reserves. [11]

Democrats' opposition to oil production is nothing new. In 1995, a bill passed by a Republican-led Congress to drill in the ANWAR area of Alaska was vetoed by President Bill Clinton. Since then, every attempt by Republicans to open ANWAR and the Outer Continental Shelf has been thwarted by Democrats. As recently as 2008, when oil prices had skyrocketed to $147 a barrel, Texas Republican representative Mac Thornberry introduced the No More Excuses Energy Act (H.R. 3089), an effort to permit drilling for oil in ANWAR, the Outer Continental Shelf and the Gulf of Mexico. Despite this unprecedented surge in the price of oil, Speaker of the House Nancy Pelosi refused for months to allow the bill to be brought to a full floor vote in the House. [12]

During the 2008 presidential election, when Democrats feared the negative political consequences of their opposition, they passed a bill allowing additional drilling. A careful look at the bill, however, revealed Democrats weren't really interested in oil production, as various provisions made drilling more difficult and more expensive.

Oil is not the only Democrat energy bogeyman. In 2009, the Obama administration threw out a Bush administration rule which made it easier to mine coal off mountaintops. [13] This despite the fact that coal currently produces about 50 percent of our electricity. The coal industry itself has an ominous future if what then-candidate Obama means what he said in an interview with the *San Francisco Chronicle*:

"So if somebody wants to build a coal-powered plant, they can. It's just that it will bankrupt them, because they're going to be charged a huge sum for all that greenhouse gas that's being emitted." [14]

The above quote underscores the essence of Democrat plans. They want to impose a green agenda on America. Their principal vehicle is a cap and trade scheme for taxing carbon emissions and creating carbon offsets.

We can look to the European Union for a preview of how this scheme will turn out. The EU instituted a cap and trade policy five years ago, and the results are dismal. The carbon-trading scheme has not-created a functioning emissions-permit market, generated revenues, nor reduced carbon-dioxide emissions as promised. What it *has* done in Europe — and you can be certain it will do the same here in the U.S. if implemented — is lead to large electricity rate increases that have to be paid for by the consumer. [15] For example, Germany's electricity bill went up by 38 percent in just one year (2007 over 2006). [16]

In the meantime, the rest of the world is moving in the opposite direction, away from renewable energy and towards nuclear power, another extremely viable energy source Democrats seem to have little interest in promoting.

The reason for their opposition? Democrats contend that America has not found a way to deal with nuclear waste. But Congress already designated Yucca Mountain in Nevada as the site where such waste can be stored. Despite this, in March 2009, Energy Secretary Stephen Chu slashed funding for building a waste site there, telling a Senate panel that the Yucca Mountain site was no longer an option. [17] In reality, Democrats simply don't like nuclear power and have no intention of expanding its use.

Outside the United States, however, the nuclear power revival is a worldwide phenomenon, including Western countries that were previously anti-nuclear. Italy and Sweden, both of which had moratoriums on building nuclear reactors going back to the 1980s, have now reversed course, and Germany will almost certainly follow shortly. Italy has started building four new nuclear plants out of eight planned, and aims to get 25 percent of its future electricity from nuclear power. [18]

Other countries that were not anti-nuclear have opted to increase their nuclear energy production as well. Great Britain is planning to refurbish eight old reactors and build ten new ones.[19] France, which currently derives nearly 80 percent of its electricity from its 58 nuclear reactors, is moving ahead with third generation reactors. Ukraine, despite Chernobyl, plans 11 new reactors by 2030. And Russia wants to double its energy from nuclear power by 2020. Poland, Finland, Lithuania, Bulgaria and Romania are either planning or have started building new nuclear power plants. [20]

China and India, economic superpowers of the future, have also decided to increase nuclear production in a significant way. India, which today produces a miniscule 3 percent of its electricity from nuclear power, intends to boost that 15-fold, with 40 new reactors by 2032, five of which are now under construction. China aims to increase their nuclear capacity by over 4-fold by 2020, and by 7-fold ten years later. And Japan intends to double its share of nuclear power by mid-century. [21]

Meanwhile, the renewable energy Democrats cherish will remain economically unfeasible for the foreseeable future without huge government subsidies. In addition, wind and solar face severe technical problems, such as building a whole new grid potentially costing trillions of dollars, and producing energy *only* when the wind blows or sun shines. This unreliability means wind and solar will have to be continually backed up by conventional energy sources such as coal–fired plants, making the green agenda self-defeating.

Unlike the U.S., subsidies for green energy in other countries are being slashed, projects are being cancelled and private capital is abandoning the sector. [22] And in China, where energy needs have vastly grown, renewable energy production as a share of total energy produced has declined over the past two years, according to Beijing's State Electricity Council. [23]

Considering the high unemployment rate, one would expect Democrats' energy policies to be at least partly focused on creating new jobs. With many states going bankrupt, it would make far better sense for Americans to buy oil from oil-rich states such as California, Alaska, Colorado, and Montana, instead of buying it from foreign countries. Such a policy would keep American dollars here, create new jobs, boost our economy, and help us become more energy independent.

Unfortunately, the green agenda is the antithesis of job creation, when compared to the oil and natural gas industries. Stifling production in the oil and gas industries which employ 1.8 million people, to favor solar and wind industries that employ only 120,000, will lead to more job losses in the former than can be replaced by the latter.

In other words, promoting America's traditional energy sources is simply common sense.

Sadly, common sense is scarce within the Democrat Party. Their energy agenda will hurt this country's economic competitiveness by driving up energy costs, while at the same time making us more dependent on imported oil. That is probably not what Americans had in mind when they voted for Democrats in 2008.

If Americans agree that this country should produce more of the energy that can actually meet our energy needs, the 2010 elections would be their best opportunity to express that preference.

(Author's note: After this chapter was written, President Obama announced in March 2010 that he will propose allowing offshore oil and natural gas exploration in a large area of the eastern Gulf of Mexico. In addition, he proposed to *study* how much oil and natural gas is buried off the coasts of Middle and Southern Atlantic states. [24]

This announcement appears to be a calculated move by the President to help him pass "cap and trade" legislation, currently stalled in the Senate. Obama knows he needs Congressional approval from Congressmen in states with energy economies, so he is using off-shore drilling as a bargaining chip. Congressional Republicans and Democrats in oil-rich states need to be aware of this subterfuge.

In reality, Obama and the Democrats don't want more oil production. At the same time he announced the aforementioned proposal, Obama also announced he wouldn't allow new oil and gas development off the coasts of Northern Atlantic states or California. Equally as important, he said he wouldn't allow drilling in Alaska's oil-rich Bristol Bay area. [25] He also announced he would delay development off Virgina's coast. [26] And in late February 2010 Obama's Interior Department leaked a memo disclosing plans to have Obama use executive power to designate 10 million acres of western land as "monuments," putting them off-limits to energy exploration. [27]

The Institute for Energy Research believes that Obama's announcement "is not a step forward, but a huge step backward." Under President Bush, the vast majority of areas in the Outer Continental Shelf were open for exploration. That is no longer the case. [28])

Chapter 16

THE ANSWER, MY FRIENDS, *AIN'T* BLOWIN' IN THE WIND

Democrats are pushing wind and solar energy as the prime movers for American energy independence.

Reality check: the wind doesn't blow and sun doesn't shine all the time. What this means is that some back-up power sources will still be necessary, even under the best of circumstances.

So why do Democrats pursue such a questionable agenda? As I discovered writing this chapter, renewable energy sources require massive government subsidies to become feasible.

Greater amounts of government subsidies equal greater amounts of government control.

Only Democrats could pitch more government dependence as more energy independence.

D
emocrats are recklessly pushing wind and solar as the solution for us to become energy independent. "We will harness the sun and the winds and the soil to fuel our cars and run our factories," promised President Obama in his inaugural address. [1]

But how feasible is wind and solar to implement given the size of our country and an economy as large as ours?

While renewable energy – wind and solar – is promoted by Democrats as superior to coal, gas and even nuclear, the technological hurdles and enormous cost make it extremely undesirable to be implemented on a national scale. Plus, there is a better alternative which Democrats half-heartedly pursue: nuclear power.

The first problem with wind power is painfully obvious: wind doesn't blow all the time. In addition, wind turbines cannot produce energy when wind speed is too low *or* too high, or if the turbine blades or other critical components are iced up. Wind is so unreliable that the Electric Reliability Council of Texas (ERCOT) estimates that only 8.7 percent of wind power's capacity would be available during summer peak hours, one of the times when electricity is most needed. [2] According to The Heritage Foundation wind power produces electricity year-round only about a third of the time.[3] In addition, because wind cannot be stored, electricity generated by it must be used immediately. [4] Even the idea to put wind turbines in the ocean where winds blow more frequently still does not solve the twin problems of unreliability and the inability to store energy.

Other countries have caught on to these daunting realities. Development of onshore wind plants in Denmark has effectively stopped, and in 2004 they decommissioned 90 turbines. Germany reduced tax breaks for wind power, and Switzerland cut subsidies due to a lack of significant benefits and high expenses. Many Japanese utilities severely restrict the amount of wind-generated power because of the instability they cause to the electrical grid. In 2003, for the same reason, Ireland halted all new wind-power connections to their national grid. And in 2005, Spanish utilities started refusing new wind-power connections to their grid as well. [5]

The unreliability of solar is equally obvious: the sun doesn't shine all the time. This means solar power is ineffective at night and/or when it is cloudy. Also, the sun is not strong in the winter months when power is needed most in many parts of the country. Unlike wind, which must be consumed as it is generated, solar can be stored, but would require a vast storage network to be used on a national scale. This technology is not currently available. The bottom line on reliability: Both solar and wind would still require conventional power plants at all time – or America would be faced with continual blackouts. [6]

The second major problem with respect to renewable energy is distribution. Both wind farms and solar power grids require enormous amounts of land, meaning the best locations would likely be in remote, thinly populated areas. For example, the upper Midwest offers the most desirable location for wind and southwestern deserts offer the best locations for solar. [7]

But, most Americans live in densely populated urban centers. This means that large amounts of power would have to be moved over long distances to satisfy our energy needs.

Unfortunately, our current 345 kilovolt (kV) transmission lines cannot transport electricity more than 300 miles without extreme losses due to heat and friction. The only way to reduce line loss is to upgrade the power grid to 765 kV. [8]

The next major problem is volume. Even if we could solve the distribution problem, creating a national grid based on renewable energy would require windmills and sunlight collectors on an almost unimaginable scale. In January 2009, while testifying about solar energy before the Senate Foreign Relations Committee, Al Gore tried to minimize this reality. Citing a January 2008 *Scientific American* article as proof, Gore claimed that we could provide all of America's electricity needs with a southwestern solar facility "100 miles on each side" (10,000 square miles). [9]

Gore came up short on both accuracy and specifics. The *Scientific American* article, "A Solar Grand Plan," actually said that to meet the 2050 projection of (electrical demand), "46,000 square miles of land would be needed for photovoltaic and concentrated solar power installations." That equals approximately one-third of the size of New Mexico, our fifth largest state.[10]

Gore also neglected to tell the Senate Committee — or the American public — that such a facility would produce electricity *only while the sun shines*. This means a system of electrical storage, both for nighttime capacity and cloudy days would still be necessary. [11]

The other "inconvenient truth" Gore failed to reveal is the aforementioned distribution problem. While it is hard to find reliable estimates on the cost of upgrading the transmission lines from 345 kilovolts to 765 kilovolts, it could easily be in the trillions of dollars. In addition, such an upgrade would involve overcoming major hurdles with regulatory laws and NIMBY (not in my backyard) public resistance. The cost of solar collectors, which would be more than $1 trillion, and the storage system, yet another $1 trillion, would be *in addition* to the cost of transmission line upgrades. [12]

A fawning mainstream media with a soft spot for Al Gore and other radical environmentalists has failed to inform the American public of these damning details.

But assuming we go forward anyway, what will we get for our more than $3 trillion investment in solar power? Many experts have concluded that the present net costs of current solar photovoltaic installations far exceed the present net benefits of the electricity they will produce—by a factor of three or four. And with a typical life span of 25 years, solar panels are simply not economical today. [13]

Another huge but rarely discussed problem is that solar panels accumulate dust, dirt and sand, diminishing their effectiveness. This means installations would have to be washed down continuously with water. [14] Question: where does one find enough water in the middle of the desert to wash down 46,000 square miles of solar panels every month?

In conclusion, Democrats are forcing us down a path that doesn't work. They are wasting our money instead of spending it on more reliable and cost-effective sources of energy.

Why are they doing this? For power — of the political kind. Renewable energy production requires massive government subsidies to be economically viable. Thus any company willing to undertake such production becomes beholden to government bureaucrats, determining who the "winners" and "losers" will be.

This chapter does not intend to completely dismiss renewable energy per se. Some of our energy needs may be met in a decentralized model where households or neighborhoods have their own energy sources. [15] Solar panels can be used in the warmer states on an individual basis. Windmills can be used by people who have enough land and live in areas with consistent wind.

But as a *nationwide* solution to our energy problems, barring a major leap in the current technology, wind and solar unfortunately are not the answer.

Most Americans understand this. Too bad most Democrats don't.

Chapter 17

DEMOCRATS' NUCLEAR NUTTINESS

Democrats appear to have a blind spot regarding nuclear energy, despite the fact that its use is becoming increasingly common around the world.

Most of their resistance centers around a variety of claims: we don't have reliable methods for disposing of radioactive waste, transporting such waste is dangerous, reactors can melt down, and/or they are subject to terrorist attacks.

This chapter demonstrates that all these claims are largely disingenuous distractions from what I consider the real reason Democrats resist nuclear power: one of their most reliable voting blocs are radical environmentalists — who have a disproportionate amount of influence over America's energy policy as a result.

It is one thing when America's enemies hold us hostage to their energy polices.

It is quite another when Democrats do the same thing.

Democrats have chosen to disregard science in favor of politics when it comes to nuclear energy. This is ironic since it is just what Barack Obama pledged *not* to do in his inaugural address, where he said he was going to "restore science to its rightful place."

To understand the irony, a little background is necessary. During the campaign trail in June 2008, candidate Obama criticized John McCain's proposal to encourage the building of 45 new nuclear reactors by 2030. Obama said McCain lacked a plan for storage of the waste. It was among several of McCain's energy-strategy ideas that Obama said were "not serious energy policies." [1] Several days later, Obama's position became more nuanced when he said, "I think nuclear power should be in the mix when it comes to energy." But he quickly added, "I don't think it's our optimal energy source because we haven't figured out how to store the waste safely or recycle the waste." [2]

Obama was being dishonest with the American people because we have already figured out how to store and recycle nuclear waste safely. His calculated disingenuousness masked the real agenda of Democrats, which is to cater to the environmentalists who oppose nuclear energy. No Democrat administration or Congress wants to go against an estimated 4 million members belonging to hundreds of groups such as the Sierra Club and Greenpeace, who provide enormous amounts of campaign financing and votes.

A brief explanation of how the rest of the world safely stores nuclear waste will allow one to understand the deception of Obama and Democrats. Most countries with nuclear energy reprocess their spent fuel rods, so the highly radioactive waste that remains is kept to a minimum. France, which has produced 75% of its electricity for 30 years with nuclear power, has stored all its waste beneath the floor of one room at La Hague. [3] By 2040, Britain will have only 70,000 cubic feet of such waste, which could be stored in a cube measuring 42 feet on each side. In addition, the British government has determined that "geological disposal" — burying nuclear waste deep underground — provides the best available method of disposal. [4]

If Obama and Democrats were genuinely honest with the American people, they would explain how there is virtually no such thing as "nuclear waste." That's because ninety-five percent of a spent rod is harmless U-238, the non-fissionable variety of uranium that exists in such things as granite countertops and stone buildings. Of the remaining 5% of a spent rod, one-fifth is fissionable U-235 which can be recycled as fuel, as most countries do. Another one-fifth is plutonium, likewise recyclable as fuel. Much of the remaining three-fifths are used for medical and industrial isotopes, a significant amount of which is used in medical diagnostic procedures. What little remains are some isotopes which have no uses but can be stored in a small space, as France and Britain have demonstrated. [5] After 10 years, these isotopes become harmless, only *one-thousandth* as radioactive as they were initially. [6]

Unfortunately, America does not reprocess spent fuel rods. President Gerald Ford temporarily suspended reprocessing in 1976, and Jimmy Carter made the suspension permanent in 1977. Carter outlawed such processing in the naïve belief that other countries would follow suit and reduce the amount of plutonium available for weapons proliferation.[7] Although the ban was later lifted, government policies have discouraged the resumption of reprocessing. [8]

The Republicans have attempted to alter this policy.   On June 10, 2009, House Republicans introduced The American Energy Act which, if passed, would have provided an avenue to recycle spent nuclear fuel in the U.S, and cut the amount of time necessary to obtain a permit for building a nuclear power plant in half. [9]

Predictably, the Democratically-controlled Congress vetoed this bill.

And despite the controversy over how much waste would be produced by nuclear power, America *does* have a viable storage location available. Nevada's Yucca Mountain, about a two-hour drive from Las Vegas, was declared by Congress in 1987 as the site where American nuclear waste can be stored. [10] According to the U.S. Geological Survey, Yucca Mountain is one of the most geographically stable locations in the country. The area's water table sits 1000 feet below where the waste would be buried, in a basin that is separate from the Las Vegas area aquifer. Yucca Mountain is so well-sealed and well-secured that there is no risk of seepage that would damage far-off population centers.[11] In fact, the U.S. government has spent nearly $10 billion on feasibility studies which have convinced government scientists that their plans for Yucca are sound.[12] These studies by the Department of Energy have calculated that exposure to the public from radiation will be no more than 0.98 millirems (mrem) per year, up to a million years into the future.[13]

To put such "exposure" into perspective, Americans are *naturally* exposed to around 360 mrem a year from background radiation.[14] In other places around the world, the background level is much higher. In Ramsar, Iran, because of the presence of natural uranium in the vicinity, residents are exposed to 26,000 mrem a year, but there is no increased rate of cancer or shortened lifespan.[15] As Professor Donald W. Miller Jr. of the University of Washington School of Medicine wrote in 2004, "(K)nown and documented health-damaging effects of radiation – radiation sickness, leukemia and death – are only seen with doses greater than 100 rem (which is equivalent to 100,000 mrem)…" [16]

Political pressure and legal challenges from environmental groups, however, have delayed even the first shovel from breaking ground to build the facility at Yucca Mountain. As a result, nuclear plants have been storing their waste in temporary facilities. There are more than 120 "temporary" locations holding nuclear waste in 39 states. Although this has kept the nuclear industry from shutting down, many of these temporary storage pools are nearing capacity.[17] California and several other states have laws which prevent nuclear reactors from being built before Yucca is completed. [18] Thus, this issue must be resolved for there to be a surge in the development of nuclear power in this country.

Democrats know that if they put Yucca Mountain off limits, they can slow down or kill nuclear expansion.

Unfortunately, that's exactly what they did in early 2009. Obama's Energy Secretary Stephen Chu told a Senate hearing that "the Yucca Mountain site was no longer viewed as an option for storing reactor waste." Instead, Chu said the nearly 60,000 tons of used reactor fuel can remain at nuclear power plants while a new comprehensive plan for waste disposal is developed. [19]

This is a trumped up controversy. We already have a facility at Yucca Mountain, and the U.S. government has spent billions of dollars in studies to prove it is safe.

Yucca Mountain has a long history as a nuclear test facility. It sits on the western edge of the Nevada Test Site, a 1,350 square mile Federal preserve that served as the testing ground for America's nuclear weapons arsenal for decades. Beginning in the 1950s, the federal government detonated close to 1,000 atomic weapons on the site, or about half of all nuclear explosions the earth has endured. About 100 of these were above-ground nuclear explosions, many more powerful than the bombs that exploded in Japan to end World War II. As Max Schulz, senior fellow at the *Manhattan Institute* points out, "other than craters formed by the atomic bombardment...southern Nevada seems none the worse off." And Las Vegas, a mere two hours away, has grown spectacularly since the 1950s. [20]

Besides waste storage, the most common concern about the safety of nuclear energy is the fear that one of the reactors is either going to blow up and cause a nuclear explosion or meltdown. This fear is unfounded. A reactor is not a bomb and can't blow up because it does not contain enough fissionable material. What a nuclear reactor can do is overheat if it loses its cooling water, the same way your car engine can overheat and break down if it loses its antifreeze. This is called a meltdown. [21] We've had over 40 years of history with nuclear energy that demonstrate this concern is no longer justified.

Despite this track record, critics cite two incidents to justify their fears: Three Mile Island and Chernobyl.

There are two important things to remember about the 1979 event at Three Mile Island: First, no one was killed or injured. Second, there was no meltdown. The system worked as designed and completely stopped the nuclear reaction within eight seconds of the initial event that led to the episode. [22]

More importantly, it was an operator error. When a valve failed, the automatic safety mechanism was overridden because a mass of flashing lights and sirens on the control panel confused the operators. That particular valve had failed nine times before in other reactors and the manufacturer had tried to keep it a secret. This was possible because, back in 1979, people in the nuclear industry were not communicating with each other, so the valve problem went unresolved. [23]

Today they do communicate and have made other changes to enhance nuclear safety. For example, nuclear operators train for five years before they can take over a control room and now spend one week out of every five in a simulator honing their skills. And today a Nuclear Regulatory Commission inspector is constantly visiting nuclear sites. [24]

As for the Chernobyl meltdown in 1985, that incident was caused by features unique to Soviet-style nuclear reactors. The Soviets didn't put a containment structure around the reactor which would have prevented radioactive material from getting out. [25] In addition they did something no American nuclear producer has ever done — they surrounded the core with carbon in the form of graphite. When the graphite caught fire, it spewed radioactive smoke similar to the way a charcoal grill releases smoke when heated. That could never happen at an American reactor site or even a Russian one today, since they now build reactors the same way we build them. [26]

There are other concerns expressed by critics. One is that nuclear power plants present an attractive target for terrorists. After the 9/11 attacks, the

Department of Energy commissioned a study into the effects of a fully fueled jetliner hitting a nuclear containment structure at maximum speed. Containment was never breached in any of the simulations. It is also unlikely that terrorists would seek to attack such a *hard* target, given the massive investment needed to compromise it. Historically, terrorists have preferred soft targets that are easier to attack and cause a greater loss of lives. [27]

Another concern is the risk of transporting radioactive materials. A staggering amount of evidence directly refutes this myth. Since 1971, over 20,000 shipments of spent fuel and high-level waste have been moved more than 18 million miles worldwide without incident. Transportation of radioactive materials is simply not a problem. [28]

The remaining reservation about nuclear energy is economic. The direct costs of building a nuclear plant, coupled with maneuvering through the maze of regulations and lawsuits filed by environmentalists, are primary factors in the high cost of construction. On the one hand, the fact that nuclear energy provides about 20 percent of America's electricity despite these burdens is a testament to its economic viability. On the other hand, these burdens have taken their toll: no new nuclear power reactors have been built in the U.S. over the past thirty years. [29]

Republicans have tried to keep the nuclear industry alive. The George H. W. Bush administration's 1992 Energy Policy Act made licensing a one-step procedure. It allowed utilities to obtain both construction and operating licenses before putting shovels in the ground. [30] The George W. Bush administration passed the 2005 Energy Policy Act, which authorized federal risk insurance for utility companies to cover costs associated with certain regulatory — or litigation-related delays — that are no fault of the company, but stall construction. It also established loan guarantees, standby support and production credits for the construction of six new nuclear reactors to be built in the U.S. [31] As a result, on June 17, 2009, four power companies were chosen to split $18.5 billion to build new reactors. [32] In 2008, the Bush Energy Department also submitted an 8,600 page license application to the Nuclear Regulatory Commission to build the repository at Yucca Mountain. [33]

Unfortunately, just as progress was being made, Barack Obama was elected and Democrats reversed course. Their 2009 budget included almost nothing related to advancing nuclear energy. Additionally, the Democrat's American Clean Energy and Security Act of 2009 (The Waxman-Markey bill) focused instead on a misguided cap and trade program.[34] Although the original Senate version of the 2009 Stimulus Bill contained an additional $50 billion in loan guarantees, the Democratically-controlled Congress stripped that provision under pressure from environmentalists. [35]

In other words, Democrats preferred to keep a special interest group happy rather than do what was best for America.

Ironically, if Democrats decide to tax carbon emissions and price coal out of the energy market through their cap and trade scheme, then nuclear would be the best energy alternative. In addition, if America wants to cure its addiction to oil, nuclear energy would be a great way to power our hybrid electric cars.

Unfortunately, based on their track record, America isn't likely to get more nuclear energy from Democrats.

Chapter 18

OBAMANOMICS: A ROADMAP TO FISCAL RUIN

The Hippocratic Oath says, "first, do no harm." It would be nice if Barack Obama and the Democrat Party took a similar pledge regarding the economy.

Ironically, one primary reason Democrats control Congress and the White House is the fiscal irresponsibility demonstrated by Republicans when they were the majority party, and deficits ballooned during the latter years of the Bush administration.

Despite this reality, Democrats have "one-upped" Republicans — by a three-fold margin. During Barack Obama's first year in office, the country endured its first-ever trillion dollar annual deficit — and the Democratically-controlled Congress has demonstrated no inclination whatsoever to curtail its spendthrift inclinations.

In short, Democrats' current fiscal polices are exactly what I have entitled this chapter: a roadmap to fiscal ruin.

While President Barack Obama did inherit an economy in deep recession, many of the policies he and his fellow Democrats have crafted to revive it will inevitably cause even greater harm.

The 10 post-World War II recessions and recoveries generally conformed to the principle that the bigger the bust, the bigger the boom, and vice-versa. Real growth in the first year following postwar recessions averaged 6.6%, and 4.3% over the subsequent five years. [1] As Barclay's chief economist, Dean Maki, wrote in *The Wall Street Journal* on August 19, 2009, "You can't find a single deep recession that has been followed by a moderate recovery." [2]

That may no longer be the case. The reasons for pessimism?

Exhibit A — The unprecedented spending splurges by the Obama administration and a Democratically–controlled Congress — with no end in sight.

Since taking office, Mr. Obama has pushed through a $787 billion stimulus bill, a $33 billion expansion of the children's health program (S-CHIP), and an $80 billion auto company bailout. [3]

In addition, Democrats passed a $410 billion omnibus appropriations bill for 2009, and another $1.1 trillion spending bill for 2010, both of which were loaded with pork. The 2010 bill represents a 12% spending hike, well above inflation. [4]

And that's just what they've spent already. Democrats are also pushing an $821 billion cap and trade bill, and yet another stimulus package for $154 billion, despite every indication that the first stimulus package has proven to be largely ineffective. They also passed a national health care bill that will dramatically increase the federal deficits even further (see Chapter 31).

In just the first year of Obama's presidency, total U.S. public debt has jumped from 41% of Gross Domestic Product (GDP) to 53%, [5] and the 2009 federal deficit reached a record $1.42 trillion. [6] (For those Americans critical of the Bush administration's deficit spending, some perspective: the highest deficit recorded by the Bush administration was $466 billion in 2008, less than one-third of the 2009 total). [7]

Reality is stark: America is on the fiscal road to ruin. Obama and the Democrats' spending spree have raised our annual baseline budget from nearly $3 trillion to a proposed $3.8 trillion for fiscal year 2011. [8]

As a result, the Office of Management and Budget (OMB) projects added deficits of about $9 trillion over the next decade. The actual amount will be much *higher*, since the OMB didn't include the aforementioned health care bill and additional spending planned by Democrats, optimistically projects $13.5 trillion of revenue increases over the next decade, and minimizes the inevitable rise in interest rates that will come with an expanding national debt. [9]

In January 2010, to accommodate their out of control spending, the Senate voted to lift the U.S. debt limit by $1.9 trillion to $14.3 trillion. [10] By 2018, at current spending trends, our nation's debt as a share of GDP will hit 85%. In 2022, it will reach 100%, and it will keep rising at least until 2038, hitting 200%. [11] According to *Investor's Business Daily*, "at that level, our fast-growing, high innovation, high wage economy begins grinding to a permanent slowdown. The accumulated debt will become a millstone around our necks." [12]

Japan is a perfect example of such fiscal irresponsibility. For much of the postwar era, it was the world's fastest growing developed economy. But it slumped in the late 1980s and started a debt-financed binge of "stimulus" packages in the 1990s and early 2000s. Today, it has the worst of all worlds: a debt load equal to 200% of GDP, and low or no growth. [13]

Why do economies slow down with such high levels of debt? "Government borrowing reduces resources available for private investment, leading to lower productivity, wages and economic growth," explained the Heritage Foundation in a recent study. [14] Left unchecked, this destructive deficit-debt cycle will force the White House and Congress to either default on the national debt or instruct the Treasury to print money at a hyper-inflationary level of output. [15]

<u>Exhibit B</u> — Job-killing tax increases.

First, expect the Democratically-controlled Congress to let most of the Bush tax cuts expire on December 31, 2010. As a result, marginal income tax rates, capital gains tax rates, dividend rates and death or estate taxes will increase significantly. The top federal tax rate will increase from 35% to 39.6%. [16]

Next, there's the health care bill the Democrats passed. ObamaCare will require employers to provide insurance to workers or pay fines for failing to do so. The penalties for non-compliance will essentially operate as tax increases. [17] Beginning in 2018, ObamaCare will also impose a 40% tax on annual insurance premiums above $10,200 for an individual and $27,500 for a family. And beginning in 2015, it will increase the Medicare payroll tax from 2.9% to 3.8% on individuals earning over $200,000 and joint filers over $250,000. Equally as important, this new payroll tax rate will apply to unearned income from interest, dividends, capital gains, and rents. [18]

The passage of ObamaCare has also forced large corporations to lose the tax subsidies they were previously receiving for providing drug plans for retirees. These losses amount to a one billion dollar price tag for AT&T, and hundreds of millions of dollars for other companies, such as Caterpillar and John Deere. [19]

Democrats also want to impose a new tax on energy. In June 2009, the House passed a cap and trade bill that will tax carbon emissions and raise prices on every product made or transported using carbon-based energy — which is just about everything. [20]

If Democrats aren't able to pass cap and trade, which is stalled in the Senate, they plan to tax carbon dioxide emissions another way — through the Environmental Protection Agency (EPA). In December 2009, Lisa Jackson, Obama's handpicked head of the EPA, formally announced the EPA's intention to regulate and tax greenhouse gases through the Clean Air Act. This was likely done to pressure Congress and the business community to support the cap and trade legislation or else face tougher EPA regulations. [21]

In December 2009, the House voted also to increase the capital gains rate from 15% to 35% on venture capitalists who invest in technology start-ups. They did this by classifying such gains as ordinary income. [22]

And the president's budget released in February 2010 includes a set of proposals to increase taxes on U.S. multinational firms. These tax increases will cost these firms an estimated $122 billion in tax increases over the next 10 years. [23]

Democrats are also considering a Euro-style Value-Added Tax (VAT) on products and services — since the taxes previously mentioned will be insufficient to pay for the trillions in new debt incurred by the government

So what happens when you raise taxes?

With respect to letting the Bush tax cuts expire, money previously invested in the private sector will be confiscated by the government. Since there is indisputable evidence that tax cuts produce greater amounts of revenue for the federal government — as proven by the three major tax cutters of recent American history, JFK, Ronald Reagan, and George W. Bush — it is logical to assume that raising taxes will have the opposite effect. Martin Feldstein, Harvard professor and chairman of the Council of Economic Advisers under President Reagan agrees: "Historians and economists who've studied the 1930s conclude that the tax increases passed during that decade derailed the recovery and slowed the decline in unemployment." [24]

Regarding the health care taxes on individuals and businesses, one can expect less investment by the wealthy and hiring freezes or job cuts by businesses, due to higher overhead. And the middle class won't escape the new increased health care costs. Many with high premium policies may have the 40% tax placed on top of their existing premiums, causing an additional financial burden.

With respect to the proposed cap and trade bill, annual job losses due to taxation on CO_2 emissions will exceed 800,000 in at least two years, and 500,000 per annum over the next two decades. [25] According to the Center for Data Analysis at The Heritage Foundation, by 2029 more than 3.5 million manufacturing jobs will have been lost. [26]

Regarding the tax on carbon dioxide emissions imposed by the EPA's Clean Air Act, raising energy prices for every decent-sized commercial building will inevitably cause businesses to shed jobs. Landlords will pass their increased energy costs on to their tenants, and businesses will also do the same with their customers or else absorb those higher costs. In any event, jobs will be lost because of higher operating costs.

With respect to venture capitalist taxes, small businesses which create the overwhelming majority of jobs in America will be adversely affected. Raising the cost on those willing to invest in new businesses — which account for most of the new jobs in this country — will be a drag on investment and job growth. [27]

How serious is this? Newer businesses, those in existence less than five years, create two-thirds of the new jobs in this country. [18] This period of time is when those businesses need venture capital the most. Companies which have been the beneficiaries of venture capital now generate more than 20% of U.S. gross domestic product. [28] Thus, this bill is the *antithesis* of economic growth and job creation.

Regarding the taxes on multinational firms, according to Matthew Slaughter, associate dean and professor at the Tuck School of Business at Dartmouth, "these tax increases will destroy jobs in some of America's most dynamic companies." [29]

With respect to a VAT tax, emulating Europe, a continent that averaged an unemployment rate twice that of the U.S. for much of the 1990s, and one used to double-digit unemployment as a routine feature of life, hardly makes sense. [30]

Even those things done with the best of intentions don't stand up to fiscal scrutiny. In July 2009, Democrats raised the minimum wage once again, which resulted in the loss of jobs for low-skilled and young workers. The hardest hit were black male teens, whose jobless rate climbed the following two months from 39.2% to 50.4%. [31] Democrats and the Obama administration have ignored the economic consensus which has long linked minimum wages with higher unemployment. In 2007, economists David Neumark and William Wascher reviewed more than 100 academic studies on the effect of the minimum wage. They found "overwhelming" evidence that the least skilled and the young suffer employment losses when the minimum wage is increased. [32]

According to the Heritage Foundation, reduced private-sector investment, as opposed to an increase in layoffs, is the primary engine driving higher unemployment: "...the main reason unemployment has risen is because job creation has fallen. As a result, those without work stay unemployed longer, thereby driving up the unemployment rate." [33]

Unfortunately, Democrats and the Obama administration have done little to address this problem, because they prefer an increase in government spending, instead of encouraging entrepreneurial activity. In a revealing example of the Obama White House's approach toward employment, the December 3, 2009 "job summit" excluded the two principal groups that represent job-creators, the Chamber of Commerce and the National Federation of Independent Businesses. [34]

Exhibit C — Protectionist policies that will hurt American exports.

Foreign trade is a mainstay of the U.S. economy, accounting for about a third of U.S. Gross Domestic Product and underpinning about 40% of U.S. jobs. [35]

The Democrats' $787 billion stimulus package contained a "Buy American" provision that required iron, steel and manufactured goods used in projects funded by the stimulus bill to be produced in the United States. [36] This provision has angered foreign governments, including Canada, who have threatened to retaliate.

In 2009, Democrats banned Mexican trucks from U.S. roads in direct violation of NAFTA, prompting Mexico to retaliate against U.S. farm and kitchen goods. [37] They also slapped a 35% tariff on Chinese tires, and China responded by threatening to retaliate against U.S. chicken and auto parts producers. [38] The threat became more of a reality, when, in February 2010, China's Ministry of Commerce proposed retaliatory duties of between 43% and 106% on imports of American poultry. [39]

Previously negotiated free trade agreements with Columbia, Panama and South Korea have been languishing unsigned in Congress because of the Democrat Party's deep alliances with unions who don't want free trade. In fact, it seems evident that the labor unions' anti-trade positions now dominate the Democratically-controlled Congress. The worry is that these protectionist policies will ignite trade wars with catastrophic consequences similar to the Smoot–Hawley tariffs enacted in 1930.

Exhibit D — The uncertainty created by the Obama administration's intervention in the GM and Chrysler reorganizations.

The Obama administration upset decades of accepted bankruptcy law by leveraging TARP funds to place *unsecured and lower priority* creditors like the United Auto Workers Union ahead of *secured and higher priority* creditors. [40]

This "redistribution of wealth" was payback to the unions who support the Democrat Party. More importantly, this intervention could stifle future investment if investors can't be certain that the rule of law will trump political cronyism.

As Warren Buffett noted at the time, "We don't want to say to somebody who lends and gets a secured position that the secured position doesn't mean anything." [41] Gary Parr, deputy chair of the mergers and acquisitions firm Lazard Freres & Co., stated the problem more precisely: "I can't imagine the markets will function properly if you are always wondering if the government is going to step in and change the game." [42]

<u>Exhibit E</u> — The Democrat Party's determination to emulate European-style socialism — vastly expanding entitlement programs, strengthening unions, and increasing government control over the private sector. [43]

The stimulus bill contained multiple provisions that burden the already strained unemployment insurance system with "new entitlements," such as paying workers who *choose* to leave their job for "family-related" reasons. [44] Imposing these entitlements on an insurance system designed to support workers who are *laid off* compromises the integrity of the program. [45] To pay for such an expanded definition of "unemployed," states will be forced to raise unemployment insurance taxes on employers. Raising taxes on employers will only lead to one thing: fewer job opportunities. [46]

With respect to unions, Democrats have proposed the "Employee Free Choice Act," commonly known as "card check." This totally misnamed bill will actually *deprive* workers of a genuine free choice by eliminating their right to a secret ballot in unionization efforts at their workplace. It will also impose a short-term deadline for companies to sign a labor contract — after which government arbitrators would *dictate the terms* of such contracts. [47]

Increased unionization will lead to one result: increased salaries and benefits for workers, even though those salaries and benefits may not be economically feasible for the company. Since the cost of doing business will increase, the inevitable consequences will be job layoffs or business closings.

Such negative consequences have already played out across the country. Public employee unions have reaked havoc on state and local government budgets, and private unions have hurt the auto, airline, steel and many other industries. Unrealistic union contracts are busting budgets in both the public and private sector. None of these negatives matter to the Democrat Party, which has long been indebted to the unions for their help in getting candidates elected. Mr. Obama himself admits his indebtedness to them:

"I owe unions," he said in 2006. "When their leaders call, I do my best to call them back right away. I don't consider this corrupting in any way; I don't mind feeling obligated toward (them)...I got into politics to fight for these folks." [48]

As for increasing government control over the private sector, in May 2009 Obama's Assistant Attorney General for Antitrust, Christine Varney, claimed that the Justice Department can aid economic recovery by prosecuting businesses that have been successful in gaining large market shares. [49] Mrs. Varney defended this change in governmental policy by arguing that our current recession reflects "a failure of antitrust" and "inadequate antitrust oversight." [50]

George L. Priest, writing in *The Wall Street Journal,* puts such nonsense in perspective: "Prosecuting successful businesses will help the recovery? ... Hard to believe." [51]

Another example of increasing government intrusion is the Democrats' meddling in the auto industry. First, they set a national mileage standard for passenger cars of 35.5 miles per gallon. Then they forced auto makers GM and Chrysler to make the types of cars that helped drive them into bankruptcy in the first place — cheap, lightweight, low mileage cars Americans don't buy. [52] To top it off, they prevented GM from sending the production of a new line of small cars to China, where labor costs are cheaper and where smaller, more fuel-efficient cars are already made. [53]　Instead, the Auto Task Force, in a concession to the United Auto Workers, decided GM should produce a class B, Yugo-like car in the United States, requiring the company to retool its domestic plants. [54] Unfortunately, Democrats found meddling insufficient. Embracing Rahm Emanuel's "never let a crisis go to waste" mentality, the Obama administration nationalized a substantial portion of the auto industry.

Writer Phyllis Schlafly puts this government takeover of the auto industry in perspective:

"Obama's takeover of the American auto industry is so breathtaking in scope and power...The takeover was followed by orders to close 789 local Chrysler dealers, notices to 1,100 General Motors franchises that they will be shut down by next year, and estimates that total dealer shutdowns will rise to 3,000. The Chrysler and GM dealership closings are estimated to eliminate 187,000 jobs, which is more than the number of people who work for the two automakers …Nearly every one of the closed local dealerships have donated to Republican candidates, almost none was an Obama contributor, and some dealerships owned by Democrats were not being told to close." [55]

European-style interventions which Democrats and the Obama administration have been pushing will not make America more competitive in the world-wide economy. Such policies will not increase growth, will not reduce unemployment, and will not increase workers' wages. Evidence of this has been apparent for decades in Europe's declining growth rates, higher unemployment, lower per capita income, and longer periods of unemployment. [56]

Ironically, the poor and middle class, the very people Obama promised to help, will suffer the most from the policies outlined in this chapter.

In 2006, Americans elected Democrats to a majority in both houses of Congress. In 2008, they voted for hope and change. However, it is very unlikely they voted for runaway spending, job-killing taxes, economic protectionism, government takeovers and a European-style socialist welfare state. It is even more unlikely they voted for unsustainable levels of debt and a bleak future for their children and grandchildren.

Such extreme policies may lead to a reckoning in 2010. One thing is certain; the romance is over. As of this writing, Americans on both sides of the political spectrum are angry and frightened.

With good reason.

Chapter 19

KEYNESIAN KRAZINESS

In 2009, Vice President Joe Biden said something that, for me, completely summarizes the Democrat Party's economic philosophy. At a meeting with the American Association of Retired Persons (AARP), he said that America has to spend money — to keep from going bankrupt.

Biden was referring to a philosophy known as Keynesian economics which posits that the government must "jumpstart" the economy when the private sector falters. Yet even Keynes himself said such spending should be followed by tax cuts once the economy begins to recover.

Democrats are adamantly opposed to such tax cuts.

The research I did for this chapter regarding economic downturns both here and abroad leads me to a far different conclusion. In virtually every case, the best thing the government can do to minimize the effect of a recession is stunningly simple:

Get out of the way and let the free market work.

Democrats and President Obama have pointed to massive government spending programs undertaken in the 1930s Great Depression as proof that the government can spend its way out of a recession. As a result, in 2009, Democrats budgeted almost a trillion dollars of new spending to stimulate the economy. Much of that money was not targeted for immediate expenditure, but for 2010 or later, thus not providing much of an immediate jolt to the economy. More troubling was that much of the stimulus spending was aimed at paying back special interest groups and advancing other political priorities, rather than stimulating the economy and creating jobs. Regardless, the question we need to ask is: can spending large sums of money pull an economy out of a slump?

Probably not.

Democrats and President Obama are pursuing economic policies first advanced by John Maynard Keynes, a noted economist from the 1930s. Keynes' idea was that, left to its own devices, an economy can fall into a slump and remain there. Self-corrective mechanisms will not necessarily work on their own; they require help. [1] Keynes believed that when businesses and people cannot or will not invest, then government must take the responsibility to fill the gap. The key, he argued, was speed. Keynes favored large public works projects *and later, tax cuts as well* — specifically in response to criticism that public works projects did not put cash quickly enough into the system. [2]

In reality, the success of an economy depends on investment, and on businesses building new plants, buying new machines, and employing more workers. Typically, when an economy slows down, businesses reduce their demand for credit. At the same time, worried consumers save their earnings in banks, and, as a result, add to the funds available for lending. These two forces – as well as actions taken by the Federal Reserve – combine to push interest rates down to levels so attractive that businesses start borrowing again, and the economy picks up. [3] This is the natural way an economy recovers.

Unfortunately, President Obama and Democrats have not learned from history. Massive government spending has been tried in the past, and the track record is discouraging. What has worked in the past are tax rate reductions, which immediately stimulate business and spending. Three presidents cut tax rates and were successful in stimulating the economy. Two of those presidents were Republicans, namely Ronald Reagan and George W. Bush. Ironically for tax and spend Democrats, one of the largest rate reductions of modern times was engineered by liberal icon, John F. Kennedy. Democrats claim they put tax cuts in the 2009 stimulus package, when in fact they were just rebates, which like government spending, merely redistributes wealth.

The Great Depression provides some insight. Despite Franklin Roosevelt's aggressive government spending, unemployment reached 25 percent in 1933, fell only to 14 percent in 1937, and increased to 19 percent in 1939.[4] Even Roosevelt's loyal Treasury Secretary confessed that New Deal policies failed. By 1939, a frustrated Henry Morgenthau concluded: "We have tried spending money. We are spending more than we have ever spent before and it does not work... I say after eight years of this Administration we have just as much unemployment as when we started…and an enormous debt to boot!" [5]

From 1929 until 1941, spending large sums of government money (fiscal stimulus) did not jumpstart the economy. According to some economists, such as Paul Krugman of *The New York Times,* government stimulus packages work. However, Krugman offers only a single dubious "success" story. He said, "The Great Depression in the United States was brought to an end by a massive deficit-financed public works program, known as World War II." [6]

Many economists believe Mr. Krugman is wrong and that the United States could not tolerate enormous budget deficits that developed during World War II, which ran more than 50 percent of gross domestic product, or about $7 trillion annually in current dollars. [7] Why? During World War II, the federal government wasn't the entitlement machine it is today, spending trillions of dollars a year in retirement and health care benefits. [8] Our current economy, quite frankly, couldn't withstand such double-barrel deficit spending.

An even more compelling argument against government stimulus spending is the case of Japan in the 1990s. In the 1980s, Japan had a spectacular boom with rapidly escalating real estate prices, as well as an incredible stock market rise. When the inevitable bust occurred, it hit hard. The Japanese stock market declined from 40,000 in late 1989 to 15,000 in 1992, and real estate prices dropped 80 percent between 1991 and 1998. [9] In 1992, the country embarked on a great Keynesian experiment, and attempted to spend its way out of its recession. In August 1992, they passed an $85 billion stimulus package, and followed it with seven larger stimulus packages: April 1993 - $117 billion, September 1993 - $59 billion, February 1994 – $139 billion, September 1995 - $137 billion, April 1998 - $128 billion, November 1998 — $195 billion, and November 1999 - $164 billion. [10]

This was enormous amount of stimulus for a country with a much smaller economy than the U.S. As a result, Japan's economy grew anemically over that decade — but its national debt exploded, reaching 128.3% of Gross Domestic Product by the end of 1999 (the U.S. equivalent today would be about $18 trillion). [11] In spite of the numerous stimulus packages, the slump *worsened.* Only when the government reinflated the money supply in the early 2000s, and more importantly, decided to privatize state assets and force banks to acknowledge their bad debts, did the economy recover. [12]

This period in Japanese history is commonly referred to as the "lost decade."

Is there an alternative to Keynesian economic solutions? The depression of 1920-1921 is especially informative. During and after World War I, the Federal Reserve began to inflate the money supply substantially, and when it began raising interest rates, the economy slowed. By the middle of 1920, the downturn in production had become severe, falling by 21 per cent over the following year. Conditions were worse than they would become in 1930, after the first year of the Great Depression. [13]

Very few Americans are aware that such a depression occurred. That's probably because, compared to the Great Depression of the 1930s, it was so brief. The federal government allowed the free markets to make the necessary corrections, instead of instituting public works spending, incurring government deficits, and instituting inflationary monetary policy. Robert A. Gordon, a Keynesian economist, admitted that "government policy to moderate the depression and speed recovery was minimal. The Federal Reserve authorities were largely passive...Despite the absence of a stimulative government policy, however, recovery was not long delayed." [14] According to economist Benjamin Anderson, "we took our losses, we readjusted our financial structure, we endured our depression, and in August 1921 we started up again....The rally in business production and employment that started in August 1921 was soundly based on a drastic cleaning up of credit weakness, a drastic reduction in the costs of production, and on the free play of private enterprise. It was not based on government policy designed to make business feel good." [15]

Unfortunately, in spite of the historical shakiness of Keynesian economic theory, President Obama has clung stubbornly to the position that spending massive sums of borrowed money will jumpstart the economy. Obama deceptively remarked that this was an issue we had "resolved a pretty long time ago" under the New Deal. [16] "There is no disagreement that we need action by our government, a recovery plan that will help to jumpstart the economy," said President-elect Barack Obama on January 9, 2009. [17]

There is, however, plenty of disagreement among economists that more government spending is the way to improve our economy. The Cato Institute ran full page ads in early 2009 that listed nearly 100 top college and university economists who concluded the president's plan was "a triumph of hope over experience to believe that more government spending will help the U.S. today." As an alternative, those economists stated that "…policymakers should focus on reforms that remove impediments to work, saving, investment, and production. Lower tax rates and a reduction in the burden of government are the best ways of using fiscal policy to boost growth." [18]

Brian Riedl, research fellow at The Heritage Foundation, states that, "if growing the economy were as simple as expanding government spending and deficits, then Italy, France and Germany would be global economic kings. And there would be no reason to stop at $787 billion: Congress could guarantee unlimited prosperity by endlessly borrowing and spending trillions of dollars. The simple reason government spending fails to end recessions is that Congress does not have a vault of money waiting to be distributed. Every dollar Congress 'injects' into the economy must first be taxed or borrowed out of the economy. No new income, and therefore no new demand, is created. They are merely redistributed from one group of people to another. Congress cannot create new purchasing power out of thin air." [19]

Riedl continues: "The mistaken view of fiscal stimulus persists because we can easily see the people put to work with government funds. We don't see the jobs that would have been created elsewhere in the economy with those same dollars had they not been lent to Washington." [20]

Walter E. Williams, economics professor at George Mason University, makes it even simpler. "A visual representation of the stimulus package is: Imagine you see a person at work taking buckets of water from the deep end of a swimming pool and dumping them into the shallow end in an attempt to make it deeper." [21]

Unfortunately, Obama and Democrats don't see it that way.

If history once again repeats itself, and their experiment in massive government spending doesn't work, Americans will be left with enormous government debt, higher taxes, potential hyperinflation and a dollar with significantly less purchasing power.

Bottom line: left alone, economies self-correct. Without government intervention, businesses that are inefficient and unprofitable close down, as consumers' needs and wants determine winners and losers. That's what free-market capitalism is all about.

Too bad Democrats don't get it.

Chapter 20

SIX FATAL FLAWS OF THE STIMULUS BILL

By now, most Americans are quite familiar with the "2009 American Recovery and Reinvestment Act" passed by Democrats in response to the 2008 fiscal crisis, but they know it by another name: the "Stimulus Bill." And they certainly know how much it cost: $787 billion dollars. (Author's note: it has since increased to $862 billion).

As I reveal in this chapter, the stimulus bill was indeed stimulating — for Democrats and their politically-connected cronies.

For the rest of America, which was promised that unemployment would be kept under 8% if it were enacted, the stimulus bill has been a colossal failure: unemployment is around 10%, the deficit is exploding, and precious few "shovel-ready" jobs have actually been created.

Maybe that works for Democrats—but it sure doesn't work for America.

"Never let a serious crisis go to waste. What I mean by that is it's an opportunity to do things you couldn't do before." — White House Chief of Staff Rahm Emanuel, in November 2008. [1]

Congressional Democrats certainly took Mr. Emanuel's advice to heart when they passed the 1,071 page stimulus package on February 13, 2009 in response to the 2008 financial crisis. It ended up as a $787 billion bill that appropriated money for practically every pent-up Democratic proposal of the last 40 years. [2]

Before delving into the substance of the bill, let's review how it was passed and who helped write it.

The stimulus package was rushed through both houses of Congress so quickly that it is likely no one had the time to read the entire bill. The final version was unveiled in the House at 1 a.m. on February 13, and passed later that day — after only *one hour* of debate. Every Republican in the House voted no. [3]

On the very same day, the bill was passed in the Senate on a party line vote with the exception of three Republicans: Olympia Snowe, Susan Collins, and Arlen Specter (who is now a Democrat). [4]

How urgent was it in theory? President Obama warned of economic calamity if the stimulus measure didn't pass:

"If we do not move swiftly to sign the (stimulus) into law, an economy that is already in crisis will be faced with catastrophe.... Millions more Americans will lose their jobs. Homes will be lost. Families will go without health care." [5]

How urgent was it in reality? President Obama and his wife took a vacation to Chicago to celebrate Valentine's Day. The President didn't sign the bill until four days later. [6] One shouldn't criticize the President's right to a vacation, but they should question why those four days could not have been used by Congress to read the entire bill and have a real debate.

With respect to the authors of the bill, Senate Majority Leader Harry Reid (D-Nev.) credited the Apollo Alliance – a coalition of left-wing interest groups – with helping write the stimulus bill and getting it passed. [7] The Apollo Alliance unites three of the most powerful elements of the political left – environmental groups, labor unions such as the Service Employees International Union (SEIU) and community organizers like ACORN – and directs them toward the goal of obtaining "green jobs." [8]

Specifically, $86 billion was earmarked for such jobs in the stimulus bill. [9] Thus, the same people who helped write the bill will be greatly enriched by it. Not coincidentally, these are the same groups which helped get Obama elected, and are part of an unholy alliance with the Democrat Party.

The green jobs agenda may serve a political purpose, but it doesn't create jobs. There is significant evidence from Spain and elsewhere that each green job created destroys more than two other jobs elsewhere in the economy. [10]

There are six major flaws with the stimulus bill:

1. *The spending bill was sold as a way to fund important infrastructure projects.*

Reality check: less than 15 percent of the bill is directed toward infrastructure building. In addition, the bill says that new spending on said infrastructure has to be directed toward "shovel ready" projects. [11] As a result, an *Associated Press* analysis in July 2009 showed that states are spending stimulus money on easier projects which require less planning and can be done quickly. [12] In other words, despite lawmakers' contentions that the stimulus package was a "historic chance to chip away at the $65 billion backlog of deficient structures," fixing America's crumbling bridges is taking a back seat to repairing or widening roads. [13] Or, as the Mayor of Charlotte, North Carolina so aptly put it, "while President Roosevelt built dams and President Eisenhower built an interstate highway system, President Obama's stimulus fills pot holes." [14]

2. *The stimulus bill involves $150 billion of "free" money doled out to states.* [15]

This money, allocated for health care, welfare and education will disappear in two years and leave states with no way to continue financing the expanded programs. [16]

A case in point is South Carolina. The stimulus will send about $2.8 billion to the state over two years. In order to spend that money, allocated for programs such as Head Start, child care subsidies, and special education, the state will have to enroll thousands of new families into the programs. [17]

South Carolina Governor Mark Sanford explains the dilemma: "There's no way politically we're going to be able to push people out of the program in two years when the federal money runs out." [18]

In a similar vein, federal contributions to the states for Medicaid is *also* a fiscal time bomb. The stimulus bill temporarily increases by two to three percent the federal government's share of state Medicaid bills — but in 2011, almost all the $80 billion of those extra federal Medicaid reimbursements disappears. [19]

The likely result? Instead of dumping one million or more people from

Medicaid at that stage, Congress will likely extend these transfer payments indefinitely. As *The Wall Street Journal* points out: "Pete Stark, David Obey and Nancy Pelosi (all Democrats) no doubt intend exactly this, which *could triple the stimulus price tag to as much as $3 trillion in additional spending and debt service over 10 years* (italics mine). But the states would still have to pick up their share of this tab for these new entitlements in perpetuity." [20] This leads directly to the third flaw in the bill:

3. *The stimulus package will force a huge and likely permanent increase in domestic spending by the federal government.*

Federal education spending is an excellent example. As part of the stimulus, Democrats nearly doubled education spending from $41 billion to $80 billion.[21] This was an obvious payback to the Democrats' most reliable group of campaign donors, the teachers unions. If Congress adds that and other stimulus spending (see prior paragraph) permanently into the baseline for future budgets, discretionary domestic spending could mushroom from $408 billion this fiscal year to $550 billion or $600 billion next year. [22]

The Congressional Budget Office estimated the impact of permanently extending the 20 most popular provisions of the stimulus bill, and found that the 10 year true cost would be $2.527 *trillion* in spending — with another $744 billion cost in debt servicing. [23] In other words, the so-called $787 billion stimulus package could end up costing $3.27 trillion.

How likely is this scenario? When has *any* Congress cut entitlement spending, much less one inhabited by a majority of liberals and radical leftists?

4. *Despite all the hoopla, only 18 percent of the monies appropriated for the stimulus bill was spent in the fiscal year that ended October 1, 2009.* [24]

Even though the stimulus bill was sold to the American public as a way to "immediately" create jobs, remarkably very little of the money was spent in 2009 when it was needed the most.

Another 56 percent of the stimulus money is projected to be spent by the end of fiscal year 2010. [25] Coincidentally, the bulk of the stimulus money (the aforementioned 56%) will be spent prior to the November 2010 mid-term elections. Are Democrats playing politics with our nation's economic recovery?

Of the $27.5 billion allotted for road construction, only $9.6 billion will be spent by 2010. [26] And of the money earmarked for renewable energy, only $2.5 billion will be spent by 2010. [27]

In fact, these programs will continue to spend the rest of the stimulus money through 2015, long after the recession is over. [28]

5. *The stimulus bill is loaded with massive amounts of wasteful appropriations in it — many are payoffs to the special interest groups which support the Democrat Party.*

It has been estimated that *half* of the stimulus money will directly benefit government employee and service unions that played key roles in Obama's election. [29]

More disturbing is the unnecessary waste in the bill. A few examples:

- $50 million for the National Endowment for the Arts.
- $400 million for global warming studies. [30]
- $800,000 to pave a runway for the rarely used John Murtha Airport.
- $3.4 million for a turtle crossing in northern Florida.
- $1.1 million for a guardrail near a man-made lake that no longer contains any water. [31]

A few more outrageous examples:

- $6 million to Hillary Clinton's pollster Mark Penn.
- $220,000 to study the sex drive of birds and rats and division of labor in ants.
- $1.5 million for fossil research in Argentina.
- $2.2 million for a failing golf course in San Francisco.
- $400,000 for malt liquor and marijuana journals.
- $500,000 to study how people use Facebook. [32]

6. *The stimulus bill will create few permanent jobs.*

From *CNNMoney.com:* "The American Recovery and Reinvestment Act (the stimulus bill) was designed to put millions of people to work, mainly for 'shovel-ready' projects. By their very nature, most of those projects last only until the work is completed or the funding runs out. That means millions of workers hired with stimulus funding are left looking for a job after the stimulus-funded program is completed." [33]

According to Peter Morici, professor at the Smith School of Business at the University of Maryland, "unemployment will remain stubbornly high because President Obama's policies don't fix what's broke.... Half the private sector jobs were lost in construction and manufacturing.... (Those industries) provide some of the best-paying jobs for workers without college diplomas. Yet President Obama has no coherent plan to bolster those sectors." [34]

Once the stimulus bill was passed, Democrats predicted that the impact would be practically instant. House Majority leader Steny Hoyer (D-Md.) claimed there would be "an immediate jolt." Director of the National Economic Council, Larry Summers, said, "You'll see the effects begin almost immediately." White House Budget Director Peter Orszag forecast it would "take only weeks or months" to be felt. [35]

All of them were wrong.

After the stimulus bill failed to stimulate, and the unemployment rate jumped to 9.5% — 1.5% higher than the 8% top predicted by the Obama administration — Vice President Joe Biden announced on July 5, 2009:

"The truth is, we and everyone else misread the economy." [36]

House Majority Leader Steny Hoyer also admitted its failure on July 5, 2009:

"I don't think anybody can say that we're honestly satisfied with results so far of the stimulus." [37]

Not only has the stimulus package failed to create greater employment, it will harm the economy in the long run. According to the nonpartisan Congressional Budget Office, the stimulus will result in so much government debt that, within a few years, it will crowd out private investment, leading to a *lower* Gross Domestic Product over the next 10 years — lower than if the government had done nothing. [38]

House Republicans offered an alternative recovery package of immediate tax cuts and safety-net measures that would have cost half as much as the Democrats' stimulus program. [39]

The bottom line: the Democrats' stimulus plan hasn't helped much because it invested too little in the private sector – where it was needed the most. True economic stimulus creates sustainable private-sector jobs by creating the conditions for investors to put more money into the economy. Tax rate cuts, less regulation and restrained government spending help accomplish that. The stimulus bill does nothing to address these factors.

That shouldn't surprise anyone. The Democrat Party believes more government is the answer to all of America's problems. Massive amounts of unsustainable debt accumulation that will burden future generations of Americans says otherwise.

Chapter 21

DEMOCRATS AND THEIR UNHOLY ALLIANCES

Part of my upbringing as a loyal Democrat included the belief that Republicans were the party of "special interest groups," while Democrats were the "party of the people."

Imagine my surprise when I discovered it was exactly the opposite.

There is nothing wrong with Democrats representing the interests of certain political groups and their wants or needs. But there is something seriously wrong with being beholden to certain constituencies — especially when those constituencies' interests are detrimental to the country as a whole.

This chapter will reveal some dubious alliances between Democrats and a variety of interest groups.

Democrats are the "party of the people?"

Make that "certain" people.

Most Americans have been brainwashed into believing that the Republican Party is the "party of special interest groups" and that such alliances affect their policymaking in ways harmful to our nation.

Nothing could be further from the truth. It is the *Democrat* Party and its deep-rooted unholy alliances with special interest groups — labor unions, teachers unions, trial lawyers, environmental groups, community organizations such as ACORN and welfare beneficiaries — that places the interests of those groups ahead of what's best for our country.

These loyal, well-organized constituencies advocate for more centralized government and thus heavily support Democrats. Supporters of the Republican Party generally desire less government, less regulation, less taxation, more traditional values, and more individual freedom. As a result, Republicans are supported by individuals and smaller groups who tend to be less loyal to the party, less organized and more focused on particular issues. [1]

Unfortunately, perception trumps reality. Republicans have been portrayed as being "in the pocket of big business" or the "party of Wall Street," yet big firms like Goldman Sachs give much more in political donations to Democrats. In fact, in the 2009-2010 election cycle, out of the top 20 entities providing political contributions, 19 have given more money to Democrats than Republicans. [2] The oil and gas industry is the one exception.

The American left would rationalize this by saying more money naturally flows to the party in power. They would be hard-pressed to explain why in 2004, when Republicans controlled both houses of Congress and the White House, 14 out of the top 20 industries still favored Democrats. [3]

Other groups, such as the National Rifle Association and pro-life organizations, support candidates who agree with their positions. They are not loyal to the Republican Party. [4]

Among special interest groups, labor unions are one of the most powerful forces in Washington. They support Democrats almost exclusively. During the 2008 election cycle, labor unions contributed $68 million to the Democrat Party — compared to only $6 million to the Republican Party. [5] Unions are the only organizations in America that can force members to pay dues as a condition of employment, and then use those dues for both direct campaign contributions to candidates and for genuine grassroots political activity. [6]

How does their alliance with labor unions affect the Democrats' agenda in Congress? The party shamelessly promotes policies that benefit unions to the detriment of the majority of Americans.

Some examples:

The Employee Free Choice Act

Commonly known as "card check," the Employee Free Choice Act, as currently proposed, will eliminate the secret ballot accorded workers when the attempt is made to unionize a workplace. By replacing the secret ballot with publicly signed cards, union organizers would be able to harass or threaten workers to unionize. The bill would also have a provision allowing federal arbitrators to impose the terms of a labor contract on a company if management and a newly established union weren't able to agree on one within a specified time frame. [7]

In other words, if you own a business, a government bureaucrat would be able to impose working terms and conditions involuntarily on your company, including *setting salaries and benefits.*

Labor unions are desperate to rig the bargaining rules because most workers don't want to be in a union. Although they promise higher wages, benefits, and more job security, workers can see what has happened to such highly unionized industries as steel, auto, airline and many others: union contracts made them uncompetitive. In addition, most workers would rather not give up part of their paycheck for mandatory dues to finance the political agenda of labor leaders. [8] And many of the original reasons for the existence of unions — safe workplaces and a limitation on working hours — are now covered by federal laws, making unions less necessary.

This bill could be a serious job killer for small and large businesses. Wages and benefits would certainly rise, but such raises increase the likelihood that many companies will either shut down or layoff employees to offset their increased costs.

When the bill came up for a vote in 2007, every Senate Democrat voted "yes" and only two Democrats in the House voted "no." While the bill passed the House, it failed in the Senate, due to a Republican filibuster. [9]

The North American Free Trade Agreement (NAFTA)

Under NAFTA, the U.S. is required to allow Mexican trucks to cross the border. However, U.S. trucking companies have argued that Mexico trucks aren't safe.

A pilot program begun in 2007 had permitted a small number of Mexican trucks to travel on U.S. highways, under rigid safety regulations. After 18 months, that program confirmed that Mexican carriers were equally as safe as their U.S. counterparts. Undeterred, the Democratically-controlled Congress ended the program in March 2009, putting the anti-competitive interests of the Teamsters Union, which represents U.S. trucking companies, ahead of the rest of the country. [10]

Mexico retaliated by imposing an estimated $2.4 billion in tariffs on 89 U.S. industrial and agricultural products, from pears to precious-metal jewelry. These 89 products will face new tariffs of 10% to 45%. With the cost of U.S. products higher, Mexicans will import substitutes from Europe, Canada and Latin America. As a result, U.S. exporters will lose market share, and that will put more American jobs, household incomes and even mortgage payments at greater risk. [11]

Other Free Trade Agreements

Previously negotiated pacts with Columbia, South Korea and Panama have languished in Congress because labor unions, particularly the AFL-CIO, are opposed to them.

Signing the Columbia Free Trade Agreement would be in our nation's best interest. Columbia's goods can already enter the U.S. duty free because of the Andean Trade Preferences Act. [12] On the other hand, U.S. goods currently face stiff tariffs when entering Columbia and this agreement would eliminate those tariffs and make our goods less expensive. U.S. exports to Columbia would be certain to increase.

It is the same with the U.S.-South Korea trade pact. While the European Union concluded negotiations of a new trade agreement with South Korea, the world's 13th largest economy, Democrats in Congress have done nothing to ratify the treaty the U.S. signed with that country — back in 2007. [13]

Around the world, other countries are moving ahead with similar bilateral trade deals, often giving their own national companies an edge over U.S. competitors. [14]

As long as the Democrat Party is aligned with their labor union friends who oppose free trade agreements, don't expect much movement on these pacts, despite the fact that protectionist policies like these harm our economy.

Protectionist Tariffs

On September 15, 2009, President Obama decided to levy three years of duties – 35 percent, 30 percent, and 25 percent respectively – on Chinese tires for automobiles and light-trucks. [15]

The reason? The United States Steelworkers Union, which represents tire factory workers, requested it. [16]

Unfortunately, this move cut off the source of nearly 17% of all tires sold in the U.S. in 2008. [17] This will hit cost-conscious consumers particularly hard, since most of the tires China sends to the U.S. are of the lower-priced variety. [18]

The U.S. Steelworkers Union believes that Chinese imports cost American jobs. In reality, the tariffs themselves will result in lost jobs. A report issued in July 2009 by Rutgers economist Thomas J. Prusa calculated that each job "saved" by the tariffs would come at the cost of at least 12 jobs lost, and possibly more than 25. [19] Most tire-related employment in America consists of workers who distribute and install tires, not workers who produce them. By depressing tire sales, these tariffs will jeopardize those jobs. [20] Because U.S. tire factories have shifted over the years to higher–grade tire manufacturing, Mr. Prusa notes that American manufacturers have little interest in, or capacity for, making substitutes for the less expensive Chinese imports. [21]

The Politicization of Government-Funded Contracts

On February 9, 2009, President Obama signed an Executive Order authorizing the federal government to require *all* companies to agree to unionization as a condition for winning a government-funded contract of $25 million or more. This order will deny every non-union contractor and worker any opportunity to work on those government construction projects. [22]

Democrats also inserted a little-known provision into the 2009 Stimulus Bill requiring all construction projects to pay Davis-Bacon prevailing wage rates. Nationwide these rates average 22 percent above market wages, and will inflate the cost of federal construction by 10 percent. [23]

Such harmful policies were obviously political payback to Big Labor for the support they provide Democrats in the form of votes and campaign contributions.

Overturning the Rule of Law

The bankruptcies of both Chrysler and General Motors illustrate how the Democrats favor special interest groups even to the point of undermining the rule of law.

Under existing bankruptcy law, *secured creditors* are entitled to *first* priority regarding repayment of debt in any bankruptcy proceeding. This legal concept is known as the "absolute priority rule." [24]

Incredibly, that's not what happened during the Chrysler and GM bankruptcies.

As payback to the United Auto Workers (UAW), the Obama Treasury Department strong-armed Chrysler's creditors. Secondary creditor, UAW, was given a 55% ownership of the company, while Chrysler's secured creditors were left with just 29 cents on the dollar. [25]

The General Motors bankruptcy was even more damning. GM's bondholders, who held $27 billion in debt, ended up with a 10 percent stake in the new company, while the UAW, owed about $20 billion, walked away with *17.5% of the company* – and $9 billion in cash. [26]

As *Barron's* so aptly wrote: "Never has an American union done so well at the expense of shareholders and creditors." [27]

The Obama administration tried to convince the American public that the United Auto Workers made "substantial concessions" as part of the bankruptcies. What were those substantial concessions? At a time when some American workers were facing stiff pay cuts, UAW workers gave up their right to overtime pay —when working less than 40 hours per week. [28]

Why such preferential treatment? Between 2000 and 2008, the United Auto Workers gave $23 million to the Democrat Party and its candidates. In 2008 alone, the UAW donated $4 million to the Democrat Party, including Barack Obama. [29]

As a result, UAW employees will have their pensions made whole by GM. [30] Such obligations usually don't survive bankruptcy — unless, perhaps, one is a major contributor to the Democrat Party.

Another large special interest group tied to the Democrat Party is the highly influential teachers unions. During the 2008 election cycle, they gave $5 million to Democrats, and only $261,000 to Republicans. [31]

How does this influence policy? At the behest of the nation's two largest teachers unions, the National Education Association and the American Federation of Teachers, Democrats killed the Opportunity Scholarship program by phasing out funding beyond 2010.[32] This extremely popular program offered vouchers to poor students in the District of Columbia. Vouchers are cash payments made to parents enabling them to send their children to better, often private schools.

Republicans passed the program in 2004. It allowed D.C. families to receive an annual payment of up to $7,500 per child and use that money to attend the school of their choice. Considering that D.C. public schools spend an average of $14,400 per pupil, this was a bargain by comparison. Furthermore, the results of the program were impressive: a 2008 Department of Education evaluation found that the participants had higher reading scores than their peers who didn't receive a scholarship.[33]

Why did Democrats kill the program? Because teachers unions don't want competition. Sadly, Democrats consider unions more important than kids trapped in failing schools.

Hypocritically, D.C. public schools weren't good enough for President Obama's two daughters to attend, so he enrolled them in a private school. Apparently Obama and Democrats believe school choice should be reserved for children of privilege.

Yet another powerful group that overwhelmingly supports the Democrat Party is the trial lawyer constituency. This group is one of the largest financial contributors to Democrat candidates and the National Democratic Party. During the 2008 election cycle, lawyers and law firms gave $178 million to the Democrats and $54 million to the Republicans. [34]

Influence on policy? Democrats consistently resist any attempt to pass tort reform measures even though they would greatly reduce frivolous and abusive lawsuits. [35] A case in point is health care. High malpractice insurance rates and the practice of "defensive medicine" are critical factors in driving up the cost of medical care. Despite this reality, neither the House nor Senate version of the health care bill still being debated at this writing contain a *single word* regarding tort reform.

Hundreds of environmental groups, such as Sierra Club and Greenpeace, are also key contributors, almost exclusively, to the Democrat Party. During the 2008 election cycle, environmental groups gave $5.3 million to the Democrats and only $305,000 to Republicans. [36]

Policy effects? Environmental groups are opposed to nuclear energy, and the Democrat Party has pursued policies intended to stifle its development. In March 2009, the Obama administration slashed funding for the proposed Yucca Mountain repository where nuclear waste was slated to be stored. [37] And the Obama administration's initial budget in 2009 included almost nothing related to advancing nuclear energy. Instead, Democrats focused on a misguided cap and trade program (see chapter 23) designed to benefit special interest groups. [38]

Environmental groups also oppose the production of energy from sources that emit carbon dioxide and Democrats have accommodated them. In 2009, they proposed legislation to remove all tax incentives to produce oil and gas;

passed a 13 percent excise tax on all energy derived from the Gulf of Mexico; increased corporate taxes on all companies that produce or process oil and gas; cancelled already issued oil and gas leases; and halted plans to allow leases on the oil shale regions in five states. They also threw out a Bush administration rule which made it easier to mine coal off mountaintops. [39]

Perhaps the worst example of politically-motivated policy can be found in California, where farmers are enduring a severe "drought:" billions of gallons of mountain water have been deliberately redirected away from farms and into the ocean, leaving hundreds of thousands of acres of arable land unplanted and/or scorched. [40] Unemployment in some farming towns is reaching 40 percent. [41]

Why is all this happening? Environmentalists want to protect a three-inch long fish known as the delta smelt.

But it gets even worse. In June 2009, the Obama administration denied the governor's request to designate California a federal disaster area as a result of the drought conditions. [42] A House amendment proposed by Devin Nunes (R-CA.) to prevent this manmade drought from continuing was defeated by the Democrats. A similar Senate amendment introduced by Jim DeMint (R-S.C.) was also defeated by a 61-36 vote, mostly on party lines. [43]

California Senators, Democrats Dianne Feinstein and Barbara Boxer? They voted for the fish over the farmers. [44]

Other special interest groups with ties exclusively to the Democrat Party are radical "community organizing" groups such as ACORN (Association of Community Organizations for Reform Now) and similar left-wing, non-profit advocacy groups.

With its vast network of more than 100 tax-exempt non-profit affiliates and approximately 400,000 members, ACORN is an insidious presence on the American political landscape. This radical activist group was previously known for its raucous protests, often held in bank lobbies or in front of bank officials' homes in the 1990s. [45] These protests, coupled with the threat of litigation, were aimed at forcing banks to increase the number of loans made to low-income borrowers.

As the 2008 financial crisis showed, many of these borrowers had no business obtaining mortgages.

Today, ACORN, despite its professed non-partisanship, is a powerful political force that organizes voter registration efforts *exclusively* for the Democrat Party. There is nothing wrong with organizations wanting to register more people to vote. The problem with ACORN, however, is that they have been charged with, or are being investigated for, voter registration fraud in many states. Larry Lomax, the registrar of voters in Las Vegas, Nevada says he believes 48 percent of ACORN's registration forms in the 2008 presidential election "are clearly fraudulent." [46] According to John Fund of *The Wall Street Journal,* there are allegations that almost *one-third* of the 1.3 million voter cards it turned in during the 2008 election are invalid. [47]

ACORN's relationship with president Barack Obama is a matter of public record. In 1992, he led a voter registration effort for Project Vote, an ACORN partner at the time. In 1995, he represented ACORN in an important case upholding the new Motor Voter Act — the law whose mandated postcard registration system ACORN uses to flood election offices with bogus registrations. And in 2008, the Obama campaign paid $832,000 to Citizens Consulting Inc., the umbrella group controlling ACORN, for get-out-the-vote efforts in key primary states. [48]

(Note from the author: as most Americans know by now, ACORN is embroiled in a huge scandal which has caused many Democrats to abandon that organization in droves. Congress has voted to cut off federal funding, and the organization is under investigation. Also, the Census Bureau severed its ties with ACORN. I decided to leave in the following two paragraphs as a way of letting readers know what was happening before the scandal.):

The Obama administration announced that the 2010 census will be taken away from the Commerce Department, which traditionally conducts the count, and put under control of the White House. ACORN was selected by the Obama administration to assist the process by reaching out to minority communities and recruiting census takers for next year's count. [49]

The Democrat Party has allocated $3 billion in federal funding from their stimulus package and set-aside an additional $5.5 billion for grants in Housing and Urban Development's 2010 budget for ACORN and similar left-wing *nonprofit advocacy groups.* [50]

As the investigations of ACORN demonstrate, taxpayer money has been used to register hundreds of thousands of ineligible voters. Republicans and other Americans are rightly concerned that such funding could be used to rig state and national elections in favor of Democrats. One need only look at the 2008 Minnesota Senate election victory of Democrat Al Franken over Republican Norm Coleman by a few hundred votes to see the possible impact groups like ACORN can have on a close election.

Chillingly, the voter registration tricks used by advocacy groups like ACORN may soon be unnecessary. Congressional Democrats are behind a bill to mandate a nationwide database which would automatically register drivers' license holders or recipients of government benefits to vote. This "would create an engraved invitation for voter fraud," says Hans von Spakovsky, a former Federal Election Commission member, who explains that these lists are filled with felons and non-citizens ineligible to vote. [51]

Finally, a major support group for Democrats includes the poor and other Americans classified as "welfare beneficiaries." This group includes the millions of people on food stamps, and those receiving housing subsidies. [52] Big government Democrats have cynically calculated that the more they can increase this voting block's dependency on government, the more likely they will vote for Democrats. Unfortunately, this divides our country, since those voting for greater government benefits are increasingly separated from those paying for them.

Perhaps like an aging athlete, Democrats are living more on past reputation than present day performance. I would not make the claim that Democrats were never the party of the people. But a party currently dominated by radical leftists bears little resemblance to the one that used to champion *genuine* social justice and American values. As has been said by many people many times before: I didn't leave the Democrat Party, the Democrat Party left me.

Chapter 22

THE GREEN JOBS FAIRY TALE

Most fairy tales have a happy ending. The green jobs fairy tale isn't one of them.

The theory behind the so-called "green" revolution is certainly seductive. Who wouldn't want a booming economy in which thousands of previously jobless Americans are employed to produce clean, efficient, domestically-generated energy?

Unfortunately, as this chapter explains, when theory gives way to reality, Americans will be sorely disappointed.

Or, as Kermit the frog once remarked, "it's not easy being green."

In early 2009, when President Barack Obama signed the American Recovery and Reinvestment Act into law, he claimed it "will lay the groundwork for new green energy economies that can create countless well-paying jobs." [1]

Despite Obama's rhetoric, renewable energy plans will *not* create new jobs, but they *will* destroy countless existing jobs, and severely hinder our ability to get out of the current economic crisis.

An examination of Spain, one of the first countries to actively engage in the creation of green jobs, reveals such policies to be *economically counterproductive:* a March 2009 study conducted by Gabriel Calzada Alvarez, an economics professor at Juan Carlos University in Madrid, Spain, revealed that the U.S. should expect a loss of at least 2.2 jobs on average for every one green job created. [2]

This study also marked the first time a critical analysis of the *actual* performance and impact of renewable energy job creation had been made.

More importantly, it demonstrated that a similar agenda now being promoted in the U.S. would most likely have a similar impact. [3]

The Spanish study's results explained how a green jobs policy has clearly hindered Spain's way out of the current economic crisis, even as U.S. Democrat politicians insist that rushing into a similar scheme will   help America emerge from its own recession. Alvarez explained that while it is not possible to directly correlate Spain's experience with exactitude, it is likely the U.S. would lose at least 6.6 million to 11 million jobs were it to create 3 to 5 million green jobs as promised. [4]

The study calculated that since 2000, Spain spent 571,138 euros ($774,000) to create each green job, including subsidies of more than 1 million euros ($135 million) per wind industry job.   Despite such expenditures, the study concluded that Spain has created a surprisingly low number of jobs — and *just-one-out-of-ten* is permanent. Permanent jobs deal with the actual operation and maintenance of renewable sources of electricity. The rest of the jobs? Temporary employment in the construction, fabrication, installation and project engineering phases. [5]

Another study published in early 2009 by the University of Illinois College of Law concurred, concluding that green jobs estimates include large numbers of clerical, bureaucratic, and administration positions that do not produce goods and services for consumption.   It further added that simply hiring people to write and enforce regulations, fill out forms, and process paperwork is not a recipe for creating wealth. That study showed that much of the promised boost in green employment turns out to be in "non-production positions" (aka, government bureaucracy) that raise costs for consumers. [6]

The results of a third study published in January 2009 by the independent non-profit *Institute for Energy Research* agreed with the other two studies cited. Their Executive Summary concluded with the following: "Unfortunately, it is highly questionable whether a government campaign to spur 'green jobs' would have net economic benefits. Indeed the distortionary impacts of government intrusion into energy markets could prematurely force business to abandon current production technologies for more expensive ones.   Furthermore, there would likely be negative economic consequences from forcing higher-cost alternative energy sources upon the economy. These factors would likely increase consumer energy costs and the costs of a wide array of energy-intensive goods, slow GDP growth and ironically may yield no net job gains. *More likely, they would result in net job losses."* [7] (Italics mine)

From an economic standpoint, renewable energy technologies are big losers. They simply cannot produce enough reliable energy at attractive prices — which is why the government needs to subsidize them. [8]

Tellingly, these subsidies are substantial. According to the U.S. Energy Information Administration, the government subsidizes solar energy at $24.34 per megawatt-hour (MWh) and wind power at $23.37 per MWh. [9] Even with these massive subsidies, in addition to numerous state-level mandates for utilities to use green power, wind and solar energy currently supply less than 1 percent of our nation's electricity. [10]

Compare the subsidies for renewables with those awarded to natural gas (25 cents per MWh in subsidies), coal (44 cents), hydroelectricity (67 cents) and nuclear power ($1.59). [11] Despite all the pie in the sky rhetoric espoused by Democrats, these sources of energy form the backbone of America's energy needs.

Furthermore, the higher subsidies required for renewable energy inevitably raise prices. The aforementioned Spanish study noted that the price of energy in Spain would have to be increased 31% to repay the historic debt generated by the government subsidies to renewables. Spanish citizens must therefore deal with either an increase in electricity rates, or increased taxes. So will Americans if we follow Spain's model. [12]

The high cost of renewable energy-generated electricity also tends to drive most energy-intensive companies and industries to countries where energy costs are lower. Manufacturing industries that are energy-intensive will inevitably gravitate to low-cost countries. For example, Acerinox SA, Spain's largest stainless steel producer, blamed domestic energy costs for deciding to expand in South Africa and the U.S., according to the Spanish study. [13] Thus, policies that drive up energy costs nationwide, as Democrats intend, will likely drive more manufacturing jobs overseas.

Meanwhile, the supposed economic benefits of green technologies are disappearing. In Germany, government subsidies for installing solar panels – presumably to create domestic manufacturing jobs – backfired when it was discovered that it was cheaper to make them in China. [14]

Investor's Business Daily explains that because there is little market for green programs, those jobs have to be financed by taking money out of the private sector, where it could be used for investments that would generate honest, non-taxpayer-subsidized jobs. [15]

Losing jobs in efficient industries to create jobs in inefficient and speculative technologies favored by special interest groups is hardly a recipe for economic success. To pay for expensive renewable energy, consumers will have less to save or spend, which will harm the economy.

How unrealistic are these Democrat-inspired policies? Vice President Al Gore:

"If we set our minds to it, we in this country could produce 100 percent of our electricity from renewable and carbon-free sources in 10 years. That is possible." [16]

Gore apparently believes the U.S. should depend solely on energy sources which currently cannot produce anything remotely resembling large volumes of reliable energy at attractive prices. Why? Al Gore has millions of dollars invested in renewable companies where he stands to make a fortune if renewable energy policies are forced down America's throat. He joins a long line of Democrats more concerned with their self-interest as opposed to what's good for the country. Moreover, pursuing renewable energy placates radical environmentalists, key contributors to the Democrat Party.

In reality, energy policy is the small picture. The big picture was addressed by the aforementioned University of Illinois College of Law study:

"Our review convinces us that the real purpose of the green jobs initiative is not to create jobs but to remake society. The sweeping changes…under the guise of greening our economy are intended to shift the American and world economies away from decentralized decision-making, in favor of centralized planning. Therefore, instead of allowing individuals to voluntarily trade in free markets in pursuit of their own ends, green jobs advocates would instead discourage trade and allow technologies to be chosen by central planners and politicians, who would determine the choices faced by consumers and workers. By wrapping these policy shifts in the green jobs mantle, those advocating the reorganization of much of life hope to avoid a debate over the massive costly changes they want to impose." [17]

In other words, today's Democrats, who believe America is a *fundamentally flawed country*, are aiming to completely remake it to conform to their "enlightened" worldview, whether Americans like it or not. Using government regulations as a club, they intend to force Americans away from independent (and viable) free-market energy solutions into centrally-planned boondoggles.

Saving the planet is their rationale, but in reality central planning is nothing more than Marxism in disguise. And what are we currently calling a Marxist solution to our energy problems?

Hope and Change.

Chapter 23

CAP AND TRADE: HANDI-"CAPPING" AMERICA'S ECONOMIC FUTURE

Of all the wrong-headed policies being pursued by the Obama administration and Congressional Democrats, cap and trade gets my nod as the absolute worst.

It is a deadly combination of economically devastating initiatives based on dubious, if not fraudulent, science.

Even if it is implemented exactly as envisioned by Democrats, it will do virtually nothing to reduce global temperatures.

On the other hand, it will enrich certain well-connected individuals and corporations who tout it as an absolute necessity to "save the planet."

Cap and trade is the epitome of over-reaching, big-government, freedom-killing legislation.

In short, it doesn't get any worse than this.

On June 26, 2009, the Democratically-controlled House of Representatives passed the 1,427 page American Clean Energy and Security Act (otherwise known as Waxman-Markey), arguably the worst piece of legislation ever enacted.[1] This boondoggle, rejected by all but eight House Republicans, is designed to address global warming by restricting and taxing the amount of carbon-based energy Americans use. [2]

Why is this legislation so harmful? Consider the words of candidate Barack Obama in a speech given on January 2008:

"...Under my plan of a cap and trade system, electricity rates would necessarily skyrocket...because I'm capping greenhouse gases, coal power plants, natural gas...you name it...whatever the plants were, whatever the industry was, they would have to retro-fit their operations. That will cost money...they will pass that money on to the consumers." [3]

If this bill becomes law, it will burden families with thousands of dollars per year in added energy costs. Consumers will also be hit with indirect costs as businesses will be forced to raise prices to cover their own increased energy costs. Equally important, millions of jobs will be lost.

The rationale for this bill? To counter global warming by sharply reducing greenhouse gases, primarily carbon dioxide. But is cap and trade really about saving the environment? Even if the bill works *exactly* as envisioned, most radical environmentalists admit that it will only slow temperature increases by a miniscule *9/100th of one degree Fahrenheit* by 2050. [4]

And that's assuming rapidly industrializing countries such as China and India sign on. The reality is that neither of those countries, which account for almost a quarter of the world's CO_2 emissions, wants to follow developed nations in burdening their economies with such measures. India's Environmental Minister Jairam Ramesh said his country "will not accept any emission-reduction target – period. This is a non-negotiable stand." China has also resisted. Thus, it makes little difference what developed countries do to limit greenhouse gas emissions if undeveloped giants such as China and India don't do the same. [5]

Still, Congressional Democrats are unrelenting in their campaign to turn this legislation into law. Why?

Perhaps Al Gore revealed the answer in a speech in England in July 2009, where he said that legislation like Waxman-Markey would be a boost for "global governance." [6]

If Obama and the Democrats really want clean air, laws already exist to achieve that goal. The original Clean Air Act and its subsequent amendments have already achieved significant pollution reductions in power plant nitrogen oxides and sulfur dioxide emissions. The Bush-inspired Clean Air Act (of 2005) requires a reduction in emissions by an additional 53 percent by 2010 and 70 percent by 2020. [7]

Waxman-Markey has been called "cap and trade" because it would place a mandatory "cap" or limit on the amount of carbon dioxide emitted by a company through a credit allowance system. That company can later sell or "trade" those credits or permits if they emit less of their allotted amount to companies who emit more. [8]

To pass the bill, Henry Waxman (D-Calif.) had to *give away* 85 percent of those carbon permits to utility companies, petroleum interests, refineries and a host of other politically-connected businesses. [9] In March 2009, White House budget director Peter Orszag told Congress that "if you didn't auction the permit(s), it would represent the largest corporate welfare program that has ever been enacted in the history of the United States." [10]

Despite Orszag's reservations, that's exactly what House Democrats did.

In reality, Waxman-Markey is a giant payoff to Democrat constituencies. Here are some of those groups who will benefit:

- Unions: The bill mandates our current infrastructure be made "energy efficient" and "green," which will require much construction work. Projects will be mandated to implement union-wage rules all the way down to the plumbing-repair and light-bulb changing level.

- Academia: College administrators will be given billions of dollars to create "Clean Energy Innovation Centers."

- Community Development Organizations: Waxman-Markey authorizes the Energy Secretary to make grants to such organizations to provide financing to businesses and projects that improve energy efficiency. As of this writing, one of those organizations is ACORN, presently under investigation for massive corruption.

- Bureaucrats: The bill will create a host of new federal agencies and sub agencies: the United States Global Change Research Program, the National Climate Change Adaptation Program, the National Climate Service, the Natural Resources Climate Change Adaptation

Strategy office at the White House and the International Climate Change Adaptation Program at the State Department. [11]

Question: Do we really need another federal government hiring binge, further enlarging the size of the government?

In addition to the permits, the bill also allows for the creation of "offsets," where one company can pay another to emit less carbon or to perform a carbon-conserving (read reducing) activity such as planting trees, so that the first company doesn't have to cut their own emissions as much.[12]

Incredibly, nearly all Waxman-Markey's carbon reduction goals can be met with *offsets alone* through 2050, meaning it will be decades before any reduction of greenhouse gases is required. This means huge new costs for small businesses and consumers in return for nearly *zero* environmental improvement. [13]

The whole point of cap and trade? To raise the price of electricity and gas so that Americans will use less of both. Unfortunately, these higher prices will show up not just in electricity bills and at the gas station, but in every manufactured good, from food to cars. [14]

The result? Consumers will cut back on spending, which in turn will reduce production. Reduced production will result in fewer jobs created and higher unemployment. [15] Making emissions in the United States costlier will force industry to move to countries with cheaper energy costs, especially if trading partners such as China and India do not have similar legislation. These regulations will have the net effect of raising the costs of producing in the U.S. relative to other countries. [16]

Despite this reality, Democrats claim this bill will result in millions of new jobs. President Obama said as much in his weekly radio address in June, 2009:

"This historic piece of legislation will not just lessen our dependence on foreign oil, but also spark a clean energy transformation in our economy that will create millions of new American jobs that pay well and cannot be outsourced. Clean energy and the jobs it creates are critical to building a new foundation for our economy." [17]

If Democrats truly believe what they are saying, perhaps they could explain a little-noticed provision in Waxman-Markey allowing workers who lose their jobs as a result of this bill to receive a weekly paycheck for up to three years, subsidies to find new work, and other generous benefits. Adversely affected employees in the oil, coal and other fossil-fuel industries would qualify for a weekly check equal to 70 percent of their current salary. [18]

Chris Tucker, a spokesman for the Institute for Energy Research, makes the implication of such a provision crystal clear: "Can you name another 'jobs-creation' bill that was so concerned about its potential impact that it preemptively included a benefits' program for the millions of workers it expected to displace?" [19]

Thus, it is highly likely that jobs created by alternative energy companies will be more than offset by job losses in traditional energy industries. (See chapter titled "The Green Jobs Fairy Tale.") In addition, the "millions" of jobs this bill is supposed to create can easily be outsourced. GE is *already importing* wind turbines from its overseas plants in China, Germany and Spain to supply wind farms in the United States." [20]

Job losses will not only come from companies moving operations offshore, but also from American companies that decide to stay in the U.S. and absorb the higher energy costs. According to *Investor's Business Daily*, across the next two decades, annual job losses due to restrictions on CO^2 emissions will exceed 800,000 in at least two years and losses for most years will be more than 500,000. Manufacturers will be especially vulnerable to CO^2 emissions limits for two reasons: the manufacturing process is energy-intensive and the demand for their products will fall as higher energy costs raise prices. [21]

According to the Center for Data Analysis at the Heritage Foundation, more than 3.5 million U.S. manufacturing jobs will have been lost by 2029. The machinery industry will lose more than 57% of its jobs, while jobs in the plastic and rubber industries will fall 54%. Other manufacturing areas in which employment will drop significantly are paper and paper products (36%), durable goods (28%) and textiles (27.6%). [22]

A reminder: these numbers don't include the potentially staggering losses from companies moving their operations overseas.

Knowing that the costs associated with cap and trade will send hard-pressed U.S. consumers and producers to purchase lower-priced imports, Waxman-Markey includes a provision that would require the president to levy tariffs against nations that don't pass similar legislation. [23] These tariffs will raise the cost of foreign products in the U.S. and may ignite trade wars, further fueling job losses here in the U.S. Trade is a mainstay of the U.S. economy, accounting for about a third of U.S. Gross Domestic Product and underpinning about 40 percent of U.S. jobs. [24]

Waxman-Markey will also significantly harm the real estate industry. In the *National Review*, authors Stephen Spruiell and Kevin Williamson explain, "The bill requires the EPA to establish environmental standards for residences, meaning a federally dictated one-size-fits-all policy for greening every home in America." [25] This will add many thousands of dollars to the cost of every home. Waxman-Markey will also affect commercial properties. All buildings would be regulated by a "national energy-efficiency building code" requiring 50 percent reductions in energy use by 2018, followed by 5 percent reductions in energy use every three years after that through 2030. [26]

Supporters of Waxman-Markey argue that these costs will pay for themselves through lower energy bills. But since cap and trade will raise the cost of energy, this claim is highly dubious. The more likely scenario is that businesses and homeowners will pay twice – once to retrofit their properties and again when their energy bills go up. [27]

Democrats cite a study from the Congressional Budget Office (CBO) which claims the cost of Waxman-Markey to the average household would be only $175 per year by 2020. As *The Wall Street Journal* explains, this analysis is "useless" because the CBO analysis looks solely at the year 2020, before most of the tough restrictions begin. The price of carbon emission permits will likely skyrocket thereafter as companies lose the opportunity to "offset" their emissions. Corporations will then pass the cost of buying these expensive permits to consumers. [28]

The Heritage Foundation analysis projects that by 2035, the economic effect of Waxman-Markey will be devastating:

- A family of four will pay an additional $4,609 per year in energy costs (including taxes).

- Total Gross Domestic Product losses will be $9.4 trillion (over half current U.S. GDP).

- Total cap and trade energy taxes will be $5.7 trillion.

- The national debt will increase an additional $12,803 per person ($51,212 per family of four). [29]

Another indicator of this bill's impact might be what's *already* happening in Great Britain. Britain's Taxpayer Alliance estimates the average family there is paying almost $1300 a year in taxes for carbon-reducing programs in effect for only a few years. [30]

One would think a bill of this magnitude would be thoroughly analyzed and debated by Congress before its passage. One would be incorrect. Congressional Democrats introduced a 309 page "amendment" at 3:00 a.m. prior to the vote being taken later that day. As explained by the *American Spectator's* Jeremy Lott and William Yeatman: "Representatives would have had all of nine hours to study the text, assuming they went without sleep. The manager's amendment made even that impossible, because you had roughly 1,200 pages of text – containing, at last count, 397 new government regulations and 1,090 new economic mandates – followed by over 300 pages of text with no index that amended the previous legislation on paragraph by paragraph basis… It would take a team of lawyers several days to sort out a mess like that." [31]

On top of that fiasco, Democrats limited floor debate to only *three hours.* [32]

The Republican minority on the House Energy and Commerce Committee put up a determined fight, attempting to set limits on the economic damage the bill could do. They offered amendments that would suspend the bill if gasoline prices reached $5 a gallon; or if electricity prices doubled; or if unemployment exceeded 15%. Each of the amendments was defeated on near party-line votes. [33] Also defeated on a straight party-line vote was an amendment to suspend the legislation if China and India don't agree to cut their own greenhouse gas emissions. [34]

Even though the premise behind the bill is invalid – the Earth's temperature has not warmed for more than a decade and has actually cooled significantly for the past few years – Democrats in Congress have raced ahead with this job-killing, growth-limiting bill that would raise energy costs for every American. It will also impose crushing competitive disadvantages on America in the global marketplace.

Let's hope that a few sane Democrats in the Senate see the folly of this boondoggle and vote against its passage. The alternative is frightening.

Chapter 24

OBAMA'S FOREIGN POLICY: ALL YOU NEED IS LOVE

I grew up believing America was the greatest country in the world. I was proud of our enormous contributions to world peace and world prosperity.

Unfortunately, for the first time in my life, this concept of American exceptionalism is being challenged — by an American president.

Barack Obama has decided that America needs to "improve" its image. He has determined we are unnecessarily belligerent, culturally insensitive, and that we owe the world an apology for our shortcomings.

I find such a perspective highly distasteful — but if it worked, I'd swallow my American pride and hop on the so-called "soft power" bandwagon.

As this chapter will show, the president's hopey-changey approach to world affairs has done little more than embolden our enemies and alienate our friends.

I'll take American exceptionalism instead — warts and all.

The Obama administration has developed foreign policy objectives designed to undercut America's global dominance and reduce its superpower status to one equal to Russia, China or the European Union. This marks a radical departure from previous presidencies.

Consider President Obama's response to a reporter's question about American exceptionalism during a recent trip in 2009 to Europe. "I believe in American exceptionalism, just as I suspect that the Brits believe in British exceptionalism and the Greeks believe in Greek exceptionalism." [1]

Reality check: if every country is exceptional, then no country is.

In his trips abroad and to the U.N. General Assembly in 2009, President Obama did paint his own picture of America — an America flawed in its moral culpability and heavy-handedness, and guilty for its treatment of other nations and peoples. He also indicted the U.S. for arrogance, for dismissiveness and derisiveness (toward Europe), for maltreatment of natives, for torture, for the bombing of Hiroshima, for Guantanamo, for unilateralism, and for insufficient respect for the Muslim world. [2]

According to columnist Charles Krauthammer, this new worldview is rooted in the left's belief that America is "so intrinsically flawed, so inherently and congenitally sinful that it cannot be trusted with, and does not merit, the possession of overarching world power.... And because we remain so imperfect a nation, we are in no position to dictate our professed values to others around the world." [3]

As Jeffrey Kuhner of *The Washington Times* explains, "promoting democracy and human rights has been abandoned in favor of improving America's standing in the world. Since the presidency of Jimmy Carter... each successive administration has understood that expanding political freedom strengthens American national interests — and values. Ronald Reagan sought to roll back Communism. George H.W. Bush encouraged the reunification of Germany and oversaw the implosion of the Soviet empire. Bill Clinton liberated Muslims in Bosnia and Kosovo from Serbian revanchism. George W. Bush imposed democracy in Afghanistan and Iraq, freeing more than 50 million Muslims from totalitarian rule." [4]

This tradition has been turned upside down by Mr. Obama. Regarding China, he and Secretary of State Hillary Clinton have deliberately put human rights and Tibetan autonomy on the back burner. The same applies to Russia, despite its war of aggression against the Republic of Georgia and its attempt to bully Ukraine. Instead of openly supporting Iran's democratic movement, Obama stood by and watched passively as peaceful demonstrators were gunned down, arrested and tortured. [5]

The President's rationale? Despite the fact that it was a widely reported fraud, Mr. Obama claimed he didn't want to "meddle" in the Iranian election.

Furthermore, although the Obama administration tripled the federal deficit in the first 10 months in office, it incredibly cut funding for several programs that would help Iranian dissidents challenging the regime's legitimacy. In October 2009, the Obama State Department cut off funding for the Connecticut-based Iran Human Rights Documentation Center — a nonpartisan group that documents Iran's human rights abuses and had received $3 million over the past five years. [6]

The Freedom House, a nonpartisan watchdog group founded in 1941, also lost State Department funding. In April, 2009 it applied for significant funds to support initiatives including *Gozaar,* its Farsi-English online journal of democracy and human rights. It was turned down in July. Since 2006, Freedom House had obtained over $2 million from the U.S. and European governments for Iran-related efforts. [7] Lastly, the International Republican Institute, which for several years received State Department support to train Iranian reformers, and connect them to like-minded activists in Europe and elsewhere, was likewise turned down for funds in 2009. [8]

Ironically, while the Obama administration decided not to interfere in the democratic aspirations of the Iranians, it tried to strong-arm Honduras into backing the anti-American, Chavez-backed autocrat, Manuel Zelaya. Zelaya was trying to establish a presidency for life (much like Chavez did in Venezuela) and was lawfully removed by his own government as a result. The U.S. cut off aid to Honduras and threatened not to recognize presidential elections previously scheduled unless Mr. Zelaya was brought back to power. [9]

Apparently, Barack Obama has no problem "meddling" when a left-wing agenda is being promoted.

The Obama administration has also sought warmer ties with other dictatorships and strategic foes of America. Iran's foreign minister visited Washington after such visits had been forbidden for a decade; the State Department announced the start of a dialogue with the Burmese dictatorship; and Syria received six visits from high-ranking American officials. [10]

In addition, President Obama is also creating antagonists among nations who were previously friends. His decision to scrap a missile defense agreement the Bush administration had negotiated with Poland and the Czech Republic angered those countries, and undermined the concept of a U.S. nuclear defense umbrella for Europe. Jan Vidim, a Czech lawmaker who voted for the missile system, expressed his anger at the Obama administration:

"If the Administration approaches us in the future with any request, I would be strongly against it." [11]

Other ostensible allies, including countries in the Middle East, now realize they might not be able to rely on the United States to protect them. Instead, some may want to follow the Israeli path and develop their own nuclear deterrent. [12] The last thing the world needs is a nuclear arms race, especially in the Middle East.

Additional antagonistic actions by the Obama administration include picking trade fights with Canada and Mexico, sitting on trade treaties with Columbia and South Korea, battling Israel over West Bank settlements, and ignoring Japan in deciding to talk with North Korea. [13]

Unfortunately, Obama's desire to improve our standing in the world has not resulted in any tangible benefits to the United States. In the Middle East, leading Arab states have repeatedly declined to move towards compromise with respect to the peace process, and show no inclination to normalize relations with Israel. [14] North Korea is still openly belligerent, testing a nuclear weapon and long range missile, withdrawing from the 1953 Armistice Agreement with South Korea and declaring it will weaponize its plutonium stocks. [15]

With respect to Russia, the Obama administration's "reset" of relations has been fruitless regarding Iran's nuclear program, as Russian Foreign Minister Sergei Lavrov declared in September 2009 that Moscow wouldn't back any new rounds of tough sanctions against Iran in the U.N. Security Council [16]

Nor has Obama's "outreach" to the Muslim world yielded a more favorable view of America. A May 2009 University of Maryland survey of the Middle East revealed that those with a very or somewhat favorable view of the United States increased only 3 percent between 2008 and 2009, from a dismal 15 percent to a still dismal 18 percent. [17]

In keeping with their naive worldview, Democrats and the Obama administration have also abandoned the idea that there is a "global war on terror" against Islamic fundamentalists. It is now called an "overseas contingency operation" against "insurgents," and terror attacks are now referred to as "man-caused disasters." And at a time when every other government department is expanding amidst the greatest domestic spending spree in American history, the Defense Department is being forced to *cut* programs — a highly-regarded F-22 fighter aircraft and missile defense being two of the victims.

As a result of this "September 10th" mindset, fighting terrorism has once again become a "law enforcement" problem. High-level al-Qaeda prisoners will now be interrogated by the FBI instead of by the CIA, and five Guantanamo Bay detainees with alleged ties to the 9/11 attacks may be tried in a civilian court. If that happens, defense lawyers will be able to argue that the defendants were not given their Miranda rights, or that everything obtained from their capture, including information on laptop computers about al-Qaeda plans and operatives, is therefore inadmissible. In other words, any terrorist tried in civilian court could be freed based on nothing more than the ostensible illegality of the evidence obtained.

This law enforcement approach to fighting terrorism was never more obvious than when the so-called "underwear bomber," Nigerian Umar Farouk Abdulmutallab, who attempted to blow up a Northwest Airlines plane headed to Detroit on Christmas Day was arrested. The opportunity to obtain crucial information about al-Qaeda was lost because the Obama administration decided to prosecute him as an ordinary criminal, rather than an enemy combatant. Abdulmutallab was "singing like a canary" until he was granted his Miranda rights, after which he stopped talking. The potential significance became frighteningly clear when it was reported that shortly after his detention, he boasted that 20 other Muslim men were being prepared for similar murderous plots by al-Qaeda in Yemen. [18]

This was not the Obama administration's first flirtation with the so-called September 10th mindset. One of its first actions was to drop charges against Abu Rahim al-Nashiri, mastermind of the 2000 USS Cole bombing in Yemen that killed 17 U.S. sailors. [19] And Binyam Mohamed — the al-Qaeda member selected by Khalid Sheikh Mohammed for a major post 9/11 attack with co-conspirator Jose Padilla — was released 17 days later to roam free in Great Britain. [20]

With respect to military strategy, the Obama administration remains determined to withdraw American forces from Iraq on a fixed timetable, as opposed to basing it on realistic political and military considerations. In Afghanistan, it is pursuing a politically calculated strategy designed to placate both liberals and conservatives: for conservatives, more troops but 25 percent less than General McChrystal requested; for liberals, a due date for withdrawal in 18 months, based on the idea that Afghanistan forces will have achieved self-sufficiency.

How sensible was the President's Afghan policy?   Charles Krauthammer explained the consequences of such a strategy:

"Does he think that such ambivalence is not heard by the Taliban, by Afghan peasants deciding which side to choose, by Pakistani generals hedging their bets, by NATO allies already with one foot out of Afghanistan?" [21]

All of these policies regarding the prosecution of terror and terrorism paint a troubling picture. By emphasizing a law enforcement approach, the Obama administration is essentially playing defense instead of offense.   In other words, they are willing to prosecute the perpetrators of a domestic terror attack, but only *after* the attack has occurred. On the other hand, the Bush administration's pre-emptive strategy of finding and prosecuting terrorists *before* an attack likely prevented another one from occurring for the remainder of his term.

Here's a brief rundown of some of Barack Obama's other questionable actions regarding foreign policy and national security:

- His first call to any head of state, as president, was to Mahmoud Abbas, leader of the Fatah party in the Palestinian territory. [22]
- His first one-on-one television interview with any news organization was with Al Arabia television. [23]
- He ordered Guantanamo Bay closed. [24]
- He ordered all military trials of Guantanamo detainees halted. [25]
- He ordered overseas CIA interrogation centers closed. [26]

There is also this catalogue of President Obama's embarrassing moments on the world stage:

- Giving England's Queen Elizabeth II an iPod containing videos of his speeches.

- Giving British Prime Minister Gordon Brown an assortment of DVDs that were not formated to the European standard (by contrast Mr. Brown gave Mr. Obama a thoughtful and historically significant gift).
- Visiting Austria and making reference to a non-existent "Austrian language."
- Bowing to the Saudi king.
- Saying the United States was "one of the largest Muslim countries in the world."
- Suggesting Arabic translators be moved from Iraq to Afghanistan where Arabic is not a native language.
- Sending a letter to French President Jacques Chirac when Nicolas Sarcozy was the current president of France.
- Referring to "Cinco de Cuatro" in front of the Mexican ambassador when it was the 5th of May (Cinco de Mayo).
- Releasing a photo of a conference call with Israel's Prime Minister Benjamin Netanyahu in which the president was displaying the soles of his shoes to the camera (an Arab insult).
- Stating "let me be absolutely clear. Israel is a strong friend of Israel's." [27]
- Returning the bust of Winston Churchill that was displayed in the White House, even though Britain had not asked for its return. [28]

The Washington Times summed up the Obama administration's foreign policy in a September 28, 2009 editorial, calling it "the worst foreign policy ever."

Sadly, they could be correct.

Chapter 25

AMERICA EXPOSED

The foremost duty of the federal government is to protect the nation from harm.

President Obama's implementation of missile defense cuts, as reflected in his first defense budget, is the latest example of why he and his fellow Democrats are dangerous when it comes to national security.

The world is full of rogue states, bloodthirsty tyrants and fanatical terrorists, all of whom share a common goal: the destruction of America.

Such evil ambitions are nothing new. But two factors make them especially troubling at the present time. First, the advancement of technology has given our enemies new and potentially devastating methods to inflict severe damage on this country — methods for which we remain largely unprepared.

Second, we are now facing terrorist enemies literally willing to be annihilated in order to kill as many Americans as possible — making deterrence all but impossible.

As I discovered researching this chapter, America remains vulnerable. Uncomfortably — and unconscionably — vulnerable.

President Obama's first defense budget for 2010 was breathtaking in its failure to adequately provide for our national defense.

While our enemies such as North Korea, Iran and Syria are proceeding with advanced missile programs that could pose an existential threat to the U.S., the Obama administration and Democrats in Congress decided to slash missile defense appropriations, cutting the budget by $1.2 billion in

2010. [1] This unilateral disarming includes reducing the number of ground-based interceptors in Alaska from 44 to 30. [2] They also cut funding for the European missile defense shield, double-crossing our allies in Poland and the Czech Republic, after those countries took major political risks to support the program.[3] The European missile shield would also protect the U.S. by providing an additional layer of defense for America's Eastern seaboard, which is a long way from our missile sites currently located in Alaska and California. [4]

Frighteningly, these are not the Democrats' most serious derelictions of duty. What's truly inexplicable is their almost complete elimination of the Airborne Laser (ABL) program. [5] The ABL is the best defense system to provide America protection against a nuclear-generated electromagnetic pulse (EMP) attack — one which could completely destroy America's electrical infrastructure. Consider what *The Commission to Assess the Threat to the United States from Electromagnetic Pulse Attack* concluded in a July 22, 2004 report to Congress:

"A nuclear-operated electromagnetic pulse is one of a small number of threats that has the potential to hold our society seriously at risk and might result in the defeat of our military forces." [6]

Few Americans can conceive of the possibility that terrorists could bring our society to its knees. But imagine this scenario: An ordinary-looking ship sails toward New York or Los Angeles and launches a nuclear-armed missile from international waters off the coast of the U.S. The missile explodes 300 miles above Chicago, and this detonation creates an electromagnetic pulse. Brian T. Kennedy, a member of the Independent Working Group on Missile Defense, explains: "Gamma rays from the explosion generate three classes of disruptive pulses, which permanently destroy consumer electronics, the electronics in most automobiles, and most importantly, the hundreds of large transformers that distribute power throughout the U.S. All of our lights, refrigerators, water-pumping stations, TVs and radios stop running." [7]

In a single moment, America would literally be sent back to the horse and buggy days of the 19th century. Without electricity, there would be no communications, modern transportation, refrigeration, water distribution, or medical resources, resulting in a crisis of pandemic proportions, one that could cripple the United States.

Judging from articles in their press, the Iranians are well aware of the devastating effects of an EMP. In March 2001, an analysis in the Iranian journal, *Siasat-e Defai* (Farsi for defense policy) weighed the use of nuclear weapons against cities in the traditional manner, as "against Japan in World War II," versus their use in "information warfare" that includes "electromagnetic pulse…for the destruction of integrated circuits." Another article published in *Nashriyeh-e Siasi Nezami* (December 1998 – January 1999) warned that "if the world's industrial countries fail to devise effective ways to defend themselves against dangerous electronic assaults, then they will disintegrate within a few years." [8]

Over the past eight years, the Iranians have practiced detonating ballistic missiles in mid-flight. [9] They have also tested high-altitude explosions of their Shahab-3 missile, a test consistent with an EMP attack. [10] In 2005, William Graham, President Reagan's top science adviser and Chairman of *The Commission to Assess the Threat to the United States from Electromagnetic Pulse Attack,* stated that he could think of no other reason for Iran to be experimenting with mid-air detonation of missiles than for the planning of an EMP-style attack. [11] And according to Jack Spencer from The Heritage Foundation, "crude weapons with low yields, such as those used against Japan in World War II, would have ample power to generate an EMP over the entire continental United States." [12]

America is not only vulnerable to the threat of an EMP attack from rogue nations like Iran, but also from a terrorist organization such as al-Qaeda. It would certainly be possible for them, especially if sponsored by a country like Iran, to acquire or construct an unsophisticated ballistic missile and use it in an EMP attack against America.

Primitive Scud missiles are reportedly available on the market for $100,000 apiece. Such missiles could be launched from a freighter in international waters. Al-Qaeda is believed to own about 80 such vessels, according to Senator John Kyl (R-AZ). [13]One Scud-type ballistic missile, detonated at an altitude of 95 miles, could degrade electronic systems across one-quarter of the United States. [14]

There are ways to protect America from an EMP attack. One is to harden our electronics infrastructure. Unfortunately, this would be difficult and very expensive. It would require encasing entire systems in a metallic shield, equipping antennas and power connectors with surge protectors, and taking other protection measures necessary to prevent any external electromagnetic pulse from entering the grid. [15]

While this avenue should be pursued, it is not the only answer. Another solution to preventing an EMP attack (or a conventional missile attack for that matter) is a multi-layered missile defense system. We currently have ground-based interceptors located in Alaska and California, but they are only able to hit incoming missiles well after the boost phase, after the separation of the warhead. By that time the target would be a cold, dark, small object hurtling through space or plummeting to earth at supersonic speeds. [16]

Fortunately, we have an even better defensive system than the ground-based interceptors, and it is known as the Airborne Laser program. The Airborne Laser Program is able to place a laser on a modified Boeing aircraft which can detect, track and destroy all classes of ballistic missiles. It can also pass on information regarding launch sites, target tracks, and predicted impact points to other parts of our missile defense system. And it is designed to reach out over 200 miles from where it is deployed. [17] Unlike the ground-based interceptors we have in California and Alaska, Airborne Laser aircraft can be deployed on short notice where needed, patrolling the Persian Gulf, the Taiwan Strait, the Korean Peninsula, and our own shores. [18] More importantly, they have the unique capability to destroy an enemy warhead in its ascent or boost stage, when it is easily identifiable, is slower, has not yet deployed decoys, and is at a point in the missile trajectory when it would fall back down on enemy territory. [19]

On September 7, 2008 the Airborne Laser was successfully fired for the first time. [20] And on August 10, 2009, the Airborne Laser successfully shot down an "instrumented" or simulated target missile, further confirming the laser works as expected. [21]

Amazingly, the Obama administration slashed the budget for the ABL in half, pulled the plug on buying a second plane, and is allowing the program only three tries to hit a live missile, or the program will be killed altogether. [22] An attempt by Congressional Republicans to restore funding for the ABL and the rest of the missile defense program in the 2010 budget was rebuffed by Congressional Democrats. [23]

The Democrat Party's policy of objecting to the weaponization of space dates back to their opposition to Ronald Reagan's Strategic Defense Initiative, which they derisively dubbed "Star Wars," in the early 1980s. [24]

Barack Obama maintains Democrats' dubious ideological consistency. Consider the comments he made to the disarmament group, Caucus for Priorities, during the presidential campaign:

"I will cut investments in unproven missile defense systems. I will not weaponize space. I will slow our development of future combat systems." [25]

Secretary of State Hillary Clinton also vigorously opposes development of defensive missile systems. She has voted to slash budget requests for missile defense and criticized President Bush for "focusing obsessively on expensive and unproven missile defense technology." [26]

Current Vice President Joe Biden is of similar mind. He considers national missile defense in general to be unnecessarily provocative. During a debate in June 2000, he said building missile defenses would be "acting on our worst fears" and would "only make those fears come true." Joe Biden, like most Democrats, voted against Reagan's Strategic Defense Initiative in 1987 in the middle of his own presidential run. [27]

Despite Democrats' continued hostility towards it, space-based missile defense is really the only conceivable way to provide cost-effective, global, around-the-clock defense against enemy missiles, and particularly against missiles in the boost phase. [28]

Missile defense has proven to be workable and successful. According to the Missile Defense Agency, there have been 37 successful hit-to-kill intercepts out of 47 attempts since 2001, a phenomenal 80% success rate. Former Missile Defense Agency Chief, Gen. Trey Obering III revealed that after dozens of successful missile intercepts, "Our testing has shown not only can we hit a bullet with a bullet, we can hit a spot on a bullet with a bullet." [29]

An effective missile defense is one of four possible ways to deal with rogue countries intending to go nuclear. The others are pre-emption, deterrence, and regime change. [30]

The world doesn't appear to have an appetite for pre-emption. Despite continued defiance by Iran and North Korea, the so-called military option looks increasingly improbable, with one glaring exception: if Israel concludes that Iran is an irreversible threat to its existence, it may very well act unilaterally.

Deterrence has a historical track record of success during the Cold War. The policy of mutually assured destruction (MAD) proved effective because both Russia and the U.S. were equally afraid of being annihilated. Deterrence may also work with North Korea because their regime is obsessed with survival.

Iran is a different story. In Iran, radical Islamists, many of whom are in positions of power in government, consider martyrdom a virtue. Thus deterrence is unlikely to be successful because that government might consider its own annihilation a reasonable tradeoff for any damage they could inflict on Western nations.

As the most recent Iranian election demonstrates, regime change is a genuine possibility. There have been ongoing demonstrations by thousands of anti-government Iranians, many of whom are decidedly pro-western and are sick of their nation's status as an international pariah.

Nevertheless, a powerful missile defense plus the threat of retaliation remains our best defense against rogue nuclear nations. Charles Krauthammer said it best:

"Deterrence plus missile defense renders a first strike so unlikely to succeed and yet so certain to bring on self-destruction that it might – just might – get us through the day the rogues go nuclear to the day they are deposed." [31]

For some reason, Democrats cannot grasp the importance of missile defense. They prefer to spend billions of taxpayer dollars on wasteful pork-barrel projects, such as the $8 billion budgeted in the stimulus bill for high-speed trains, or the $3 billion spent on the Cash for Clunkers program. Neither these nor a host of other expenditures will mean much if Americans are forced to endure months or years of living without electricity due to an EMP attack — one that might have been thwarted by the missile defense Democrats casually dismiss.

It is distorted priorities such as these and others that have earned Democrats their well-deserved reputation as being weak on national security.

Chapter 26

DEMOCRATS WAGE WAR — AGAINST THE WAR ON TERROR

One of the main reasons I am no longer a Democrat has to do with the party's insistence that Islamic terrorism can be treated as a "law-enforcement problem."

For me, such an approach demonstrates a disturbing disconnect from reality. It's as if 9/11 never happened — or worse, that Democrats apparently consider it an insufficient level of violence and bloodshed to define it unequivocally as an "act of war."

I firmly believe in the Constitution. But unlike the Democrat Party, I don't believe it applies to non-citizen, non-uniformed enemy combatants. I also don't believe rights exist in a vacuum; for example, given a trade-off between saving thousands of Americans and protecting a terrorist's rights, I'll take saving my fellow countrymen — every time.

Democrats might think we're engaged in, as the Obama administration likes to characterize it, an "overseas contingency operation" to combat those who would commit "man-caused disasters."

I think we're engaged in an all-out war against suicide-bombing religious fanatics who will do anything and everything they can — including using our own Constitution against us — to bring this country to its knees.

And I'd bet dollars to doughnuts most Americans feel exactly the same way.

Unfortunately for Americans, Democrats have elevated political gamesmanship over keeping Americans safe. That they are placing our nation at greater risk is troubling at best or negligent at worst. More to the point, Democrats are waging war against the War on Terror.

Their misguided approach to the danger of Islamic Jihad is three-fold: Democrats are demoralizing the CIA, making it less capable of protecting America; they are undermining our efforts to get valuable intelligence from captured terrorists; and they are determined to close America's most viable facility for incarcerating enemy combatants.

Let's start with the Democrats' attempt to undermine the CIA.

In mid April 2009, President Obama overruled the advice of his CIA director, Leon Panetta, and four prior CIA directors by releasing the details of the "enhanced interrogation program" (or "torture memos" as commonly referred to by the left) used against senior al-Qaeda suspects in 2002 and 2003. It was not necessary for Obama to release the memos, because members of Congress from both parties had been fully aware of them since the program began in 2002, and Congress repeatedly approved and funded this program on a bipartisan basis. [1]

For many Americans, the release of these memos may have been seen as an exercise in open government, honoring the public's right to know. They would be mistaken: the public was given only a portion of the truth. The released memos were carefully edited to leave out references to what our government learned through these interrogation methods. Other memos, laying out specific terrorists plots that were thwarted, apparently were not even considered for release. [2]

This selective disclosure by the Obama administration reinforced the perception for many that this was a political stunt designed to make the Bush administration look bad. A request by former Vice President Dick Cheney to release more CIA records showing that "enhanced interrogations" — including waterboarding — produced intelligence enabling us to prevent other terrorist attacks was turned down. [3]

Could the release of the memos jeopardize our national security? At the very least, terrorists are now aware of the absolute limit of what the CIA can do to extract information, and this will allow them to train accordingly, thus diminishing the effectiveness of these techniques.

More disturbing was the Obama administration's decision on April 21, 2009 to investigate Bush administration lawyers for possible criminal and ethics violations regarding the memos drafted in 2002. [4] This was the President's payback to the anti-war faction in his party, despite the fact he and Chief of Staff Rahm Emanuel had assured Americans they did not intend to prosecute those lawyers. These were the very same attorneys the Bush administration asked for guidance regarding the legality of using harsh interrogation techniques.

Such political gamesmanship is dangerous. It will likely discourage intelligence professionals from offering frank opinions in future counterterrorist cases for fear that they will be prosecuted by a subsequent administration.

Equally damaging to CIA morale was the Obama Justice Department's decision to appoint a special prosecutor to investigate for possible criminal prosecution CIA operatives who interrogated terrorists in overseas locations. This despite the fact that several years ago independent prosecutors examined the allegations of torture, conducted an inquiry, and made a determination not to proceed. [5] Again, this political gamesmanship will result in a more risk-adverse CIA less willing to protect America.

Democrat Speaker of the House Nancy Pelosi also contributed to undermining the CIA's morale. In an April 23, 2009 news conference, Pelosi denied she had been briefed by the CIA in September 2002 on the fact that waterboarding had been performed on detainees:

"We were not ... told that waterboarding or any of these other enhanced interrogation methods were used...And any, any contention to the contrary is simply not true." [6]

On May 5, the CIA refuted Pelosi's allegations. They released an account of the briefing that she was given on EIT's (Enhanced Interrogation Techniques), including the use of them on Abu Zubaydah, and a description of the particular EIT's that had been applied. [7]

And then came a shocker. At a May 14 news conference, a reporter accused Pelosi of complicity in waterboarding detainees because she hadn't done anything to stop it. Ms. Pelosi's response: she accused the CIA of "misleading the Congress." [8]

The following day, CIA Director Leon Panetta — a former Clinton White

House Chief of Staff and a partisan Democrat — fired back: "It is not our policy or practice to mislead Congress. It is against our laws and our values." [9] Porter Goss, the only other member of Congress present at the September 2002 briefing with Pelosi, confirmed Panetta's assessment in a *Washington Post* editorial published on April 25, 2009:

"We understood what the CIA was doing. We gave the CIA our bipartisan support. We gave the CIA funding to carry out its activities. On a bipartisan basis, we asked if the CIA needed more support from Congress to carry out its mission against al-Qaeda. I do not recall a single objection from my colleagues.... After the events of this week (disclosure of enhanced interrogation techniques), *morale at the CIA has been shaken to its foundation.*" [10] (Italics mine)

Apparently, Nancy Pelosi's public objection to waterboarding in 2009 — after seven years of silence — occurred when it became politically advantageous for her to do so. Responding to Pelosi's claims, Peter Hoekstra (R-Mich.) offered an amendment requiring the CIA to publicize an unclassified version of its records. House Intelligence Committee Democrats defeated the Hoekstra amendment on a party line vote in an apparent attempt to protect Mrs. Pelosi. That vote followed Democrat rejection of a resolution by Utah Republican Rob Bishop to begin a bipartisan investigation into Pelosi's accusation. One would think the same Democrats who demanded a "truth commission" when George W. Bush was president would have welcomed setting the record straight. [11]

Democrats continued their ideological assault on the CIA. On June 24, 2009, CIA Director Leon Panetta told the House Intelligence Committee about a dormant classified program CIA counterterrorism officials wanted to activate. [12] The program was designed to assassinate al-Qaeda leaders, but it never made it past the planning stages, and was put on hold in 2004. No CIA teams were dispatched and no terrorists were killed utilizing this unlaunched operation. Panetta told the committee he didn't like the program and had just cancelled it. [13]

That didn't stop Democrats from totally misleading Americans about it. Senator Dianne Feinstein (D-CA.), *Fox News Sunday:*

"I think if the intelligence committees had been briefed, they could have watched the program, they could have asked for reports on the program, they could have made judgments about the program as it went along. That was not the case, because we were kept in the dark." She declared the failure to brief Congress "outside the law." [14]

Senator Dick Durbin's (D-Ill.) echoed Senator Feinstein's comments, telling ABC's *This Week* that "Congress should investigate whether Cheney or others ordered the secrecy…. To have a massive program that is concealed from leaders in Congress…could be illegal." [15]

On July 24, 2009, despite Panetta's insistence he had terminated the program, Democrat Silvestre Reyes, chairman of the House Intelligence Committee, announced he would be undertaking a formal investigation of the CIA. [16]

This was nothing more than political grandstanding. Even Dennis Blair, Barack Obama's Director of National Intelligence, told *The Washington Post* that the CIA was not required to brief Congress about a program that *was never implemented.* [17]

In addition, details of the "secret" program were well-reported in the press. In October 2001, *The Washington Post* ran a front page article by Barton Gellman entitled, "CIA Weighs 'Targeted Killing' Missions." [18] In December 2002, James Risen and Dave Johnston provided details of the target list on the front page of *The New York Times,* and noted that "the President has given broad authority to the CIA to kill or capture operatives of al-Qaeda around the world." [19]

Democrats continued their attack on the CIA. In July 2009, House Intelligence Committee Democrats passed a new requirement that the spy agency videotape all detainee interrogations. [20] This was yet another payback to the radical left anxious to prosecute CIA members who had destroyed interrogation videos of al-Qaeda terrorists years earlier. The CIA believed destroying those tapes was necessary because they might be leaked and compromise our interrogation methods.

As a result of this new requirement, CIA agents can and likely will be second-guessed years later. The message to CIA operatives: taking risks for your country could result in prosecution by a new administration with a different political ideology.

More importantly, our country is now less safe.

The second element of Democrats' misguided approach to national security centers around intelligence gathering.

Intel is one of the most critical elements in any war, especially one against Islamic terrorism.   Terror cells defy normal military and diplomatic countermeasures. As a result, their evil intentions can only be thwarted by obtaining *information:* identifying their operatives, hideouts, motivations, targets, and methods. Unless covert agents can infiltrate the terror networks, which are extremely difficult to do, the best source of obtaining such intelligence is the interrogation of captured terrorists. [21]

Unfortunately, Democrats don't seem to understand this.   Soon after he was sworn in, President Obama signed an executive order suspending the use of enhanced interrogations and restricted all U.S. agencies – including the military and the CIA – to the limits set in the Army Field Manual. [22] President Obama did this even though *half* of the government's knowledge about the structure and activities of al-Qaeda came from those enhanced interrogations. [23]

At this juncture, a fundamental question must be asked: did enhanced interrogation save lives? George Tenet, CIA director under Presidents George W. Bush and Bill Clinton, on CBS' *60 Minutes*, April 2007:

"I know this program has saved lives. I know we've disrupted plots. I know this program alone is worth more than the FBI, Central Intelligence Agency and the National Security Agency put together have been able to tell us." [24]

Democrats have expressed fake outrage over the use of enhanced interrogation techniques such as waterboarding. Why do I make that claim? The CIA waterboarded only *three* high-value detainees. [25] And Democrat Congressmen were *fully informed* that they were doing it. [26]

Ironically, these same "high-minded" Democrats and their media allies have no problem with unmanned predator drones in Pakistan being deployed to kill al-Qaeda members —along with friends, family and innocent civilians that may be nearby. This successful strategy, which dates back to the Bush administration, has been kept in place by the Obama administration.

One has to wonder why it's acceptable to use drones to bomb terrorists and innocent civilians, but not be allowed to waterboard captured terrorists. Despite Democrats' objection to waterboarding, one is hard-pressed to believe it is in fact torture.

It is even harder to believe since for many years waterboarding has been part of the training course for U.S. military special operators, including Navy SEALS. [27]

Are Democrats and the American left contending that we torture our own military personnel?

More incredibly, in May 2009, the Obama Justice Department quietly ordered FBI agents to read Miranda rights to high value foreign fighters captured on the battlefield. [28] Providing suspects Miranda rights requires them to be advised of the right to remain silent and to have an attorney provided at America's expense during questioning.

Rep. Mike Rogers (R-MI.) told *Fox News Thursday* that this new policy is causing "chaos, confusion and frustration in the field." [29]

That's a gross understatement. A law enforcement approach to terror in an American courtroom is highly questionable. The same approach on a battlefield in a middle of a shooting war with American troops in harm's way is an absurdity of the highest order.

The final element of the Democrats' wrong-headed approach to national security involves the demonization of the Guantanamo Bay prison facility.

In November 2001, President Bush announced the establishment of Guantanamo Bay as a detention center to hold al-Qaeda terrorists captured after the October 2001 invasion of Afghanistan. At that time, Bush's approval rating was in the mid-80s and Democrats were looking for an issue they could use to undermine public support for him. [30]

Michael Ratner, a lawyer with the Center for Constitutional Rights, immediately began organizing an effort to offer pro bono legal counsel to the first detainees. The Center for Constitutional Rights was founded by the late William Kunstler, a radical leftist lawyer who had served as defense attorney for the Chicago Seven, the Black Panthers and other violent groups. Ratner himself had represented members of Hamas and Omar Abdel Rahman, the blind sheikh who had organized the original bombing of the World Trade Center back in 1993. [31]

The initial focus of Ratner and his allies was not torture or the interrogations at Guantanamo Bay. Instead, they wanted to plant the idea in the public's mind that most, if not all, of the inmates might be innocent victims, picked up on the battlefield by mistake. [32]

Nothing could have been further from the truth. The military captured more than 70,000 people and put *all of them* through a rigorous screening process. Ten thousand were released immediately, and by the time the military's work had been completed, only 800 remained in custody. These prisoners were the ones the military had deemed hard-core, well-trained terrorists who could not be released without running the risk they would rejoin the war. [33]

The question confronting the Bush administration was what to do with them.

The answer was Guantanamo Bay. The purpose of "Gitmo" was not to have inmates serve sentences for crimes, but to prevent enemy combatants from continuing their fight against the U.S. and its allies. Gitmo was selected because it was under U.S. control, but not on U.S. soil. Terrorists could be detained and processed without the involvement of U.S. civil courts and their time-consuming procedures.

Ratner's claims gained little traction until revelations about the Iraqi prison, Abu Ghraib broke in the spring of 2004. The exposure of abuses at Abu Ghraib originally came, not from a reporter or a human rights advocate, but from the *Department of Defense* itself. [34]

The Bush administration's "culpability" for Abu Ghraib was the perfect campaign issue for the Democrats looking to derail President Bush's re-election chances in 2004. Senator Edward Kennedy (D-Mass.) was the first to "rise" to the occasion:

"We now learn that Saddam's torture chambers (are) reopened under new management: U.S. management." [35]

Senator Dick Durbin (D-Ill.) was not far behind. He compared Gitmo jailors to the Nazis and the Soviets in the gulag, henchmen of some "mad regime – Pol Pot and others – who have no concern for human beings." [36]

Democrats were attempting to create an invidious comparison between Guantanamo Bay and Abu Ghraib to make it appear the Bush administration was creating torture chambers at Gitmo.

The reality was far different. A total of *twelve separate investigations* left no doubt: Gitmo is safer and less abusive than any detention facility anywhere in the U.S., military or civilian. A 2005 report commissioned by the Defense Department was unequivocal: "No torture occurred." [37]

And in yet another reality check for radical leftists, a 2004 Pentagon commission headed by former Defense Secretary James Schlesinger cleared the Defense Department and Bush administration of any responsibility for what happened at Abu Ghraib. [38]

A *Washington Times* article written January 15, 2009, exposed the hypocrisy of Democrats regarding the treatment of captured terrorists. "Extraordinary rendition," which involves capturing a terrorist suspect in one country and sending him to another without formal judicial proceedings, "took place dozens of times under the Clinton administration…" According to human rights organizations and former U.S. officials, Barack Obama's CIA director, Leon Panetta "served as White House Chief of Staff during the time the Clinton administration accelerated a practice of kidnapping terrorist suspects and sending them to countries with records of torturing prisoners…" [39]

Does anyone recall the same Democrats complaining about torture when Bill Clinton was president?

The moral dilemma posed by rendition was the reason Gitmo was created in the first place. Unlike the Clinton administration, the Bush administration preferred to reign in the CIA and other interrogators by clarifying the rules under which they could operate. [40]

Democrats and the mainstream media have turned this reality upside down. They continue to falsely assert that torture at Gitmo was routine, and that the prison's very existence was counter-productive to the war on terror.

The result? On January 21, 2009, President Obama's first executive order was to close Guantanamo Bay within one year. An unresolved issue? How to deal with the 240 or so inmates still detained there. Europeans, so firmly opposed to Gitmo during the Bush years, refused to take them, and countries that might have such as Yemen, couldn't be trusted to prevent them from returning to the battlefield. Obama wanted to relocate the prisoners into U.S. prisons — but even his own party denied him the funding to do so. [41]

Even more telling, Obama decided to stick with Bush's idea of military commissions for some detainees, adding some procedural changes as political cover to justify his past opposition. [42] Ironically, although Obama accused Bush of making "decisions based upon fear rather than foresight," he is now doing the same thing for which he criticized Bush. [43] *(Author's note: as most Americans know, other detainees may be getting civilian trials, most notably the perpetrators of 9/11, who may be tried in New York City. See chapter 24 for more details.)*

As for the warrantless wiretapping Democrats spent years denouncing as "spying on Americans" and "illegal," the Obama Justice Department adopted a stance identical to, if not more aggressive than, that of the Bush administration. They argued in court that the disclosure of surveillance programs would cause "exceptional harm to national security" by exposing intelligence sources and methods. [44]

Where was the mainstream media regarding this hypocrisy? Conspicuously silent as usual when it comes to Democrat duplicity.

In conclusion, it is worth reminding Americans of something they may have forgotten: one of the enduring strengths of our democratic republic is its *flexibility*. Throughout the course of our history, rights have never been sacrosanct to the point where circumstances are completely irrelevant. For example, during the Civil War, Abraham Lincoln suspended the Constitutionally-protected concept of habeas corpus, and during WW II, Franklin Delano Roosevelt had six German spies tried by military tribunal — after which they were executed.

After both conflicts, Constitutional rights were completely restored.

The Democrats' approach to the war on terror completely ignores this history. They believe in the sanctity of rights, *per se,* even if such a dogmatic approach hampers our ability to keep Americans safe.

If America is attacked again because of Democrats' ideological rigidity, they will be hard-pressed to justify such deadly stubbornness to a country once again consumed by national mourning.

Chapter 27

A ROGUE'S GALLERY OF RADICALS

The adage, "you can judge a man by the company he keeps" speaks volumes about the political leanings of the Obama administration.

In short, this president and his supporting cast are the most radical group of leftists who have ever been elected and appointed to run the country.

Many of these people share a common vision: America is a fundamentally flawed nation in need of an extreme make-over, which can only be achieved if we adopt European-style socialism.

Toward that end, they believe dissent must be silenced, wealth must be "re-distributed," national sovereignty must give way to global governance, and American customs, culture and tradition must give way to a new world order, where "fairness" is determined by government bureaucrats seeking "social justice."

If that's "hope and change," count me out.

Throughout his life, Barack Obama has maintained close associations with radical leftists, given them as much power and prominence as possible, and disavowed them only when it is politically advantageous to do so.

The seeds of his far-left ideology were formed in his teenage years in Hawaii. A close reading of Obama's first book, *Dreams from My Father*, shows that his childhood mentor up to age 18 — a man he referred to as "Frank" — was the late communist Frank Marshall Davis, who fled Chicago after the FBI and Congress began investigations into his "subversive" and "un-American activities." [1] A 1951 report by the Commission on Subversive Activities to the legislature of the Territory of Hawaii identified him as a Communist Party USA member. [2] According to Herbert Romerstein, a former minority chief investigator of the House Committee on Internal Security, FBI files also confirm Davis was a member of the Communist party. [3]

During that time, Davis gave Obama several pieces of advice. The most telling? Never trust the white establishment. [4]

In college, Obama hung around with Marxist professors and took in socialist conferences for "inspiration." After college, he followed in Davis' footsteps, becoming a community organizer in Chicago. [5] But as *Investor's Business Daily* points out, "Some community organizers are well-meaning and harmless. But not the ones Obama threw in with. They intimidate and agitate for more government home loans, more government job programs, a ban on police profiling, more benefits for illegal aliens, felon voting rights, minimum wage hikes, 'environmental justice' and so on." [6]

One of those community organization groups with whom Obama has had a long history of ties? The Association of Community Organizations for Reform Now, aka ACORN. (See chapter on "Democrats and Their Unholy Alliances")

As part of his community organizing efforts, Obama attempted to mobilize churches for political protest. During this time he met Reverend Jeremiah Wright, pastor of the Trinity United Church of Christ. [7]

As Stanley Kurtz reveals in a *National Review* article, Wright's church was not only thoroughly politicized, but arguably the most radical black church in the country. [8] The Rev. Wright preached a Marxist version of Christianity called "black liberation theology." Founded by James H. Cone, black liberation theology seeks an alliance with Marxists and adopts a fundamentally Marxist viewpoint and critique of capitalism. [9] In his 1969 book *Black Theology and Black Power,* Cone writes: "Together black religion and Marxist philosophy may show us the way to build a completely new society." [10]

Within this context, Wright's sermons — including comments calling on God to damn America, accusing the U.S. government of intentionally spreading HIV among blacks and blaming 9/11 on America's allegedly terrorist history and foreign policy — become easily understood. [11]

When Wright's comments became national news during the 2008 election campaign, Barack Obama sought to distance himself from the Reverend. Certain facts, however, are indisputable:

- Barack Obama attended Wright's church for twenty years.[12]
- Wright helped Obama become a Christian, officiated at his marriage, and baptized his two daughters. [13]
- Obama has called Wright his "spiritual adviser" and mentor. [14]
- Obama was aware of Wright's incendiary views — the title of his second book, *The Audacity of Hope,* was taken from the first sermon he heard at Trinity Church. The theme of Wright's sermon? "White folks' greed runs a world in need." [15]

Obama also became deeply involved with Bill Ayers, a former head of the terrorist group Weather Underground, which specialized in bombing government buildings in the late 1960s. Ayers escaped conviction on the grounds that the government had used an illegal wiretap to monitor his activities. [16]

Ayers is totally unrepentant regarding his terrorist past. In 2001, he told *The New York Times,* "I don't regret setting bombs. I feel we didn't do enough." [17]

According to Sol Stern, senior fellow at the Manhattan Institute, Ayers was "one of the leaders of a movement for bringing radical social-justice teaching in our public school class rooms... He still hopes for revolutionary upheaval that will finally bring down American capitalism and imperialism..." Ayers' own words confirm this point:

"I'm an agnostic about how and where the rebellion will break out, but I know I want to be there and I know it will break out..." [18]

The mainstream media tried to minimize the relationship between Obama and Ayers. The facts tell a different story. When Obama decided to run for the Illinois state senate in 1995, his first fund-raising event was held in the home of Ayers and his long-time companion, Bernadine Dohrn, also a former Weather Underground member. [19] In 1997, Ayers wrote a book about juvenile justice, *A Kind and Just Parent,* which Obama endorsed as "a searing and timely account." [20] Both men were also members of the board for the leftist Woods Fund from 1998 to 2001. [21]

A release of records in 2008 from the University of Illinois, Chicago shows that Ayers was instrumental in starting the Chicago Annenberg Challenge in the 1990s, securing a $50 million grant to reform the Chicago Public Schools. Ayers named Barack Obama Chairman of the Board. Obama ran the fiscal arm that distributed grants to schools and raised matching funds, while Ayers ran the operational arm. [22]

How "casual" could the relationship between Ayers and Obama have been? Ayers relinquished control of the aforementioned $50 million grant (which became $160 million because of matching grants) to Obama. Who would do that for a person he did not know well and trust thoroughly? [23]

Barack Obama also has ties to other dubious characters. Syrian-born Tony Rezko, a real estate developer and convicted felon, had several shady financial transactions with then-Senator Obama. [24] Robert Malley, former advisor to Obama, quit after the press found out he was having regular contact with Hamas. [25] Father Michael Pfleger, who also espoused the anti-white, anti-capitalist black liberation theology of Reverend Wright, was another of Obama's self-admitted "spiritual advisors." [26]

Considering Obama's ties to these political radicals as well as his relationship with radical community organizing groups, it is no surprise that he would surround himself with similar-minded appointees to his administration. The following is a *partial* list:

Green Jobs Czar — *Van Jones*

Van Jones was selected in March 2009 by President Obama as Special Adviser for Green Jobs, Enterprise and Innovation at the White House Council on Environmental Quality. [27] Jones was a founding member of the Apollo Alliance, a radical group consisting of a coalition of environmentalists, unions and community organizers that helped write the $787 billion stimulus bill. [28] Jones' job allowed him to control the green jobs-related cash in that bill — estimated to be approximately $86 billion. [29]

On September 5, 2009 Van Jones resigned from his position after exposure by conservative activists, lawmakers and a media campaign led by Fox News'

Glenn Beck. The pressure on Jones reached a peak after weeks of video clips and interviews of Jones revealed his "radical" views.

What views?

Jones described his radicalization in a 2005 interview with the *East Bay Express:*

"(In jail) I met all these young radical people of color — I mean really radical, communists and anarchists. And it was, like, "This is what I need to be a part of.... I spent the next ten years of my life working with a lot of those people I met in jail, trying to be a revolutionary.... I was a rowdy nationalist on April 28th, and then the verdicts (Rodney King police trial) came down on April 29th... By August, I was a communist." [30]

The same interview also revealed that Van Jones formed a communist organization, Standing Together to Organize a Revolutionary Movement (STORM) in 1994, which held study groups on the theories of Marx and Lenin and harbored dreams of a multiracial socialist utopia. [31]

Van Jones also signed a "9/11 Truth Petition" alleging that the "current administration (the Bush administration) may have deliberately allowed 9/11 to happen, perhaps as a pretext for war." [32] In keeping with many of Barack Obama's anti-white associates, Van Jones also claimed that "white polluters and the white environmentalists are essentially steering poison into the people-of-color communities." [33]

Ironically in 2008, *Time* Magazine named Van Jones as one of its "Environmental Heroes." [34] This is another example of a mainstream media either incapable of doing its homework — or *unwilling* to do it.

Regulatory Czar — *Cass Sunstein*

Cass Sunstein was selected by President Obama as the head of the Office of Information and Regulatory Affairs, and confirmed by the U.S. Senate on September 10, 2009. [35]

Sunstein's confirmation should alarm every American. He is a fanatical proponent of the belief that the government should control virtually every aspect of human activities.

His book, *The Second Bill of Rights: FDR's Unfinished Revolution and Why We Need it More Than Ever* documents his enthusiasm for socialism and his desire to increase the size and scope of government:

"My major aim of this book is to uncover an important but neglected part of America's heritage: the idea of a second bill of rights. In brief, the second bill attempts to protect both opportunity and security, by creating rights to employment, adequate food and clothing, decent shelter, education, recreation, and medical care." [36]

Sunstein also wants the government to control and regulate talk radio. From his 2007 book, *Republic.com 2.0:*

"A system of limitless individual choices, with respect to communications, is not necessarily in the interest of citizenship and self-government." [37]

Unfortunately for Mr. Sunstein, but fortunately for the rest of America, the First Amendment to the Constitution says otherwise.

Controlling the radio waves is not the only medium Sunstein wants to regulate. In his new book, *On Rumors: How Falsehoods Spread, Why We Believe Them, What Can Be Done,* Sunstein claims that bloggers have been running wild and that new laws need to be written to control them. [38]

Ed Lasky of *American Thinker* explains that "Sunstein's book is a blueprint for online censorship as he wants to hold blogs and web hosting services accountable for the remarks of commentators on websites while altering libel laws to make it easier to sue for spreading 'rumors.' " [39]

Currently bloggers and commentators are immune, but under Sunstein's plan they would be forced to remove any comments unless those comments could be proven. The expenses associated with compliance and potential litigation could be overwhelming and time consuming. The mere threat of retaliatory actions could be enough to discourage many web sites from issuing any words of criticism or skepticism, thus chilling freedom of speech. [40]

Perhaps Sunstein's most radical view is revealed in a book he co-edited in

2004 entitled, *Animal Rights: Current Debates and New Directions*. In the introduction, he wrote that *animals should have legal rights and be able to file lawsuits in court.* [41]

<u>Science Adviser</u> — *John P. Holdren*

John Holdren was confirmed by the U.S. Senate on March 19, 2009 for the position of Director of the White House Office of Science and Technology Policy. [42]

In 1977, he co-authored the book *Ecoscience: Population Resources and Environment* with Paul and Anne Ehrlich. In the chapter entitled "Changing American Institutions," Holdren and the Ehrlichs call for a "considerably more equitable distribution of wealth and income" in the United States, praising an economist's plan to limit the level of compensation to a $100,000 annual salary, or just under $350,000 in 2009, adjusted for inflation. [43]

Holdren's quest for economic redistribution goes much further. In the same book, he proposed the "surrender of sovereignty" to a "comprehensive Planetary Regime" that would control all the world's resources, direct global redistribution of wealth, oversee the "de-development" of the West, control a World Army and taxation regime, and enforce world population limits. [44]

Holdren and the Ehrlichs also embraced "compulsory abortion" if the population crisis became sufficiently severe to endanger the society. [45] How would Mr. Holdren do this? His plan:

"Add(ing) a sterilant to drinking water or staple foods is a suggestion that seems to horrify people more than most proposals for involuntary fertility control. [46]

Or as an alternative: "A program of sterilizing women after their second or third child, despite the relatively greater difficulty of the operation than vasectomy, might be easier to implement than trying to sterilize men." [47]

Ironically, when Barack Obama nominated Holdren as his Science Adviser in December 2008, the president said that "promoting science isn't just about providing resources," but "ensuring that facts and evidence are never twisted or obscured by politics or ideology." [48]

Holdren's track record? In 1986, he predicted that a billion people would die before the year 2020 from "carbon dioxide-induced famines." [49] He repeated this opinion in *Newsweek* just two years ago, and confirmed it again in his Senate confirmation hearing on February 2009. [50]

In 2007, Holdren wrote that current quantities of carbon emissions could cause a 13 foot rise in sea levels. Under cross-examination by Senator David Vitter (R-LA) during his confirmation hearings, Holdren admitted that the alarming scientific estimates are now half as much as he predicted just two years ago. [51] A subsequent estimate by the U.N.'s own Intergovernmental Panel on Climate Change placed the figure at a maximum of 59 cm (or 23.2 inches) by the year 2100. [52]

Senator Vitter also grilled Holdren about his 1973 opinion that 280 million people would be "too many" for the United States. Holdren's response:

"When I wrote those lines in 1973, I was preoccupied with the fact that many problems the United States faced appeared to be being made more difficult by the rate of population growth that then prevailed." [53]

William Yeatman of the Competitive Enterprise Institute warned the Senate that Holdren had a "40 year record of outlandish scientific assertions, consistently wrong predictions, and dangerous public policy choices" that made him "unfit to serve as White House Science Adviser." [54]

Incredibly, no senator from either party voted against his nomination. This so-called "expert" will now have the ear of the president in setting scientific policy.

Diversity Czar — *Mark Lloyd*

On July 29, 2009, Mark Lloyd was appointed by President Obama to be the new Chief Diversity Officer at the Federal Communications Commission (FCC). [55]

There never was a "diversity officer" at the FCC before Mr. Lloyd's appointment. [56]

Lloyd is a long-time Democrat activist who has proposed ways to cripple conservative media under the pretense of "local accountability." [57] A Saul Alinsky disciple, his 2006 book entitled *Prologue to a Farce: Communication and Democracy in America* calls for an all-out "confrontational movement" against private media, and replacing them with public broadcasters. [58]

In 2007, while working at the George Soros-funded Center for American Progress, Lloyd co-wrote a report entitled "The Structural Imbalance of Political Talk Radio," in which he suggested ideas to combat conservative dominance of talk radio. These include diversity rules to ensure that more progressive voices get on the air, and enforcing "localism" rules to guarantee that more minorities and local leaders own broadcasting licenses and stations. If private broadcasters don't follow the "diversity" and "localism" rules, they will face fines. [59]

Lloyd also wants private broadcasting companies to pay licensing fees equal to 100% of their total operating costs. These fees would then be redistributed to create and subsidize more liberal public radio stations. [60]

Lloyd's radicalism was revealed at the National Conference for Media Reform in 2008, where he praised the "really incredible revolution" led by socialist Hugo Chavez in Venezuela, despite the fact that Chavez has shut down almost every independent radio and television station in that country. [61]

Energy Czar — *Carol Browner*

Carol Browner was selected by the Obama administration to head a newly-created position as "Director of the White House Office of Energy and Climate Change Policy," more commonly known as the "Energy Czar." [62]

Until January 2009, Mrs. Browner was one of the leaders of the climate change arm of the anti-capitalist organization, Socialist International, which calls for "global governance" and says rich countries must shrink their economies to address climate change. [63]

According to its own principles, Socialist International favors nationalizing industry, questions the benefits of economic growth and wants to establish a more "equitable international economic order." [64]

Less than a week after Mrs. Browner was exposed as a Socialist International member, the group removed her name, position and biography from its website. [65]

As the Energy Czar, Carol Browner has played a key role in pushing cap and trade legislation. If such legislation becomes law, it will represent the largest tax increase in the history of the world, and one of the largest transfers of wealth from consumers to big business and special interest groups. [66]

Chief Legal Adviser to the State Department — *Harold Koh*

On March 23, 2009, Harold Koh was nominated to be legal adviser to the State Department. He was subsequently approved by the U.S. Senate. [67]

Koh is an advocate of the dangerous concept known as "transnationalism." Transnationalism would elevate foreign law above the U.S. Constitution. [68]

Koh doesn't see the United States as an independent nation with its own sovereignty. Under the transnationalist approach he advocates, treaties the U.S. has not ratified would be given the force of law.[69] This would allow the United Nations to enforce foreign law within America. A few examples of the potential consequences:

- U.S. troops could be put on trial by foreign judges for "war crimes."
- The United Nations could impose a global tax on American citizens.
- The United Nations could control oil, gas and mineral rights in the world's oceans through the Law of the Sea Treaty.
- The United Nations could also abrogate the right to bear arms, and require alien enemy combatants to be tried in civilian federal courts.

Andrew McCarthy, writing in the *National Review,* also believes Koh would "require federal and state courts to give effect to the rulings of the International Court of Justice, which in recent years has, among other things, attempted to invalidate death sentences in Texas and held that Israel's security fence — which reduced suicide bombings by more than 90 percent — is a violation of international law." [70]

How far could such rulings go? New York lawyer Steven Stein says that, in addressing the Yale Club of Greenwich in 2007, Koh claimed that "in an appropriate case, he didn't see any reason why Sharia law would not be applied to govern a case in the United States." [71] Sharia law is an Islamic system of laws virtually incompatible with our judicial system, or any democracy for that matter.

Safe School Czar — *Kevin Jennings*

Kevin Jennings was appointed by President Obama as the Safe School Czar. Jennings founded the Gay Straight Alliance (GSA) and the Gay Lesbian Straight Education Network (GLSEN) which have imparted his propaganda model to thousands of staff members presently indoctrinating children in grades K-12 in every state. [72]

What is his "propaganda model?" Creating a series of several buzz words or phrases to surreptitiously promote the homosexual agenda in public schools. A few examples: "safe school," "hate-free," "respect differences," "free to be fully me," "day of silence," etc. [73]

As a school teacher in Massachusetts, he refused to report the sexual victimization of a student to the proper authorities, school officials, or the child's parents. Instead, he offered the child this advice: "I hope you knew to use a condom." [74]

White House Communications Director — *Anita Dunn*

Anita Dunn was appointed as the White House Communications Director. Speaking to high school students in June 2008, she cited Mao Tse Tung, the Communist Chinese leader who killed tens of millions of his own people, as one of her two "favorite political philosophers" and one of the "two people I turn to most." [75] Unsurprisingly, she also admitted that the Obama campaign strategy during the 2008 presidential race was to rarely communicate anything to the press unless it was "controlled." [76]

In November 2009, Anita Dunn resigned from her post due to similar exposure from the same conservative forces that forced Van Jones' resignation.

Auto Task Force (Car Czar) and Manufacturing Czar — *Ron Bloom*

Ron Bloom was appointed as both the head of the Auto Task Force (Car Czar) and as senior counselor for manufacturing policy. [77] Speaking at the 6th Annual Distressed Investing Forum Union Club in New York in February 2008, he stated, "We know that the free market system is nonsense... We kinda agree with Mao that political power comes largely from the barrel of a gun." [78]

Judged by these personal associations and political appointments, Barack Obama is arguably the most radical president ever elected in the history of our republic. While each of the individuals mentioned in this chapter have their idiosyncrasies, when put together, like a jig-saw puzzle, their overall motivations are revealed: Every one of these people believe America is a fundamentally flawed nation in need of radical transformation.

The vehicle for that transformation? An ever-expanding government aimed at diminishing individual liberty and, for all intents and purposes, doing away with our capitalist system.

Chapter 28

THE DEMISE OF DISSENT AND DEMOCRACY

On my journey from the left side to the right side of the political spectrum, I have discovered an enduring irony: the most intolerant, judgmental and ideologically rigid people are those who claim to be exactly the opposite.

The Democrat Party is the standard-bearer of such hypocrisy.

This chapter will reveal policies and tactics being used by Democrats to undermine free speech and the democratic process — from attempts to limit conservative talk radio to damaging the integrity of American elections.

This is quite a leap for a party which once considered dissent, as characterized by Hillary Clinton, to be the "highest form of patriotism."

Too bad she and her fellow Democrats don't really mean it.

The First Amendment of the Constitution guarantees freedom of speech, the most important building block of our democratic republic. Every American should be alarmed that this right is under attack by Democrats and the Obama administration.

Their main target is talk radio, one of the media's few remaining conservative outlets.

Most Americans are unaware of a dangerous amendment to the D.C. Voting Rights Bill, called the Durbin Amendment. In February 2009, it was passed 57-41 by our Democratically–controlled Senate. This bill will force the Federal Communications Commission (FCC) to "promote diversity in communication media ownership and ensure broadcast licenses are used in the public interest." [1] The FCC will be able to pull licenses of radio stations who fail to meet arbitrary guidelines for race and gender at their companies. [2]

The Durbin Amendment masquerades itself as something that will "promote diversity" and be "race-neutral," when in reality it's nothing more than an attempt to stifle free speech. It is intended to push the radical left-wing agenda by shutting down legitimate conservative dissent. It will clamp down on conservative talk radio by allowing the FCC to arbitrarily pull the licenses of conservative station owners and replace them with ones operated by female and minority owners, who the Democrats believe are more likely to broadcast liberal political talk shows. [3]

President Obama and the Democrats are keenly aware of how to use the "public interest" façade, which the FCC refers to as "localism," as a way to silence conservative dissent. The Durbin Amendment's language is modeled after a 2007 report by the left-wing group, Center for American Progress. [4] Their report, *The Structural Imbalance of Political Talk Radio,* complained that there was too much conservative talk on the radio because of the "absence of localism in American radio markets" and urged the FCC to "(e)nsure greater local accountability over radio licensing." Unsurprisingly, the President and CEO of Center for American Progress is John Podesta, who was the head of Obama's transition team. [5]

The Durbin Amendment's sponsor was Dick Durbin (D-Ill.), who three years ago told The Hill: "It's time to reinstitute the Fairness Doctrine." [6] For those unfamiliar with the Fairness Doctrine, it was regulation enacted in 1949, at a time when there were a limited number of broadcast outlets. The Fairness Doctrine required broadcasters to provide opposing viewpoints when discussing political topics. The consequences were just the opposite: radio stations, under the threat of random investigations and warnings for perceived lack of compliance, stopped producing *any* shows with political content. As a result, political talk radio hardly existed until the Fairness Doctrine was overturned by the FCC in 1987 during the Reagan administration. [7] From that point on, talk radio exploded, and it became a medium dominated by conservative talk show hosts, even though liberal shows had equal broadcasting opportunities. Such dominance demonstrated that free markets were working and Americans were making their choices. Polls have shown more Americans, whether Democrat or Republican, consider themselves to be conservative rather than liberal.

Today, with the Internet, 500 channels on television, and a plethora of radio stations, there is little prospect of opposing viewpoints not being heard.

That's what makes this "diversity" legislation so dubious.

The appointment by the Obama administration of Mark Lloyd as the FCC's *first-ever* diversity chief also lends much credibility to fears that Democrats want to silence conservative talk radio. Lloyd is a long-time Democrat activist who has proposed ways to cripple conservative media under the pretense of "local accountability." A Saul Alinsky disciple, his 2006 book entitled *Prologue to a Farce: Communication and Democracy in America* embraces the idea that private broadcasters (read: conservative broadcasters) should pay huge licensing fees in order to fund left-leaning public radio. He also wrote an article several years ago encouraging liberals to challenge conservative media moguls and station owners. [8] Lloyd has also praised Venezuelan dictator Hugo Chavez, calling his regime an "incredible revolution, a democratic revolution," that "began to take very seriously the media in the country" after a rebellion against his rule. This is the same Chavez that, as of August 2009, had revoked the licenses of 34 radio stations in his country. [9]

How "fair" do you think Mark Lloyd will be as our "diversity czar" in light of the fact that he admires how Chavez silenced opposition voices in Venezuela?

Liberals also use other tactics to silence those with whom they disagree. Glenn Beck, a conservative radio and television host, exposed the radicalism of Van Jones, a former special adviser to the Obama administration, by playing video clips of him making radical statements. Beck was then targeted by a racially-charged activist group called "Color of Change," who called for a boycott of his TV advertisers. Using racism as a pretext, they successfully bullied some of his advertisers to pull their ads from his program. Who founded Color of Change? Van Jones, of course. [10]

Another target was the supermarket chain Whole Foods. Its CEO, John Mackey, wrote a 2009 op-ed in *The Wall Street Journal* explaining how his company has successfully reduced health care costs using free market principles. The left immediately organized a boycott of Whole Foods because Mackey didn't endorse government-run health care.

With regard to personal attacks, Former Republican Vice Presidential candidate Sarah Palin, ordinary American citizen Joe the Plumber, and Miss USA runner-up Carrie Prejean, are three recent examples of people thoroughly vilified for daring to defy liberal dogma.

Even news organizations are not immune. The Obama administration has defamed Fox News as "not being a real news network." [11] Ironically, the nonpartisan Pew Research Center found that Fox News' coverage of the 2008 election campaign was the most balanced of any network. [12]

Today's liberals and Democrats also attempt to squelch freedom of speech in other ways. Their proposed "card check" legislation would abolish secret ballot elections at workplaces trying to determine whether or not employees are to be represented by unions. At colleges and universities, administrators, "armed with speech codes, have for years been disciplining and subjecting to sensitivity training any students who dare to utter thoughts that liberals find offensive. The campuses that used to pride themselves as zones of free expression are now the least free part of our society." [13]

Liberal students are equally guilty of speech suppression. When conservative author David Horowitz attempted to speak during Islamo-Fascism Awareness Week at Emory University in 2006, protestors forced him from the stage. The same thing has happened to other conservatives such as author Ann Coulter at the University of Connecticut, columnist Bill Kristol at the University of Texas, and the Minutemen founder, Jim Gilchrist, at Columbia University. [14] On the other hand, there was no outrage whatsoever from these same liberal students when Iranian President Mahmoud Ahmadinejad spoke at Columbia University in 2007.

Furthermore, there are no recorded instances in which conservatives have similarly violated the freedom of speech of liberal speakers.

Democrats are also subverting the principles of democracy. The census, a Constitutionally-required population count undertaken every 10 years, determines the number of representatives each state sends to the House. House representation determines the composition of the Electoral College, which in turn determines the winner of the presidential election.

The census has always been controlled by the Commerce Department. Yet in 2009, the Obama White House moved control of the census from the Commerce Department to the Executive Office of the President. [15] Americans should question why, for the first time in our history, the White House would suddenly take control of this effort.

An indication of how politicized the census would have been was the White House's intention to make the community organizing group ACORN an integral part of the process, in spite of the fact that it is under investigation in many states for voter registration fraud. Due to a corruption scandal, the White House subsequently announced they were rescinding ACORN's role. [16]

Democrats attempt to undermine our democratic process in other ways. They are heavily invested in increasing voter registration by any means necessary — even if it raises the possibility that thousands of illegal voters will be enfranchised. Once again the aforementioned ACORN is at the heart of these ongoing attempts. In the last election alone, of the 1.3 million voter registration applications submitted by that organization, *400,000 were rejected.* [17]

Even the common sense requirement of photo identification for voting has been consistently opposed by Democrats in state after state.

The Democrats' desire to register as many voters as possible began with their passage of the National Voter Registration Act of 1993, aka the Motor Voter Act. This act allowed people to register to vote at the same time they applied for a driver's license, either by mail or in person. [18] Liberal states like California have made it illegal to require documentation regarding an applicant's immigration status. They use the honor system. [19] John Sample of the CATO Institute, testifying before Congress on March 14, 2001, said it best: "Mr. Chairman, judged by its purpose, the National Voter Registration Act should be judged a failure. The Act has brought a substantial increase in the number of registered voters. However, that increase has been bought at a high price. Specifically, the Act has made it difficult if not impossible to maintain clean registration rolls, a major purpose of the law. Moreover, the inaccuracy in the rolls caused by the Act has thrown into doubt the integrity of our electoral system." [20]

Voter intimidation is also part of the anti-democratic mix. During the 2008 presidential election, members of the New Black Panther Party decided to "patrol" election sites in a Philadelphia precinct. Their effort to scare voters was caught on videotape and broadcast nationwide. [21]

In the first week of January 2009, the Justice Department filed a civil lawsuit against the New Black Panther Party and three of its members, claiming they violated the 1965 Voter Registration Act. Although the three defendants never showed up in court to deny the allegations, the Obama Justice Department incredibly dismissed the lawsuit against all but one defendant, who received *only* an injunction against carrying a weapon in a polling place *only* in Philadelphia, and *only* until 2012. [22]

Democrats even subvert democracy amongst themselves. While the Republican Party's presidential primaries are conducted in a truly democratic fashion — one vote for each voter — Democrats employ super-delegates who control nearly 40 percent of the total number of votes needed to determine their presidential candidate. Even the ultra-liberal MSNBC called this aspect of the Democrat Party "at odds with grass-roots democracy." [23]

Why are the Democrats so invested in restricting speech and undermining democracy?

Author David Horowitz aptly explains: "We are in the midst of a political war in which one side is seeking to eliminate the other. This is a war begun by the left, and in fact waged only by the left...Seven years ago the left set out to destroy George Bush and did — because he didn't fight back." [24]

Most Americans have been led to believe the greatest threat to democracy and freedom of speech comes from the right. As this chapter demonstrates, the real threat comes from the left and the Democrat Party.

Chapter 29

THE COMMUNITY ORGANIZER'S COMMUNITY ORGANIZER

Context, it has been said, is everything. And nothing puts President Barack Obama's political viewpoint in better context than discovering the source of its inspiration: radical leftist Saul Alinsky, the "godfather" of community organizers.

The "Alinsky Method" is a blueprint for engineering social revolution without its victims even realizing it's happening. Toward that end, the method contains specific strategies for dealing with one's enemies, including deception to pursue one's radical goals, and creating a Fifth Column to undermine the existing system from within.

Barack Obama was both a dedicated disciple and a teacher of the Alinsky Method in his early years.

What this chapter reveals: despite the death of its author, the Alinsky Method lives on.

"We are five days away from fundamentally transforming the United States of America." — candidate Barack Obama five days before the 2008 election. [1]

Although candidate Obama claimed to be a moderate who wanted to bring Americans together and govern from the center, the words uttered above were an unmistakable hint of something far different to come.

To understand the president's true intentions, one needs to become familiar with a Chicago radical named Saul Alinsky and the strategy of deception he developed to promote "social change."

Alinsky developed the concept of confrontational political tactics, which he termed "organizing," that characterized the 1960s. [2] His mission was to teach radicals to disguise their ideology. [3]

The change he advocated was the complete remaking of society — in other words, revolution.

Obama never met Alinsky. But he was trained by the Alinsky-founded Industrial Areas Foundation in Chicago, a training institute for community organizers. As *Investor's Business Daily* points out, "In the 1980s, Obama spent years as director of the Developing Communities Project, which operated using Alinsky's strategies, and was involved with two other Alinsky-oriented entities: Acorn and Project Vote." [4]

He became an adept practitioner of Alinsky's methods.

On the Obama campaign website was a photo of him teaching in a University of Chicago classroom with "Power Analysis" and "Relationships Built on Self Interest" written on the blackboard beside him. Both are key phrases used in the Alinsky method. [5] Obama himself taught workshops on the Alinsky method for several years. [6]

Immediately after the 2008 Democratic National Convention in Colorado, the *Boston Globe* published a letter from L. David Alinsky, in which he boasted about how Barack Obama had made extremely effective use of his father's training methods:

"Barack Obama's training in Chicago by the great community organizers is showing its effectiveness. It is an amazingly powerful format, and the method of my late father always works to get the message out and get the supporters on board. When executed meticulously and thoughtfully, it is a powerful strategy for initiating change and making it really happen. Obama learned his lesson well." [7]

What training method did Barack Obama use so successfully?

The one Alinsky set forth in his 1971 book *Rules for Radicals: A Primer for Realistic Radicals*. In that book, originally entitled *Rules for Revolution*, "organizing" is a euphemism for "revolution" — "a wholesale revolution whose ultimate objective is the systematic acquisition of power by a purportedly oppressed segment of the population, and the radical transformation of America's social and economic structure. The goal is to foment enough public discontent, moral confusion, and outright chaos to spark the social upheaval Marx, Engels, and Lenin predicted..." [8]

As Alinsky put it, "A reformation means that the masses of our people have reached the point of disillusionment with past ways and values. They don't know what will work but they do know that the prevailing system is self-defeating, frustrating, and hopeless. They won't act for change but won't strongly oppose those who do. The time is then ripe for revolution." [9]

John Perazzo, writing for FrontPageMag.com, says that "though Alinsky is generally viewed as a member of the political left, and rightfully so, his legacy is more methodological then ideological. He identified a set of specific rules that ordinary citizens could follow, and tactics that ordinary citizens could employ as a means of gaining public power." [10]

The most fundamental aspect of Saul Alinsky's methodology? Deception. Author David Horowitz explains: "The most basic principle of Alinsky's advice to radicals is to *lie* to their opponents and disarm them by pretending to be moderates and liberals.... Instead, advance your radical goals by camouflaging them; change your style to appear to be working within the system.... Even though you are at war with the system, don't confront it as an opposing army; join it and undermine it as a fifth column from within.... In other words, it is first necessary to sell the people on change itself, the 'audacity of hope' and 'yes we can.' You do this by proposing moderate changes which open the door to your radical agendas." [11]

Barack Obama's former "green jobs czar" Van Jones, an Alinsky disciple and self-described communist, expressed the concept of deception in a 2005 interview with *East Bay Express:*

"I'm willing to forgo the cheap satisfaction of the radical pose for the deep satisfaction of radical ends." [12]

How far was Alinsky willing to go with his tactic of deception? In the preface of his biography of Alinsky, *Let Them Call Me Rebel* author Sanford Horwitt provides an anecdote that illustrates Alinsky's method. In the anecdote,

Alinsky shares his strategy with students who wanted to protest the appearance on their campus of George H. W. Bush, then-U.S. representative to the U.N. during the Vietnam War:

> *"College student activists in the 1960s and 1970s sought out Alinsky for advice about tactics and strategy. On one such occasion in the spring of 1972 at Tulane University's annual week-long series of events featuring leading public figures, students asked Alinsky to help plan a protest of a scheduled speech by George Bush, then U.S. representative to the United Nations, a speech likely to be a defense of the Nixon Administration's Vietnam War policies. The students told Alinsky that they were thinking about picketing or disrupting Bush's address. That's the wrong approach, he rejoined — not very creative and besides, causing a disruption might get them thrown out of school. He told them instead to go hear the speech dressed up as members of the Ku Klux Klan, and whenever Bush said something in defense of the Vietnam War, they should cheer and wave placards, reading 'The K.K.K. supports Bush.' And that is what the students did with very successful, attention-getting results."* [13]

Fast forward to today. Democrats and their media sycophants are using similar methods to discredit America's newest political movement, the Tea Partiers. Theirs is a carefully orchestrated and ongoing campaign to mislead the public into believing this grass-roots phenomenon — encompassing Americans of every ethnic background and political persuasion — is nothing more than a fringe group of ignorant, bigoted, radical extremists with potentially violent tendencies.

Unfortunately for the left, the Tea Partiers are not cooperating. Their protests have been overwhelmingly orderly and their central themes of reduced government spending, greater individual freedom and a desire to re-embrace Constitutional values are gaining popularity. However, keeping Alinsky's tactics in mind, Americans shouldn't be surprised if there is a sudden outbreak of racist or violent behavior at one or more Tea Party rallies. The left has learned this tactic of infiltration/deception very well, they have used it before, and there is every reason to expect they will use it in the future.

Alinsky also endorsed the idea of community organizer's "agitate(ing) to the point of conflict." [14] Such agitation includes picketing, demonstrating and general hell-raising. ACORN, the Alinskyite grass-roots political organization, embraced this concept — its protests in bank lobbies and at homes of bank presidents for more minority mortgages were regular occurrences in the 1990s.

Unfortunately, these tactics proved greatly effective. Banks loaned billions of dollars in mortgage money to previously unqualified applicants, leading to the subprime mortgage crisis of 2008.

Alinsky also believed that the organizer's task was to cultivate in people's hearts a negative, visceral and emotional response to the face of the enemy. [15] Alinsky summarized it this way:

"Pick the target, freeze it, personalize it, and polarize it." [16]

True to Alinsky's principles, the Obama administration has cultivated several "enemies." Wall Street bankers are "fat cats who don't get it," health insurance companies are "discriminatory for refusing to cover pre-existing conditions," doctors will "take out tonsils just to make more money," and Fox News is "not really a news network." Even conservative radio talk show host Rush Limbaugh has been singled out: "You can't just listen to Rush Limbaugh and get things done," Obama warned a group of Republican lawmakers.

Despite Alinsky's radical prescriptions for community organizers, Barack Obama is proud of his days working as one. In a debate held in February 2008, he boasted, "I can bring this country together. I have a track record, starting from the days I moved to Chicago as a community organizer." [17]

Barack Obama is not the only powerful Democrat who is an Alinsky follower. Hillary Clinton was so impressed with Alinsky's theories and tactics regarding social change that, during her senior year at Wellesley College, she interviewed Alinsky personally and subsequently wrote a 92 page thesis based on his ideas:

"If the ideals Alinsky espouses were actualized the result would be social revolution. Ironically, this is not a disjunctive projection I considered in the tradition of Western democratic theory. In the first chapter it was pointed out that Alinsky is regarded by many as the proponent of a dangerous socio/ political philosophy. As such, he has been feared — just as Eugene Debs (the five-time Socialist Party candidate for U.S. President) or Walt Whitman or

Martin Luther King has been feared, because each embrace the most radical of political faiths — democracy." [18]

Democracy?

Van Jones, Obama's former handpicked green jobs czar, summed up the Alinsky philosophy far more appropriately:

"This movement is deeper than a solar panel! *We're gonna change the whole system!* We're gonna change the whole thing, We're not gonna put a new battery in a broken system. We want a new system. We want a new system!" [19]

Barack Obama's new system, aka "Change We Can Believe In," is simply socialism — imposed by subterfuge because Americans have never believed in Marxist economics. Capitalism is considered the enemy. The free market system is disparaged as a "winner-take-all" economy, where one man's gain is another's loss. And big tax increases are imposed as "restoring fairness to the economy." [20]

When candidate Obama told Joe the Plumber that he wanted to "spread the wealth around," he was merely expressing the fundamental belief of Alinsky that "Mankind has been and is divided into three parts: The Haves, the Have-Nots, and the Have-a-Little, Want Mores." [21] Alinsky's purpose was to teach the Have-Nots how to take power and money from the Haves by creating mass organizations to seize power and redistribute wealth. [22]

Americans went to the polls in 2008 and did indeed vote for change. Little did they know that the change they were voting for was Saul Alinsky's radical blueprint.

Chapter 30

ABORTION: PRAGMATIC AMBIVALENCE

It is probably impossible to write a comprehensive book about politics without mentioning abortion. Yet it is nearly as impossible to say something about the subject that hasn't been said before — without driving either the pro-choice or the pro-life side up the wall.

As a result, this chapter is the shortest one in the book. Nevertheless, it touches on an idea that I would like Americans to seriously consider when they enter the voting booth on Election Day.

I don't expect to change Americans' long-held beliefs on abortion — but perhaps I can get them to re-order their priorities.

In America, there is probably no other issue as polarizing as abortion. And if truth be told, far smarter people than me have tried — unsuccessfully — to find a middle ground between the Democrat Party's staunchly pro-choice position and the Republican Party's commitment to the pro-life position.

Yet ironically, while both political parties are ideologically polarized, most Americans are not.

Yes, there is the abortion-on-demand faction of the Democrat party for whom any restrictions whatsoever constitute an unacceptable assault on their rights. Sadly, many on the far left have absolutely no conscience about late term abortions, or "disposing" of an aborted fetus that was still alive after the abortion.

And yes, there is the pro-life faction of the Republican Party for whom any abortion at all — even one for victims of rape or incest, or to prevent the birth of a severely deformed fetus — constitutes murder, no ifs ands or buts.

Yet most Americans — including me — fall somewhere in the middle. They accept neither the wholesale slaughter of the unborn, nor the dogmatic rigidity that would force women to carry an unwanted fetus to term. Perhaps the best way to describe such Americans is to call us "pragmatically ambivalent." I don't like abortion, but I grudgingly recognize the need to keep it legal. No doubt such "wishy-washiness" offends ideologues on both sides of the aisle, but I believe it's where the overwhelming majority of Americans stand on the issue.

So why bring abortion up at all? Because for far too many Americans, abortion is the *only issue that matters* on Election Day.

By now, readers understand that I am no longer a Democrat, not so much because I left the party, but because I believe the party left me. I also believe that their tilt to the extreme left has put this country on a path towards Euro-style socialism, which is completely at odds with our economic and cultural history, and our commitment to individual freedom and prosperity.

So here's all I have to say about abortion: *just remember the strings that come attached to it.* If you're willing to accept all the other aspects of the Democrat agenda, i.e., treating terrorism as a "law enforcement problem," tripling the Bush administration's worst deficit spending, or having government-run healthcare — for no other reason than keeping abortion legal — then by all means vote Democratic.

But don't say you weren't warned.

This is a critical time in American history. And while there will always be "one-issue" voters, I would respectfully suggest that abortion is not *the* one issue that should be the ultimate litmus test for determining which candidate to vote for in the next few elections. Not when the future of our nation is at stake.

It's time to put abortion on the back burner, and re-visit it after we've dealt with the far more pressing issues that need to be addressed.

Lastly, I feel something needs to be said about an aspect of Roe v. Wade that confuses millions of Americans: if Roe v. Wade were overturned, abortion would *not become illegal.* Its jurisdiction would be returned to the states, each of which would determine how loose or restrictive the laws concerning abortion would become.

Obviously some states would make it more restrictive, some not restrictive at all. As one who believes democracy works best when it aligns itself with as many people as possible, making abortion a states' rights issue may serve the peoples' interests far more effectively than the current one-size-fits-all federal statute.

Maybe nothing will change anyone's position on abortion. But abortion is just one issue. Perhaps now more than ever before, America is ill-served by one-issue voters.

Chapter 31

OBAMACARE: PRESCRIPTION FOR AN UNHEALTHY AMERICA

Perhaps the most divisive political event of the Obama administration's brief tenure in office was the enactment of the health care "reform" bill by a Democratically-controlled Congress. It was passed without a single Republican vote in either the House or the Senate — and in complete defiance of a substantial majority of the public.

Why would Democrats do such a thing? Because the health care bill has virtually nothing to do with health care. It has far more to do with the accumulation of power by a political party which believes America is a fundamentally flawed nation requiring a wholesale transformation. It is merely one plank of an agenda dedicated to the continued expansion of a command-and-control federal bureaucracy — with radical Democrats in command and control.

For Americans who still believe in freedom, fiscal sanity and quality of care, there's nothing remotely "healthy" about it.

Few issues illuminate the difference between Democrats and Republicans more than health care. While both parties were in agreement that America needed health care reform, the way each approached the issue demonstrated the stark difference between the parties: Democrats wanted more government control, Republicans wanted reform that incorporated free market solutions — and wouldn't create another large entitlement America couldn't afford.

Democrats won the day. The Senate health care bill passed on March 21, 2010 through a reconciliation vote of 220 to 211 in the House of Representatives, with no Republican support whatsoever.

The majority of the American public rejected it as well.

How did we get to this place? Americans were rightly concerned about the exploding cost of health care, so let's begin there.

Health care costs have risen dramatically due to eight primary reasons:

1. *Diseases and chronic conditions are more prevalent.*

Because Americans are living longer, they become more susceptible to various illnesses such as heart disease, obesity, osteoarthritis, cancer, osteoporosis and cognitive diseases such as Alzheimer's. Treating these illnesses is expensive. How expensive?

Chronic illnesses account for *85 percent* of all U.S. health care spending. [1]

Another reason for the increased prevalence of disease is an increase in unhealthy lifestyles. Factors such as lack of exercise and poor diet have contributed to increased obesity. And increased spending on obesity-related illnesses has accounted for 27 percent of the health care cost increase between 1987 and 2001. [2]

2. *An increased number of Americans have health insurance coverage.*

In 1960, insurance and government health care programs covered only 46 percent of total medical costs. By 2000, the percentage had grown to nearly 78 percent. [3] Increased coverage has led to greater usage of health services. In addition, because 60 percent of Americans receive their insurance tax-free through their employer, employees are unaware of the true cost of health care. As a result, they use more of it. [4]

3. *Technological advances.*

The Congressional Budget Office has attributed about half the increase in health care spending to technological innovation. [5]

Cutting-edge drugs, medical devices, and other treatments are usually high-priced when introduced, due to the high cost of research and development.[6]

4. *Wasteful spending.*

Wasteful spending on health services and operational costs in the Medicare program could account for as much as 40 percent of Medicare expenditures, according to Arnold Milstein, chief physician at Mercer Health and Benefits and medical director of the Pacific Business Group on Health.[7]

Most experts agree that Medicaid is also riddled with fraud and misspending. Fraud alone is frequently estimated to account for at least 10 percent of Medicaid outlays. [8]

In addition, malpractice insurance and liability concerns have prompted physicians to practice defensive medicine, ordering more procedures and tests than they would otherwise. According to a study by the Pacific Research Institute, this costs $124 billion annually and causes premiums to rise, resulting in 3.4 million Americans being uninsured. [9]

5. *A third party payment system which often leaves the physician and patient insulated from, and even unaware of, the costs of different treatment options.* [10]

The percentage of health care spending paid "out-of-pocket" by patients fell from 52 percent in 1965 to only 12.6 percent in 2007. At the same time third-party payments by insurance companies and the government have increased from 48 percent in 1965 to almost 88 percent.[11]

Since patients pay so little of their medical costs, and physicians are reimbursed for their services by someone other than the patient, no market incentives exist to reduce spending and pricing.[12]

In other words, no one has much incentive to spend health care dollars efficiently.

6. *State-mandated requirements severely limit the ability to offer inexpensive insurance plans.*

Responding to special interest groups, state governments have passed laws forcing insurance companies in their state to cover a wide range of conditions and treatments —whether a customer wants them covered or not. For example, some states mandate all health plans cover treatments such as massage therapy, marriage therapy, hormone replacement therapy, hearing aids, in-vitro fertilization, breast reduction and hair prosthesis (wigs). [13]

The consequence is that premiums rise for everyone, and people are unable to obtain low premium, catastrophe-only policies. And once premium levels increase, more people decide to go without any coverage at all. [14]

These state mandates have grown spectacularly — from only 252 mandate laws in force in 1979 (an average of five per state) to 1,901 by 2007 (an average of 38 mandates per state). [15]

According to the Council for Affordable Health Insurance, state mandates can easily increase the cost of a basic health insurance policy by up to 50%, depending on the number of mandates it has and what they cover. [16]

7. *Other state-level regulations drive up the cost of insurance.*

One of the most common is "guaranteed issue," which requires insurers to cover everyone, even those very sick. These policies force insurers to take on clients *certain* to cause them a financial loss. Such losses raise the cost of premiums for everyone else. As a result, many people decide to purchase coverage only when they become sick. [17]

Imagine if there were such regulations for fire insurance — no one would purchase coverage until their homes were on fire. [18]

Another regulation is "community rating," which prevents insurers from charging premiums based on a person's existing medical condition. This also forces insurers to raise the premiums for everyone.[19]

8. *Low reimbursement rates from Medicare and Medicaid cause doctors and hospitals to shift costs to private insurers.*

Medicare reimbursements to health care providers are at rates about 20 percent less than those paid by private insurers, [20] and Medicaid pays only 72 percent of Medicare rates on average.[21]

These shortfalls are paid for with revenue from private insurance. In other words, everyone with private insurance pays more because of low Medicare and Medicaid reimbursements. Both programs underpay doctors and hospitals so much that the average family in a private PPO health plan pays an additional $1,788 a year to compensate for underpayments by Medicare and Medicaid.[22]

◆◆◆

One of the primary criticisms leveled at our health care system is the idea that many countries spend much less on health care than the United States and have better health outcomes. The critics say the United States should follow the example of those countries and adapt a government-run, national health care system. [23]

In reality, *no single model* is used by other countries for health care. Each system varies significantly in the degree of central control, regulation and cost sharing they impose, and the role of private insurance. [24]

Yet Michael Tanner, director of health and welfare studies of the Cato Institute, notes that *overall trends* from national health care systems around the world provide some important lessons:

1. Having health insurance does not mean one has *access* to health care. Many countries promise universal coverage, but have extremely long waiting lists for treatment or they ration care.

2. Rising health care costs are not just an American phenomenon. Even though other countries spend considerably less than the United States on health care, costs are increasing almost everywhere, leading to budget deficits, tax increases and benefit reductions.

3. Countries whose systems are weighted heavily toward government control are most likely to have waiting lists, rationing, restrictions on doctor choice, and other obstacles to obtaining care.

4. The more effective national health care systems, such as France, the Netherlands, and Switzerland, are successful to the extent that they incorporate free market mechanisms such as competition, cost-consciousness, market prices and consumer choice, and avoid centralized government control.

5. Discontent and dissatisfaction with a country's health care system seems to be universal.

6. While no nation with a national health care system is considering giving up universal coverage, the trend is to move away from centralized governmental control and to introduce more market-oriented features. In other words, while the trend in the U.S. has been toward a more European-style system, the trend in places like Europe is toward a system that looks more like America. [25]

But there's an even more important lesson Americans need to learn. Despite our system's flaws, shortcomings and inefficiencies, if you have a serious ailment, or your goal is to live longer, *your chances of survival are better when treated by American doctors in American hospitals than anywhere else in the world.* [26]

Perhaps that's why around 400,000 foreign patients come to the U.S. every year for medical care. "Not too many people get on a plane and fly to Cuba or to France (for health care)," says Dr. Stanley Goldfarb, associate dean of clinical education at the University of Pennsylvania School of Medicine and an expert on worldwide health care systems. [27]

When Italian Prime Minister Silvio Berlusconi needed heart surgery in 2007, he didn't go to a French, Canadian, Cuban or even Italian hospital — he went to the Cleveland Clinic in Ohio. Likewise, Canadian MP Belinda Stronach had breast cancer surgery at a California hospital. And *one out of every three* Canadian doctors sends a patient to the United States for treatment each year. [28]

Why? More than any other country, America provides timely access to the latest cutting-edge technology, along with the latest drugs and the top medical specialists. For example, the United States has 27 MRI machines per million Americans, compared to 6 per million for Canadians and Britons. We also have 34 CT scanners per million compared to 12 per million in Canada and 8 per million in Britain. [29]

Another little known fact: Out-of-pocket expenses by Americans in 2007 averaged 12.6 percent of total national health spending, one of the lowest percentages of private, out-of-pocket spending among the world's industrialized nations — lower than Canada, Germany and Japan, and most countries in Europe, including those with government-run health care. [30] In Switzerland, which spends only 11 percent of GDP on health care, out-of-pocket expenses equal about 31 percent of total spending. [31]

Why do Americans receive more and pay less? Because American insurance policies provide broader coverage than most government plans, says Tom Miller of the American Enterprise Institute. [32] Private insurance, Medicare and Medicaid cover most of the huge cost of treating life-threatening illnesses, such as cancer and heart disease. [33]

More importantly, the survival rates for cancer and heart disease in the United States are significantly higher than in Europe or other countries. Dr. Scott Atlas, senior fellow at the Hoover Institute and a professor of radiology and chief of neuroradiology at Stanford University Medical School, explains how America compares more favorably to European systems when it comes to common cancers:

"Breast cancer mortality is 52 percent higher in Germany than in the United States, and 88 percent higher in the United Kingdom. Prostate cancer mortality is 604 percent higher in the United Kingdom and about 457 percent higher in Norway." [34]

The American system also has better outcomes than even the much-admired Canadian system. "Breast cancer mortality in Canada is 9 percent higher than in the United States, prostate cancer is 184 percent higher, and colon cancer among men is about 10 percent higher," according to Dr. Atlas. [35]

Americans have better access to preventive cancer screening than Canadians as well, with a greater percentage of patients receiving recommended tests for breast, cervical, prostate and colon cancer. For example, 30 percent of Americans have had a colonoscopy, compared with only 5 percent of Canadians. [36]

Another study by Samuel Preston and Jessica Ho of the University of Pennsylvania found that "death rates from breast and prostate cancer declined during the past 20 years by much more in the U.S. than in 15 comparison countries of Europe and Japan." [37]

As critically important as outcomes, Americans spend less time waiting for care than patients in Canada and the United Kingdom. "Canadian and British patients wait about twice as long — sometimes more than a year — to see a specialist, have elective surgery such as hip replacements, or get radiation treatment for cancer," says Dr. Atlas. [38]

Bottom line: despite its flaws, the American healthcare system is still the best in the world. Rather than change the entire system, perhaps we should have fixed only that which doesn't work.

Unfortunately, that's not how Democrats decided to solve our health care problems. They chose to pass a bill without a shred of bipartisan support, largely unpopular with the public.

♦♦♦

Americans were well aware that our heath care system needs reform. But re-ordering one-sixth of the American economy should have generated a debate on the merits of that reform based on *factual* information. What Americans got instead was a carefully orchestrated campaign of lies and deceptions from Democrats aided by the mainstream media. Here are ten of those lies:

Lie # 1: "Republicans haven't offered any alternatives to Democrat health care plans."

Reality: Democrats and their media allies have branded the Republicans as "the party of no" on health care policy. This claim is utter nonsense. In fact, over the years Democrats have defeated many Republican health care proposals — proposals that would have helped solve many of the current problems regarding health care.

The following is a rundown of recent reform bills offered by Republicans and defeated overwhelmingly by Democrats in Congress — including then-Senator Barack Obama who voted against all of them:

1. Allowing Americans the Opportunity to Purchase Health Insurance Across State Lines. This amendment was offered by Sen. Jim DeMint (R-S.C.) and rejected by a vote of 62-37 on August 2, 2007.

2. Allowing Americans to Deduct Their Health Care Cost. This amendment wass offered by Sen. Jim DeMint (R-S.C.) and rejected by a vote of 51-45 on March 13, 2008.

3. Allowing Americans to use Their Own HSA Funds to Cover Health Insurance Premiums. This amendment was offered by Sen. John Ensign (R-NV) and rejected by a vote of 48-47 on January 25, 2007.

4. Preventing the Erosion of Private Health Coverage. This amendment was offered by Sen. Jon Kyl (R–AZ) and rejected by a vote of 62-37 on August 2, 2007.

5. Requiring Health Insurance for Illegal Immigrants. The amendment was offered by Sen. Jim DeMint (R-S.C.) and rejected by a vote of 55-43 on June 6, 2007. [39]

In 2009, the Republicans also introduced three additional bills that contained genuine health care reform, all of which were rejected by Democrats. These bills addressed the need to reform the current tax code which favors people who get their health coverage through their employers. These bills also would have created the conditions for portability so employees could take their insurance with them if they decided to change jobs, and provided people with pre-existing conditions the ability to purchase coverage at affordable rates, through high-risk pools and reinsurance mechanisms. [40]

Here's a rundown of those bills:

The Patients' Choice Act of 2009 would have replaced the current system of tax breaks for employees with a universal system of tax credits. Regardless of income or employment, families would have received a credit of $5,700 and individuals would have received one equal to $2,300. Low-income families would have obtained further help through a supplemental debit card with roll-over funds. The Patients' Choice Act also would have required the federal government to work with states to create exchanges which would have prevented insurance companies from discriminating against pre-existing conditions. [41] The bill also addressed tort reform — something Democrats have refused to consider because of their unholy alliance with the Trial Lawyers Association. [42]

The other two bills, The Improving Health Care for All Americans Act and The Empower Patients First Act both offered similar reforms that would have allowed Americans to keep their insurance if they lose or change their jobs, and provided insurance to Americans with pre-existing conditions. The Improving Health Care for All Americans Act would also have allowed churches, alumni associations, trade associations, and other civic groups to set up new insurance pools that offered affordable health care packages to their members. [43]

Democrats and the mainstream media have deliberately kept most Americans in the dark about Republican attempts to reform health care. They realize it's more effective politically to brand the Republicans as the "party of no."

Lie # 2: *"46 million Americans are without health care."*

Reality: According to the 2007 Census Bureau report, 45.6 million Americans were uninsured that year. [44] The actual number of *chronically uninsured* is far less.

A closer look at the Census Bureau data shows that 9.7 million of the uninsured are not citizens of the United States. [45]

Another problem with the 46 million number cited is that many of those uninsured are eligible for existing government programs — *but never bother to enroll.* A 2003 Blue Cross Blue Shield Association study estimated that about 14 million of those uninsured were eligible for programs such as Medicaid and SCHIP. [46]

Furthermore, the Census Bureau estimate was based on a survey question that asked respondents if they "were not covered by any type of health insurance at any time in that (past) year." As a result, a person switching jobs who goes temporarily without coverage is considered uninsured, even if he or she quickly obtains coverage for that year. [47]

In addition, many people who can afford health coverage choose not to purchase any to save money. This is especially the case for the 18.3 million uninsured under 34 who have decided they are healthy enough to go without insurance. [48] It is also the case for many of the 17.6 million uninsured who have annual incomes of more than $50,000, and the 9.1 million who earn more than $75,000. [49]

Naturally, there's some overlap in these numbers. But when all of these factors are taken into account, the aforementioned 2003 Blue Cross Blue Shield study determined that "8.2 million Americans are actually without coverage for the long haul, because they are too poor to purchase health care but earn too much to qualify for government assistance." [50]

And even those 8.2 million have access to health care. They can walk into any hospital in America and be treated for an injury, accident or disease. Because of the Emergency Medical Treatment and Active Labor Act of 1986, hospitals cannot deny treatment to patients who don't have health insurance. In addition, there are no reimbursement requirements. [51]

Sensible health care reform would have addressed those 8.2 million people without changing the *entire system*. Merely raising the minimum income requirement for government assistance could have solved this problem.

Lie # 3: *"People who go without health insurance raise premiums significantly for the rest of us."*

Reality: Proponents of universal coverage frequently invoke this idea. Nonpartisan analysts, including the Congressional Budget Office, believe the actual premium increase as a result of treating the uninsured is very small, perhaps $220 per year. [52] According to an estimate by the Kaiser Family Foundation, the total cost of uncompensated care at hospitals, physicians' offices, and community providers was $56 billion in 2008 — which represented about 2 percent of America's overall health expenditures. [53]

Naturally, expanding coverage to millions of uninsured *will* reduce the costs of providing free care. But those "savings" are minimal compared to the greater expense of insuring more people. [54]

Lie # 4: *"According to the World Health Organization, the United States ranks 37th in the world in health care."*

Reality: This ranking is based on a misleading report released nearly a decade ago by the World Health Organization (WHO), and relies on statistics that were even older and incomplete. [55]

The WHO report based its conclusions on highly subjective measures and other criteria not related to a country's health care system, such as "fairness" and "tobacco control." The United States was penalized for not having a sufficiently progressive tax system, for not providing all its citizens with health insurance, and for having a general lack of social welfare programs. In fact, much of the poor rating of the United States was due to its ranking of 54th in the category of fairness. The U.S. was also penalized for adopting Health Savings Accounts and because, according to the report, patients pay too much out of pocket. As Michael Tanner, director of health and welfare studies at the Cato Institute explains, "Such judgments clearly reflect a particular political point of view rather than a neutral measure of healthcare quality." [56]

Philip Musgrove, the editor-in-chief of the WHO report that created the rankings, called the figures that resulted in those rankings "so many made-up numbers," and the result a "nonsense ranking." He says he was hired to edit the report's text, but didn't fully understand the methodology until after the report was released. In 2003, after he left the WHO, he wrote an article in the medical journal *Lancet* criticizing the rankings as "meaningless." [57]

Notably, the World Health Organization ranked the United States number one for "responsiveness to the needs and choices of the individual patient." [58]

Question: Isn't responsiveness one of *the* most important factors in health care?

Lie # 5: "*The U.S. ranking of 30th in the world regarding infant mortality is evidence of a bad system.*"

Reality: The key reason for the low U.S. ranking in infant mortality is methodological: other countries compile their statistics for infant mortality differently than we do. In the U.S. we count the death of *every* child before the age of one year, even if it dies within hours. [59] Other countries, like Japan, don't count infants who die within 24 hours. [60] Still others register babies below a certain weight as stillborn. [61] And in many of the single-payer nations, if babies are born under 30 weeks, they are not counted as born. [62]

Premature births are another reason the U.S. ranks 30th in the world. "Premature babies born before 37 weeks tend to be more fragile and have undeveloped lungs," said the lead author of a new report, Marian MacDorman of the U.S. Centers for Disease Control and Prevention. [63]

Why are there so many more premature infants born here in the U.S.? Fertility treatments and other forms of assisted reproduction likely play a role because they often lead to twins, triplets or other multiple births. [64] Also, the number of American teenage mothers is disproportionately high in the U.S., running three times the Canadian rate. These pregnancies are less healthy and produce more premature, low-weight babies. [65]

Bottom line: the factors that cause infant mortality — adolescent pregnancies, drug abuse, smoking, drinking, and obesity — will not change even if we alter the way health care is delivered in the U.S. [66]

Lie # 6: "Despite the U.S. spending more money on health care than other countries, we have inferior care."

Reality: It is true that the American health care system spends more per person on medical care, but there's a reason for that: government-run systems like Great Britain and Canada *set budgets* on how much the government will spend and then *ration* care to the sick. Tests such as CT scans and MRIs routinely performed in the U.S., are limited in most other systems. [67]

In addition to a lack of available procedures, countries such as Canada, Britain, and Sweden also report longer wait times for treatment. [68] Equally as important, Americans receive more of the latest improvements in medical treatments, drugs, and technology than government-run systems. These medical innovations raise the cost of health care for all of us — but also increase our life expectancy when we do get sick.

The bottom line: Americans have the easiest access, the shortest waiting times, the largest choice of doctors and hospitals, and the consistent availability of health care for the elderly. [69]

As Dr. Mark Constantian wrote in *The Wall Street Journal*, "perhaps it's not that America spends too much on health care, but that other nations don't spend enough." [70]

Lie # 7: *"The U.S. has a lower life expectancy than other industrialized nations."*

Reality: The U.S. ranks 42nd in the world in life expectancy, according to international numbers provided by the Census Bureau and domestic numbers from the National Center for Health Statistics. [71]

Yet this statistic is not a reliable indicator of the quality of American health care because life expectancy is affected by factors unrelated to the quality of a health care system.

Diet, lifestyle, obesity, lack of exercise, violent crime and automobile deaths greatly affect average life expectancy. [72] And, as previously mentioned, the U.S. reports infant mortality rates differently from most other industrialized nations. [73]

The truest test of a health system's effect on life expectancy occurs when a person gets seriously ill — and in that regard, the U.S. has no equal. Survival rates for treating critical illnesses such as cancer and heart disease are significantly higher here than in Europe or other countries. [74]

Lie # 8: "Corporations based in the U.S. are at a competitive disadvantage against foreign competitors who don't have to pay their employees' health insurance."

Reality: The Congressional Budget Office disagrees, concluding that "the costs of providing health insurance to their (a corporation's) workers are not a source of competitive disadvantage for U.S. based firms." [75]

What matters to most U.S. businesses is the total cost of an employee, and health care benefits are as much a part of compensation as wages. When health care costs rise, firms reduce wages, or wages rise more slowly than they otherwise would. [76] In other words, when a company pays for an employee's health care, that compensation generally comes out of the employee's wages, rather than the company profits.

A 2009 study from the White House Council of Economic Advisers agrees, stating that if medical spending continues to accelerate, it expects take-home pay to stagnate. [77] The exception to this argument is heavily unionized businesses such as the auto makers, where adjusting health costs and wages are more difficult. [78]

The irony is that the same people who want to lift the obligation from businesses to provide health benefits now want to impose this burden on other firms that don't offer this benefit.[79] ObamaCare mandates U.S. firms provide health insurance for their employees or pay a fine.

Lie # 9: *"We need a public plan to keep the private plans honest."*

Reality: The best way to keep private insurers honest is to provide real competition for their services.

We can provide real competition for private insurers by changing laws that ban the purchase of health insurance across state lines.

America has nearly 1,300 private health insurance companies.[80] Yet, in some states one large insurer controls 80% of the market. In others, companies have little or no competition — Rhode Island has one insurer, and Vermont and North Dakota have only two. [81]

A government-run health care system would produce even less competition. That's because a government-run system, subsidized by tax dollars, could offer artificially low rates without regard to profitability — which would ultimately push private insurers out of business.

Make no mistake: eliminating private insurance is the ultimate ambition of anti-capitalist, anti-competitive progressives who believe a government bureaucracy making Americans' health care choices for them is superior to Americans making their own health care choices.

Lie # 10: *"The cost of healthcare is the leading cause of bankruptcy in America."*

Reality: This idea was expressed by President Obama in March 2009 as a justification for the Democrat's dramatic healthcare overhaul efforts. Speaker of the House Nancy Pelosi, along with House Majority Leader Steny Hoyer, both Democrats, also cited medical bankruptcy as a justification for health care reform in a July 2009 hearing of the House Judiciary Committee. [82]

Democrats have been influenced by a 2008 study by authors David Himmelstein, Deborah Thorne, Elizabeth Warren, and Steffie Woolhandler claiming that nearly two-thirds of personal bankruptcies in the United States resulted from uninsured medical expenses or loss of income due to illness. An earlier 2005 edition of their research asserted that just over half of all personal bankruptcies were due to these "medical causes." [83]

The authors also argued that the problem of "medical bankruptcies" would be solved by adopting a government-run health care system like Canada's. [84]

Those studies have been strongly refuted by several researchers, including a critique published by David Dranove and Michael Millenson in *Health Affairs,* and an analysis by the American Enterprise Institute's Aparna Mathur. [85]

Dranove and Millenson analyzed the research in the 2005 edition and found that medical spending was a contributing factor in only 17 percent of U.S. bankruptcies. They also reviewed other studies, including one by the Department of Justice which found medical debts accounted for only 12 to 13 percent of the total debts among American bankruptcy filers who listed medical debt as one of their reasons for bankruptcy. [86]

Furthermore, Himmelstein et al were also incorrect in claiming that universal coverage in Canada would result in lower bankruptcy rates. In 2006, personal bankruptcy filings as a percentage of the population in the United State were 0.20 percent, and stayed relatively constant at 0.27 percent in 2007. They were 0.30 percent for both years in Canada. [87]

$$\blacklozenge\blacklozenge\blacklozenge$$

Many Democrats rationalized their desire for national health care based on these lies. Unfortunately for them, as Founding Father John Adams put it, facts are "stubborn things." Here are six stubborn facts that should concern every American:

1. *ObamaCare will explode our national debt by creating huge future deficits.*

At a press conference on March 3, 2010, President Obama claimed that ObamaCare will be "fully paid for," and it "brings down our deficit by up to $1 trillion over the next two decades." [88]

According to a preliminary Congressional Budget Office (CBO) estimate, ObamaCare will cover an additional 32 million Americans by 2019. Budget analysts estimate the health care expansion will cost $940 billion over the next decade. Yet the Congressional Budget Office "estimated" that ObamaCare will cut the deficit by $138 billion over the next decade and as much as $1.3 trillion by 2029. [89]

How can something that costs $940 billion cut the deficit? Democrats propose to pay for this expensive health care program with a series of tax increases and Medicare spending cuts. [90]

So why will ObamaCare will explode our national debt?

According to Congressman Paul Ryan (R-WI), ranking Republican on the House Budget Committee, the Congressional Budget Office was obligated to calculate the cost of ObamaCare based on what was "placed in front of them." What was placed in front of them was a bill "full of gimmicks and smoke-and-mirrors." [91]

According to Ryan, the budget gimmicks consisted of 10 years of tax increases of about $500 billion, along with 10 years of Medicare cuts, another $500 billion, to pay for six years of spending [92] Most of the spending on benefits will begin in 2014, four years after the tax increases and Medicare cuts take effect.

According to James C. Capretta of The Heritage Foundation, the *true* ten-year cost of *fully-implemented* ObamaCare would be $2.5 trillion over the period of 2014 to 2023.[93]

Other budget gimmicks have distorted the CBO's estimate of ObamaCare's real costs and will likely increase the true ten-year cost well beyond the $2.5 trillion figure:

• Democrats counted a 21 percent or $371 billion reduction in Medicare physician fees starting in 2011. This is highly unlikely to occur because every year for the past seven years Congress has stopped those cuts from occurring. [94]

• Democrats included $52 billion in higher Social Security tax revenues and counted them as offsets — even though those revenues are reserved for future

Social Security benefits. [95]

• ObamaCare collects $72 billion of premiums over the next 10 years for a separate long-term services program known as the Community Living Assistance Services and Supports Act, or CLASS Act and counts them as revenues. Those premiums are set aside to pay *that* program's future claims, yet the Democrats counted them as revenue offsets for health care reform — which means they are being double-counted. [96]

• The new excise tax on "high cost" insurance plans is unlikely to occur. Democrats postponed the implementation of that tax until 2018, well after any potential second term of Barack Obama. Yet, they claim that hundreds of billions of dollars in revenue will come from this tax in the second decade of the program.[97]

If Democrats are unwilling to impose this tax for the next 8 years, it is hard to see another President or Congress doing so later. [98]

• Democrats claim there will be $500 billion in savings from Medicare cuts over the next 10 year period. The chief actuary of the Medicare program has repeatedly said that these cuts are not realistic because they would push many hospitals and providers into serious financial distress. Yet, the Obama administration claims those cuts will save hundreds of billions of dollars from 2020 to 2030. [99]

History also warns us that government estimates are usually inaccurate. Perfect examples are Medicaid and Medicare, both established in 1965. At that time, the House Ways and Means Committee estimated Medicaid would cost $238 million the first year it was implemented. Actual cost? $1 billion.[100]

The estimate for Medicare had a longer timeline. Its first-year cost was $4 billion, projected to be $12 billion by 1990. Actual cost in 1990? *$90 billion.*[101]

Their costs as of 2009? $251 *billion* for Medicaid and $428 billion for Medicare.[102]

Bottom line: the costs for ObamaCare will grow exponentially once implemented. The Congressional Budget Office estimates it will grow by 8%

a year.[103]

History also teaches us other lessons. The U.S. Postal Service, Social Security, AMTRAK, and the aforementioned Medicare and Medicaid programs are *all* insolvent, or will be — unless they are kept on life support with further taxpayer funding, creating huge financial burdens for future generations. The government has a poor track record in being fiscally responsible.

Furthermore, three state programs — Tennessee, Maine and Massachusetts — have mirrored ObamaCare's Medicaid expansion in one way or another. And the results have been a financial disaster:

The Tennessee experiment began in 1994 with the attempt to reduce the number of uninsured people through a major expansion of Medicaid. The state thought they could curb the rise in health care costs by squeezing savings out of its traditional Medicaid program through the use of managed care, while still increasing the number of insured. [104] In a decade, spending jumped from $2.5 billion to $8 billion. [105] Calling the program a "disaster," Tennessee's Democrat Governor Phil Bredesen was forced to restructure TennCare dramatically starting in 2004, stating he would not "let TennCare bankrupt our state." [106] The state was forced to cut the number of enrollees and reduce benefits, and yet TennCare *still* consumes a higher share of the state budget then any Medicaid program in the country. [107]

The Maine experiment began in 2003. The state decided to cover the uninsured by expanding the state's Medicaid program and creating a government-run "public option" with subsidized premiums. [108] The state believed that controls on hospital and doctor costs would lead to reduced premiums without tax increases. By 2008, "the system that was supposed to save money has cost taxpayers $155 million and is still rising," reported *The Wall Street Journal.* The program has been such a disaster that enrollment in the public plan has been capped. [109]

And in Massachusetts "universal" coverage was enacted in 2006 in conjunction with a requirement that everyone be insured or pay a fine ($1,068 by 2009). At that time the claim was similar to Obama's today — costs would decline once everyone was covered. [110] While 97 per cent of its residents are now covered by insurance, costs have soared to such a point that *The New York Times* has described them as "runaway." [111] A special state commission was established to address the cost problem and its report stated that continued cost growth "threatens the viability" of the program. Annual subsidies for low-income residents are estimated to carry a price tag of $1.3 billion by 2011, double the cost in 2007. [112] Moreover, average Massachusetts insurance premiums are now the highest in the country. Since 2006, they have soared at an annual rate of 30 percent in the individual market. [113]

Judging by these examples, expect ObamaCare to significantly increase health care costs, further bankrupting our country.

2. ObamaCare will lead to rationed care and a severe decline in the quality and choice of health care.

Having health insurance is not the same as having *access* to health care. Under ObamaCare, many patients will have health coverage, but won't be able to find a doctor, or will have to wait a lot longer to see one.

Why do I make that prediction?

ObamaCare will add roughly 32 million Americans to the number of insured. The question Americans should ask themselves is: How can our existing system effectively treat that many new patients with no extra doctors? The answer is it can't — *not without rationing.*

ObamaCare will make this problem even more severe since it creates new mandates for insurers to provide broader coverage with low co-payments. [114] At first glance that sounds great for consumers, but low co-payments coupled with an additional 32 million eligible Americans will result in far greater consumption of health-care services. Estimates indicate that each newly insured person will approximately double his or her health spending. [115]

A shortage of doctors will inevitably lead to rationing of medical care. The experience in Massachusetts confirms this. Their experiment with "universal coverage," which began in 2006, has led to what the Massachusetts Medical Society calls a "critical shortage" of primary care physicians. Expanded insurance increased demand for medical services, but many of the newly insured are unable to find a doctor. "Fifty-six percent of Massachusetts internal medicine physicians no longer are accepting new patients," according to a 2009 physician work-force study conducted by the Massachusetts Medical

Society. And for those fortunate enough to be accepted by a primary-care doctor, the average wait time is 44 days, the Medical Society study found. [116] There will be a shortage of doctors as a result of the flood of new patients. In addition, nearly one-third of all practicing physicians may leave the medical profession, according to a survey published in the March and April editions of the *New England Journal of Medicine* by the Medicus Firm, a leading physician search and consulting firm. [117]

Doctor shortages won't be the only cause of rationing — our exploding federal deficit as well as Medicare's roughly $35 trillion unfunded liabilities will force the federal government to set limits on what kinds of treatment options patients are allowed to receive, and which patients get priority with respect to those options.

Bottom line: the sick and elderly will be the first to suffer.

Why? The inevitable medical rationing will be *in addition* to the $500 billion in Medicare cuts that are part of the plan to finance ObamaCare. These proposed Medicare cuts raise the probability that more doctors will refuse to accept Medicare patients, worsening the doctor shortage among the elderly, the group that needs them most.

To cut medical spending, ObamaCare gives broad power to the agency, Centers for Medicare and Medicaid Services, to unilaterally write new rules on when medical devices and drugs can be used, and how they should be priced. [118]

Moreover, to reduce the number of expensive procedures, primary-care doctors who refer patients to specialists will face financial penalties under ObamaCare. Physicians will have a 5% reduction in their Medicare pay when their "aggregated" use of resources is "at or above the 90th percentile of national utilization," according to the chairman's mark of Section 3003 of the bill. Translation: doctors will be under financial pressure to limit referrals to costly specialists such as surgeons, since these penalties will make the referring physician liable for the cost of the referral and perhaps any resulting procedures. [119]

3. *ObamaCare will wreak havoc on state budgets.*

ObamaCare will expand Medicaid coverage to anyone making less than 133 percent of the federal poverty level — $29,326 for a family of four. [120] Estimates of new Medicaid enrollees range from 15 million to 18 million Americans. Although the federal government will pay for all the costs of this expansion for the first three years starting in 2014, states will begin paying in 2017, reaching a full 10 percent of the cost beginning in 2020. [121]

As a result, states, most of which already have huge shortfalls in their 2010 budgets, will incur enormous additional costs to cover new Medicaid patients beginning in 2020. For example, according to a report by the Agency for Health Care Administration, Florida alone will have an additional expense of $1.05 billion per year. [122]

Unlike the federal government, states can't print money, so they will have to either raise taxes or cut services, or both, to pay for these increased outlays.

4. ObamaCare will financially harm businesses — and cause job losses.

Soon after ObamaCare passed, large U.S. corporations announced major write-downs as a result of the bill. AT&T announced a $1 billion charge against earnings, John Deere $150 million, Caterpillar $100 million, 3M estimates $85 to $90 million, and AK Steel Holding $31 million. [123]

Why the write-downs? When Congress passed the Medicare prescription drug benefit in 2003, it provided corporations with a small tax subsidy to encourage them to continue providing drug plans for retirees, instead of dumping them on the government. According to the Employee Benefit Research Institute, this subsidy will cost taxpayers $665 per retiree in 2011, while the same Medicare coverage would cost $1,209. ObamaCare eliminates the deductibility of this benefit, resulting in one-time charges against earnings. [124]

The consulting firm Towers Watson estimates that corporations will have to write off nearly $14 billion in 2010, unless they cut retiree drug benefits when their labor contracts expire. [125]

Caterpillar said the additional costs will put the company "at a disadvantage versus our global competitors that are not similarly burdened." [126] That will be true of most companies who pay these retirement benefits.

ObamaCare requires all employers to offer their employees insurance by 2014, or pay fines for failing to do so. The employer is not required to pay one hundred percent of the costs of that insurance, but if they don't pay at least 60 percent of the costs—or the cost of insurance exceeds 9.8 percent of a worker's income — employees may qualify to buy government-subsidized insurance on newly-created health care exchanges.[127]

Here's the kicker: if a company's employees get subsidized insurance, companies are fined the lesser of $3000 for each employee receiving a subsidy — or $750 for *every employee in the company,* if more than a quarter of the employees are subsidized.[128]

Employers with 50 or more workers who currently *don't* offer health coverage will be required to do so — or pay a $2000 fine for each employee who receives subsidies to buy insurance through newly-created state-based exchanges. The first 30 employees would be exempt from this fine. [129]

Who will qualify to buy insurance in the aforementioned exchanges? Low to moderate income workers who earn between $14,404 and $43,320 per year or whose health insurance premiums exceed 9.8 percent of their income. [130] Unfortunately for those workers, ObamaCare severely penalizes employers if employees purchase subsidized insurance in the insurance exchanges. [131] Thus companies which currently offer health insurance to their employees have a strong disincentive to hire low and moderate wage workers.

The requirement to offer employees health coverage will financially affect many businesses. For example, ObamaCare may cost New Hampshire's major ski resorts as much as $1 million in fines, because they employ large numbers of seasonal workers who don't receive health benefits, according to John DiStaso of the *New Hampshire Union Leader.* "The choices are pretty clear, either increase prices or cut costs, which could mean hiring fewer workers next winter," he wrote. [132]

The Congressional Budget Office estimates that up to 10 million American workers will no longer be covered by their employers as a result of ObamaCare. [133] It will simply be easier or more cost effective for companies to pay the fines, and offload their employees' insurance costs on the government — which many Americans suspect is the Democrats first step towards eliminating private insurance and force-feeding Americans single-payer, government-run health care.

5.   ObamaCare imposes regulations on insurers that will significantly raise premiums in the individual market.

Insurers will be forced to cover everyone at any time, even if one is sick. Known as "guaranteed issue," this requirement will prevent individuals from being denied coverage because of any pre-existing medical condition. [134]

The other mandate is that premiums will have to be the same, regardless of one's sex, health status, or age. (ObamaCare does cap the age-based difference, though.) This is known as "community rating." [135]

The problem with guaranteed issue is that many people will choose to obtain insurance only *after* they become ill. An apt analogy is a homeowners insurance policy which would allow people to buy fire insurance while their home is burning down. Who would purchase a policy like that beforehand? This is precisely the reason only five states — Maine, Massachusetts, New Jersey, New York and Vermont — allow guaranteed issue today.   New Hampshire and Kentucky repealed such laws after finding such policies caused insurance companies to flee those states. [136]

Why? Because insurers need the premiums from healthy people who consume less health care services to offset the cost of insuring older, sicker people who consume disproportionately more. If enough healthy people don't purchase insurance, the pool of insured customers will be weighted toward those less healthy who need more health care services. Insurance companies can't be profitable enough to operate in that environment, which leaves them two real-world choices: raise premiums or leave.

Community rating also creates serious problems that raise the cost of insurance. If insurance companies aren't allowed to calculate rates based on some individuals' greater likelihood of getting sick, then they will subsidize that risk by charging more for *everyone.* When premiums are increased, many healthy people decide not to buy insurance — which raises premiums once again because the insurer then has fewer healthy people in its pool paying premiums to offset the costs of insuring the less healthy.

It becomes a vicious cycle, similar to one that occurs with guaranteed issue.

This vicious cycle is precisely the reason why thirty-five states today impose no limits whatsoever on how much insurers can vary premiums, and why six allow wide variation. [137]

Three states — New York, New Jersey and Massachusetts — have *both* guaranteed issue and community rating. The results have been disastrous. Those three states now have the most expensive individual insurance markets among all fifty states, with premiums roughly *two to three times greater* than the rest of the country. [138] ObamaCare will expand nationally the very same regulations that have already proven to significantly raise insurance premiums on the state level.

According to the Congressional Budget Office, premiums in the individual market will be 10 to 13 percent higher under ObamaCare than under current law. [139] Yet that pales in comparison to the large premium increases young people will encounter. Although ObamaCare lets insurers set premiums based on age, it is only at a three to one ratio: i.e., the oldest people will pay only three times as much for health insurance as the youngest people (versus the real world ratio of five to one). As a result, 20 year olds could see their premiums increase by as much as 50 percent according to insurer Blue Cross and Blue Shield. [140]

Wellpoint, another insurer, estimates that a healthy 25 year old in Milwaukee who buys coverage on the individual market will see his premiums increase by 178 percent. [141] Thus, younger, healthier people will essentially be subsidizing the premiums of older, less healthy people.

To ensure that young people purchase health insurance, ObamaCare includes a provision that *requires* every American to buy health insurance — or pay a yearly penalty of $695, or 2.5 percent of their income, whichever is larger. [142] An analysis by the Center for Data Analysis at the Heritage Foundation, however, estimated that roughly 93 percent of uninsured households under 35 will forgo buying insurance altogether, opting to pay the penalty instead. [143]

This will result in yet another vicious cycle. If fewer younger adults purchase insurance, insurance costs will be certain to increase substantially for everyone else. The consulting group, Oliver Wyman prepared a report for Blue Cross and Blue Shield that estimates overall premiums would increase by 54 percent in the non-group market as a result of many young people opting out. [144]

6. *ObamaCare imposes new tax increases in the present and massive tax increases in the future.*

Already discussed are the individual mandates to buy insurance and the employer mandates to provide insurance to workers. The penalties for non-compliance essentially operate as tax increases, hurting both employees and employers.

In addition new annual taxes will be levied on pharmaceutical companies (roughly $2.7 billion), health insurers (roughly $6 billion), and medical device-makers (roughly $2 billion). [145]

It would be naïve for one to think that those industries will not pass those tax increases on to the consumer.

ObamaCare also includes a new tax on high-value health insurance plans, aka the "Cadillac tax." A 40 percent levy will be imposed on every dollar of a policy whose cost exceeds $10,200 annually for an individual premium, and $27,500 for a family premium. To appease the unions, Democrats pushed the start date on this tax back to 2018. [146] Nevertheless, this tax on insurers will also likely be passed on to consumers — and since the dollar limits are not indexed to inflation, more and more Americans will eventually be subject to it.

Currently, medical expenses that exceed 7.5 percent of one's adjusted gross income can be deducted for tax purposes. ObamaCare raises that threshold to 10 percent of adjusted gross income, resulting in fewer tax deductions for someone with high medical costs. [147]

Beginning in 2015, ObamaCare also will increase the Medicare payroll tax from 2.9% to 3.8% for individuals earning over $200,000 and joint filers over $250,000. Equally as significant, this new payroll tax rate will apply to unearned income from interest, dividends, capital gains, annuities, royalties and rents — an historical first.[148] And it will apply to *every dollar* of a taxpayer's investment income, if they earn only a single dollar over the $200,000 figure. [149]

According to the Institute for Research on the Economics of Taxation, this tax on unearned income will depress Gross Domestic Product by about 1.3%

and reduce capital formation for the nation by 3.4%. [150] Unfortunately, this tax is just another item on a long list of liberal Democrat policies that are harming our country.

The most devastating tax effects of ObamaCare will come further in the future, when its costs to the federal government escalate to the point where Congress will have to raise taxes in a desperate attempt to keep federal deficits from increasing beyond hope. Look for the Democrats to impose a national consumption tax known as a Value-Added Tax, on top of all the other taxes they've imposed, as one way to pay for ObamaCare. Those tax increases will financially hurt *every* American.

◆◆◆

Because of misrepresentations by Democrats and the media regarding this massive new entitlement program, many Americans might be unaware that there were alternative, *viable* proposals for *genuine* health care reform — without the budget-busting spending.

What were those better low and no-cost solutions Democrats rejected?

1. *The implementation of tort reform.*

Our current system of malpractice lawsuits results in massive and random settlements that increase everyone's insurance premiums and causes physicians to practice defensive medicine, ordering more procedures and tests than they would otherwise do.

According to a study by Daniel Kessler and Mark McClellan, because doctors pay more for malpractice insurance, patients pay nearly $2000 a year in extra health care expenses for an average family. [151]

Texas is an excellent example of tort reform's effectiveness. In 2003, the state enacted caps on non-economic damages (pain and suffering) and imposed a requirement that lawsuits be approved by a panel of medical experts. Over the following four years, premiums fell 21 percent, the exodus of doctors out of the state was halted, and 7,000 new doctors set up practices. [152]

Yet tort reform was rejected by Democrats as a way to lower healthcare costs; the Senate bill they approved avoided it completely. And, according to a November 2009 *Wall Street Journal* editorial, the House version of the health care bill was written to discourage other states from emulating the successful Texas model.[153]

Other sensible ideas include allowing defendants to pay large settlements in periodic payments, moving to a system of binding arbitration, and placing reasonable limits on attorneys' fees. [154] We could also adopt an English-style "loser-pays" legal system which would likely minimize frivolous lawsuits.

Or we could abolish the entire medical malpractice system altogether by creating a new monetary pool, funded by a small tax on all health insurance premiums from which people injured in medical errors or accidents could draw. The adjudication of guilt would be done by medical experts, not lay juries. [155]

Reality check: as long as trial lawyers remain one of the Democrat Party's most reliable sources of campaign donations — and Democrats remain in control of Washington, D.C. — tort reform will not be addressed.

2. *Reforming the tax code.*

It is an historical accident that people get their health insurance from their employer. During World War II, government-imposed wage and price controls prevented employers from rewarding their workers with salary increases. Companies responded by offering health care benefits as a way to circumvent the law. [156]

Workers who receive their health care from their employer receive their health benefits tax-free, costing the government a quarter-trillion dollars annually. [157]

Employer-provided health coverage also handicaps the economy in other ways. It makes it more difficult for people to leave their jobs — since they will lose their insurance in addition to their job. As a result, competition for workers is reduced, putting downward pressure on wages. [158]

In addition, because workers don't directly pay for their own health care, they don't have a clear understanding of what it actually costs (many think of it as "free"), they don't bother to shop for the best deal, and end up with coverage that their employer provides for them. This disconnect between the provider and consumer allows insurance companies to become insulated from normal market pressures that would lower prices and force them to keep customers satisfied. [159]

Equally as important, the current system is also unfair because it penalizes the unemployed and individuals who are unable to purchase their health insurance with pre-tax dollars.

A sensible reform would be to tax employer-provided health care benefits and return the money to the employee with a government check to purchase his own medical insurance. [160] Consumers would then be cost-conscious in shopping for health insurance, just like they are when they buy their own car or home insurance.

Incidentally, only the Republican Party offered this solution by including such tax code reform in several of the bills it introduced in 2009.

3. *Repealing all state laws which prevent insurance companies from competing across state lines.*

State regulations vary so widely that a standard insurance policy in one state can cost more than five times a standard policy in other states. [161]

Consider the case of a hypothetical 25 year-old man from New Jersey. Based on current rates, he would have to pay $5,580 per year for a standard health insurance policy. A similar policy purchased in Kentucky — a state which has fewer mandated coverage benefits than New Jersey — would cost him only $960 annually. [162]

Being able to shop across state lines for insurance would also create competition among insurers from different states, which would reduce costs even further.

According to a study by the University of Minnesota, *12 million more Americans* would be able to purchase coverage if this no-cost solution were enacted into law. [163]

4. *Reducing costly government regulations and mandates.*

As explained earlier, state regulations such as "guaranteed issue" and "community rating" increase the cost of health care.

In addition, state-mandated coverage requirements which force insurers to include items such as massage therapy, breast reduction, in-vitro fertilization and hair prosthesis, which aren't critical components of a good health insurance policy, significantly increase the cost of everyone's health insurance. [164]

Removing mandates would allow consumers to pick exactly what they wanted covered by their policy. For example, men could choose to not have gynecological coverage included as a required benefit, thus reducing the cost of their policies.

5. *Making health care costs transparent.*

For practically every good or service in our economy, consumers know the total cost of what they are buying *beforehand.*

That is not the case with health care. If costs and fees were made more transparent, the downward price pressure from such transparency would reduce health costs. Transparency works in virtually every other industry — why not health care?

6. *Reducing regulations on Health Savings Accounts.*

Health Savings Accounts (HSAs) are tax-free, interest-accruing savings accounts that can be used to pay for routine medical expenses. They are purchased in conjunction with inexpensive, qualified, high-deductible insurance policies structured to cover major health care costs. [165]

HSAs have four positive aspects to them:

    a. Individuals can spend their money tax-free on health care as they desire, without asking permission from their health insurance company.
    b. The funds deposited into HSAs accumulate over time if one is healthy, and thus can function like a retirement savings plan.

    c.   HSAs continue providing insurance when a person is between jobs.

    d.   When an individual encounters an extremely expensive health emergency, the insurance policy kicks in — and the HSA covers the deductible. [166]

Since the creation of HSAs in 2003, about 8 million Americans have purchased such plans, according to the Treasury Department. [167] Unfortunately, as of 2010 the maximum contributions to HSAs for an individual were only $3,050, and $6,150 for families. [168] Congress should raise the limits and reduce some restrictions such as the size of the highest allowable deductible. [169]

ObamaCare will likely end the existence of HSAs, one of the most successful products in our current health care system. Since all future insurance polices will be mandated to provide low-deductibles, ObamaCare will eliminate all high deductibles policies, one of the primary features of HSAs.

7. *Supporting retail health clinics.*

Across the country, health clinics are springing up in large retailers such as Wal-Mart and Target, and also in pharmacies like CVS. Patients normally don't need an appointment, and they usually don't have to wait more than a few minutes for treatment. [170]

These clinics typically charge around $50 per visit, and have been effective at helping the uninsured gain access to medical care. They also allow people with insurance to obtain medical care on weekends and after business hours, when doctors' offices normally are closed. [171]

Many doctors are requesting the American Medical Association to push Congress to ban these clinics. [172] Lawmakers in Washington should resist those calls.

8. *Removing the legal and regulatory barriers to the development of insurance policies that insure against drastic changes in one's health status.*

A huge problem with American health insurance is the risk that a person will develop a chronic health condition that will prevent them from obtaining insurance when they change jobs or insurance companies.

One of the most innovative proposals is to remove the legal and regulatory barriers preventing insurance companies from developing policies that would cover the risk of premiums rising as people get older and their health conditions deteriorate.[173]

For people who already have pre-existing conditions and have difficulty obtaining or affording insurance, a solution is to adequately fund high-risk pools that would subsidize their cost of health care.

These are eight ideas that would have *truly* reformed health care — without creating another massive entitlement America can't afford. Considered separately or enacted together they would have reduced costs for those who have coverage and enabled others to afford it.

◆◆◆

In conclusion, genuine health care reform should involve *less* government encroachment — not more. Only the federal government could create a system in which, if you lose your job, you also lose your health insurance. A free-market approach to health care could have achieved the goal of lowering costs and thus insuring more people.

Lasik corrective eye surgery demonstrates the superiority of this free-market approach. Most private insurers and government programs don't cover Lasik corrective eye surgery. As a result, the market for this procedure isn't distorted by excessive regulations and mandates. Lasik providers operate in a free market where the technology is constantly improving, price competition is intense, and the consumer is king. Those companies grow or fail according to their ability to satisfy the consumer. [174]

In the past decade, over three million Lasik procedures have been completed. During that period, the average price of Lasik eye surgery has dropped nearly 40 percent, from $2,200 to $1,350 per eye. [175]

The key to lowering costs and thus expanding coverage is to expand the Lasik model. That means promoting competition by minimizing government's role in the health care marketplace. [176]

In light of their complete rejection of these far less costly and far less federally-intrusive ideas, it is reasonable to conclude that the Democrats' Senate health care bill was ultimately *not* about health care reform.

So what was it about?

John Cassidy, a staff writer at the *New Yorker* magazine, candidly expressed the Democrats' real political motivation on his company's Web site. According to Mr. Cassidy, ObamaCare serves the dual objectives of "making the United States a more equitable country" and furthering the Democrats' "political calculus." *The Wall Street Journal* explained what this really means: "The purpose is to further redistribute income by putting health care further under government control, and in the process making the middle class more dependent on government. As the party of government, Democrats will benefit over the long run." [177]

Or as Hoover Institution Senior Fellow Victor Davis Hanson wrote: "The bill was not really about medicine; after all, a moderately priced, relatively small federal program could offer the poorer not now insured, presently not on Medicare or state programs like Medicaid or Medical, a basic medical plan…" [178]

ObamaCare is only the first step for the progressives in the Democrat Party. Once the bill is implemented, they are sure to make incremental changes to ObamaCare, moving it closer and closer to a full-blown, government-run program — or as Speaker of the House Nancy Pelosi put it, "My biggest fight has been between those who wanted to do something incremental, and those who wanted to do something comprehensive. We won that fight, and once we kick through this door, there'll be more legislation to follow."[179]

Unfortunately for America, Ms. Pelosi isn't only referring to additional measures on health care reform. Progressives aim to completely transform America, and the health care bill is the proverbial nose under the camel's tent. That is why Democrats passed it, even though 54 percent of Americans objected to it.[180] It is why they cut special deal after special deal, even when such "negotiations" enraged the American public.

It is also why they are willing to endure potentially large losses in the 2010 elections. Despite threats by many Republicans to repeal ObamaCare,

Democrats know that once an entitlement program is enacted, it is forever.

Many Americans are unaware that two things *completely* unrelated to health care were included in the bill. One was a complete government takeover of the student loan program. The other was the establishment of a civilian "ready reserve" corps. Both have the same objective: to expand the size and scope of government. College students needing loans will now be beholden to the bureaucracy, and legions of young Americans will be organized and trained to further the ends of progressive politics.

Despite all the misrepresentations by Democrats and the media, Republicans and the overwhelming majority of the American public also wanted health care reform.

What they didn't want was a government-expanding, freedom-killing, unconscionably expensive boondoggle furthering an already over-bloated sense of entitlement that is running this country into the ground. And they certainly didn't want "reform" that will result in the severe decline in the quality of healthcare due to the inevitable rationing that will be the result of ObamaCare.

Something fundamentally immoral is occurring in Washington, D.C. Throughout its history, America has always been a country where people worked hard and sacrificed to make life *better* for their children. Yet for the first time since the inception of the country, there is a distinct possibility that younger generations will be forced to cope with a future of *diminished* expectations and lesser opportunities — all of which can be traced back to the irresponsibility of our political ruling class.

America was on an unsustainable fiscal path *before* the health care bill was passed. That Democrats were willing to severely exacerbate that condition — especially when far more affordable alternatives for health care reform were available — is indefensible.

That they would do it for nothing more than the accumulation of political power — is *reprehensible*.

EPILOGUE

After reading this book, some people might think that I am unfairly picking on the Democrats. For those people, I want to remind you that I was a liberal Democrat for most of my life.

So what changed?

The Democrat Party did. They have been hijacked by radical leftists, and it happened while many of us weren't paying attention.

Although the Democrat leaders of yesterday stood up to and defeated the evil of Adolph Hitler, I consider today's Democrats an ineffective party of appeasers. They are seemingly incapable of even defining the fight against Islamic terror as a war. The current Democrats believe that "enemy combatants" should be considered "defendants" and be entitled to Constitutional protections and civil trials. Most Americans strongly disagree.

It takes strength to keep America safe. The pacifist approach of Jimmy Carter didn't defend democracy and defeat the Soviet Union; it was Republican President Ronald Reagan who fought the spread of Communism, even though the American left in this country called him a "warmonger."

I believe we are in the greatest struggle of our time against radical Islamic jihadists. The Democrats do not share my belief. We all witnessed how they pushed Senator Joe Lieberman out of their party because he took an aggressive stance in dealing with Islamic terrorism.

These days, only the Republican Party is calling for strong action against the enemies of the free world.

I understand that many people would prefer to believe we can resolve all problems through peaceful negotiations. But I know that way of thinking is not realistic. There are many brutal and relentless enemies who will accept nothing short of our demise.

Another huge difference between the parties comes down to one simple idea: Republicans believe Americans should be largely responsible for their own lives and Democrats believe government should solve most of peoples' problems for them.

It has become increasingly apparent that government "solutions" boil down to inefficiency, cronyism, multi-generational levels of debt and more and more Americans depending on government. Democrats seem to have forgotten that ours is a country built by men with uniquely American traits such as self-reliance, and a "can-do" attitude.

These traits, among others, have made us the greatest nation on earth.

Unfortunately, today's Democrats don't think so. In their America, our history, culture and traditions are not important. What matters to them is a complete transformation of our country into a socialist utopia. If they could just get the American people to shut up long enough to allow them to re-order our society, all would be well. It has often been pointed out to Democrats that Eastern Europe endured seventy years of a Soviet government promising to bring a "workers paradise" to that part of the world. We all know it never worked, and the Berlin Wall was eventually torn down — from the inside, not the outside.

So why do progressive Democrats persist? Believe it or not, they insist that socialism failed, not because it was an inherently flawed system, but for one simple reason:

The wrong people were in charge.

Such arrogance does not bode well for the future of the country. As a result, we must be vigilant in exposing the agenda of these radicals, also known as "progressives." They have not only taken over the Democrat Party, but they have started to infect the Republican Party as well. Thankfully, not too many are in the Republican Party yet.

These progressives are really socialists and Marxists, who need to be voted out of office, or at the very least, reduced to a small minority of our representatives. After all, according to a 2009 Gallup poll, the majority of Americans consider themselves more conservative than liberal. That majority is currently under-represented in Washington.

We the people and our government have never been further apart from each other than we are right now. It's as if Washington, D.C. is completely disconnected from the concerns of ordinary Americans.

It is time for all Americans to rally around the *ideas* that made this nation the envy of the world.

Although most of us only vote in the presidential election every four years, it is time to change that trend. The 2010 mid-term elections in November would be a good place to start. Soon the mainstream media will begin to bombard us with their "spin" on who to vote for, as there are many Democrats up for re-election.

Please do your homework to stay informed of the truth. Remember, it is not what politicians say or how well they say it that counts, but what they do. Don't be fooled. Learn about the issues and check to see how your representatives voted on the ones that are important to you. I have listed some resources in the back of the book as well as some websites to check and see how your representatives have voted.

In this book, I have taken on many issues, in as much detail as I could. I hope those who read this book learn as much reading it as I did writing it.

Nothing keeps politicians more on their toes — and government in check — better than a well informed public.

LETTER TO THE DEMOCRATIC NATIONAL COMMITTEE

In addition to writing this book, author Richard Bernstein sent the following letter to the Democratic National Committee. As a former lifelong Democrat, Mr. Bernstein wanted the Democrat Party to clearly understand the reason for his defection to the Republican side of the aisle...

April 13, 2010

Tim Kaine, Chairman
Democratic National Committee
430 S. Capitol Street S.E.
Washington, D.C. 20003

Gentlemen:

As a lifelong Democrat, it is with much anger and frustration that I have left your party. But if truth be told, you gave me no choice. Your ideological shift from the center-left to the far-left has alienated me completely. The party of JFK or Harry Truman has transformed itself into one populated by radicals beholden to special interest groups — groups to whom you cater at the expense of every other American.

Below is a partial list of policies advocated by the Democrat Party that I and many Americans strongly oppose. I now firmly identify with the Republican Party, as they stand opposed to these ridiculous policies you embrace.

ON NATIONAL SECURITY

I don't agree with your policy of eliminating enhanced interrogations of captured terrorists. We need to get every ounce of actionable intelligence to prevent any further domestic terror attacks.

I don't agree with giving Miranda rights to terrorists — especially those captured on the battlefield. Allowing captured terrorists the right to remain silent eliminates our ability to gain valuable information that might prevent the next attack against Americans.

I don't believe in diminishing our missile defense capabilities.   Your missile defense cuts are inexcusable.   Your party is spending billions of dollars in wasteful projects while ignoring your primary job — to protect the American people.

I am against your attempt to criminalize the actions of CIA interrogators and Defense Department attorneys who defended our country during the Bush administration.   This politically-motivated nonsense will undermine morale, and make our agents extremely hesitant to risk their careers and/or lives attempting to protect us.

I don't agree with trying terrorists in civilian courts. Giving non-citizen, non-uniformed enemy combatants the same Constitutional rights as American citizens is absurd. You obviously don't realize that we are at war.

I don't believe in appeasing our enemies.   Please stop apologizing for America's sins while ignoring all the good we have done. This country has always stood for democracy in the world, but your party recently stood silent when the people of the democratic resistance movement in Iran were being jailed and slaughtered.

ON YOUR ENERGY POLICIES

I don't agree with your policies that eliminated tax incentives to produce oil and natural gas, passed tax increases on energy production, and canceled existing oil and gas leases.   America is still dependent on traditional sources of energy, and will be for the foreseeable future. Your actions will stifle energy production of our abundant domestic resources, lead to higher fuel costs and cause greater dependence on foreign energy sources, some of whom are anti-American.

I don't like how the Democrat Party caters to radical environmentalists regarding nuclear energy. The expanded use of nuclear energy would meet a substantial portion of America's future energy needs. Your rigid opposition to the use of Yucca Mountain for nuclear waste storage is a roadblock preventing further development of nuclear energy, even though billions of dollars in research has proven its safety.

I don't believe we should rely on alternative energy sources like wind and solar for our energy future. Again, you are ignoring the realities: countries that have already gone in this direction are now reversing course because wind and solar are unreliable, ineffective and extremely expensive.

I don't buy into the idea that green jobs will boost the economy. Your refusal to look at the damning evidence from countries such as Spain, where 2.2 jobs were lost for every one created in the "green" energy sector, is ideologically-inspired blindness.

I don't believe we should consider carbon dioxide, which is what we exhale when we breathe, a "pollutant," or give the Environmental Protection Agency or Congress the power to regulate it. Your EPA's outrageous threat to tax carbon-usage and your devastating cap-and-trade bill will hurt financially-strapped Americans. Either one of these new policies will raise energy costs, cause further job losses, and make American industries less competitive worldwide.

YOUR ECONOMIC POLICIES

I don't like how you are bankrupting our nation. You are using a largely discredited model of massive stimulus spending to "jumpstart" the economy. Keynesian economics has never worked, and yet you persist in ignoring historical reality.

I don't believe real tax cuts are harmful like you do. Once again, you ignore history. Tax cuts by JFK, Reagan and Bush helped stimulate the economy and brought us out of recessions. Real tax cuts, not the tax rebates you gave us, puts more money in peoples' pockets and encourages investment and risk-taking. I *know* that each time tax cuts were enacted, *more* money, not less, flowed into federal coffers.

I don't believe your plans to raise taxes will help the economy. Increasing taxes on everyone and everything to finance your reckless spending is terrible policy. Higher taxes will hurt job creation, and will prolong — or possibly prevent — our economic recovery.

ON YOUR VERY SPECIAL INTEREST GROUPS

I don't agree with eliminating the secret ballot for workers deciding whether or not to unionize. Your so-called Card Check legislation is the antithesis of the democratic process. Doing it to placate union interests is disgraceful.

I don't believe in protectionist economic policies. Your failure to sign previously negotiated agreements with foreign trading partners because once again, your union allies don't want them, is harming our country.

I am angry that you are standing in the way of tort reform. Your unholy alliance with trial lawyers has prevented any significant tort reform which, among other things, keeps the cost of health care much higher than necessary.

I don't believe in catering to radical environmentalists. Farmers are starving to death in California because your party, beholden to the environmentalists, is redirecting water to help the three-inch delta smelt fish rather than direct it to the farmers who desperately need it. How shameful.

I don't believe in encouraging more Americans to go on welfare. Your policies to undo the welfare reforms of the 1990s take away the incentive of recipients to be self-sufficient. Sadly, I understand your motive: people dependent on government for their well-being vote for the party of more government — which is you.

Furthermore, I am thoroughly disgusted with your brazen attempt to take over the best health care system in the world, your attempt to redistribute wealth in the name of "social justice," your naive approach to worldwide terror and your abandonment of the concept known as American exceptionalism.

Despite what far too many of you think, this is still the greatest nation on earth, and the last thing it needs is a complete make-over — courtesy of a political party which thinks it knows what Americans want, better than Americans themselves do. You don't!

You've lost your way. And as a result, you've lost me.

Sincerely,

Richard Bernstein

Richard Bernstein

RESOURCES

One of the realities of writing a political book is that it must end somewhere, even as political developments themselves continue to evolve. For those Americans interested in remaining well-informed, I recommend the following resources, which I have divided into three categories: newspapers, magazines and the worldwide web.

Newspapers:

Investor's Business Daily (free online editorials at Investors.com editorials)
The New York Post (nypost.com)
The Wall Street Journal (free editorials at wsj.com – click on opinion)
The Washington Times (washingtontimes.com)

Magazines: (Available in print or online)

American Spectator (spectator.com)
Commentary (commentarymagazine.com)
Human Events (humanevents.com)
National Review (nationalreviewonline.com)
Newsmax (newsmax.com)
The Weekly Standard (weeklystandard.com)
Townhall Magazine (townhall.com)

Worldwide Web:

American Enterprise Institute for Public Policy Research (aei.org)
American Thinker (americanthinker.com)
Accuracy in Media (aim.org)
Big Government (biggovernment.com)
Business and Media Institute (businessandmedia.org)
Canada Free Press (canadafreepress.com)
Cybercast News Service (cnsnews.com)
Drudge Report (drudgereport.com)
Fox News (FoxNews.com)
Front Page Magazine (frontpagemag.com)
Great American Journal (greatamericanjournal.com)

Judicial Watch (judicialwatch.org)
Lucianne (lucianne.com)
Media Research Center (mrc.org)
The Cato Institute (cato.org)
The Heritage Foundation (heritage.org)
The Patriot Post (patriotpost.com)

Check How Your Representatives Voted:

Govtrack.us
Votesmart.org
Clubforgrowth.org (to find out how fiscally conservative your
representatives are)

For those who have the time, I also recommend reading the Constitution, which exemplifies the brilliance of our Founding Fathers and their unique understanding of human nature.

If you liked *Duped America,* you can sign up at my website, www.dupedamerica. com, to receive information about a future newsletter. It is my hope to keep readers informed about what's *really* happening—much of which won't be found in mainstream media sources.

NOTES

Chapter One: *The Democrats Are Dangerous When it Comes to National Security*

1. Joseph Lieberman, "Democrats and Our Enemies," *The Wall Street Journal,* May 21, 2008.
2. David Horowitz, Ben Johnson, *Party of Defeat, How Democrats and Radicals Undermined America's War on Terror Before and After 9/11 (Dallas: Spence Publishing Company 2008),* p.44.
3. History.com.
4. Michael Kranish, "With Antiwar Role, High Visibility," *Boston Globe*, June 17, 2003.
5. Ibid.
6. Lt. Col. Robert Patterson, *Reckless Disregard, How Liberal Democrats Undercut Our Military, Endanger Our Soldiers and Jeopardize Our Security (*Washington, D.C.: Regnery Publishing Company 2004*),* p.8.
7. Ibid., p.29.
8. Ibid., p.27.
9. Ibid., p.11.
10. David Horowitz, Ben Johnson, *Party of Defeat,* p. 26.
11. Ibid., p.26.
12. *Investor's Business Daily,* "Just Why Democrats Are 'Dangerous' When It Comes to America's Defense," October 20, 2006.
13. David Horwitz, Ben Johnson, *Party of Defeat,* p. 27.
14. *Investor's Business Daily,* "Just Why Democrats Are 'Dangerous' When It Comes to America's Defense," October 20, 2006.
15. David Horowitz, Ben Johnson, *Party of Defeat,* pp. 27, 29.
16. *Investor's Business Daily,* "Just Why Democrats Are 'Dangerous' When It Comes to America's Defense," October 20, 2006.
17. Ibid.
18. David Horowitz, Ben Johnson, *Party of Defeat,* p. 28.
19. Patterson, *Reckless Disregard*, p.11.
20. Ibid.
21. Herbert Romerstein, "Ted Kennedy Was a Collaborationist," *HumanEvents. com*, December 5, 2003. (Mr. Romerstein is a former government official).
22. Patterson, *Reckless Disregard,* p. 11.
23. Ibid.
24. David Horowitz, Ben Johnson, *Party of Defeat,* p. 44.
25. *Investor's Business Daily,* "97 Reasons Democrats Are Weak on Defense and Can't Be Trusted to Govern in Wartime," October 2, 2006.
26. David Horowitz, Ben Johnson, *Party of Defeat,* p. 31.

27. Lt. Col. Robert Patterson, *Reckless Disregard*, p. 13.
28. Herbert Romerstein, "Ted Kennedy Was a Collaborationist," *Human Events.com*, December 5, 2003.
29. Lt. Col. Robert Patterson, *Reckless Disregard*, pp.8, 9.
30. *Investor's Business Daily,* "97 Reasons Democrats Are Weak on Defense and Can't Be Trusted to Govern in Wartime," October 2, 2006.
31. Lt. Col. Robert Patterson, *Reckless Disregard*, p. 14.
32. *The Washington Times,* "Aloha, Star Wars," June 29, 2009.
33. *Investor's Business Daily,* "97 Reasons Democrats Are Weak on Defense and Can't Be Trusted to Govern in Wartime," October 2, 2006.
34. John Miller's 1998 interview with Osama bin laden, available at www.freerepublic.com/focus/news/833647/posts.
35. *Investor's Business Daily,* "97 Reasons Democrats Are Weak on Defense and Can't Be Trusted to Govern in Wartime," October 2, 2006.
36. Dick Morris and Eileen McGann, *Because He Could* (New York: ReganBooks 2004), p. 109.
37. Michael Scheuer interview with Nora O'Donnell on *MSNBC's* "Hardball," August 18, 2005.
38. Lt. Col. Robert Patterson, *Reckless Disregard*, p. 132.
39. *Investor's Business Daily,* "97 Reasons Democrats Are Weak on Defense and Can't Be Trusted to Govern in Wartime," October 2, 2006.
40. Ibid.
41. Lt. Col. Robert Patterson, *Reckless Disregard*, pp. 115, 116.
42. Ibid., p.117.
43. David Horowitz, Ben Johnson, *Party of Defeat,* p. 42.
44. Ibid., p.44.
45. Ibid., p.45.
46. Ibid., p.48.
47. David Horowitz, Ben Johnson, *Party of Defeat,* p. 45.
48. Richard Poe, "The Idiot's Guide to Chinagate," *NewsMax.com*, May 27, 2003.
49. Charles R. Smith, "Kerry's Chinagate-Loral Money Going to DNC, *FreeRepublic.com*, July 7, 2004.
50. Meng vs. Schwartz, Judicialwatch.org.
51. Charles R. Smith, "Kerry's Chinagate-Loyal Money Going to DNC, *FreeRepublic.com*, July 7, 2004.
52. David Horowitz, Ben Johnson, *Party of Defeat,* pp. 45, 46.
53. Ibid., p.38.
54. Kenneth R. Timmerman, *Shadow Warriors, The Untold Story of Traitors, Saboteurs, and the Party of Surrender* (New York: Crown Forum 2007), p.7.
55. Ibid.
56. Lt. Col. Robert Patterson, *Reckless Disregard*, p. 135.

57. *FoxNews.com,* "Sandy Berger Probed Over Terror Memos," July 20, 2004.
58. *Investor's Business Daily,* "Just Why Democrats Are 'Dangerous' When It Comes to America's Defense," October 20, 2006.
59. pbs.org, "Democratic Fallout," November 7, 2002.
60. Susan Jones, "Democrats' Real Security Plan," *CNSNews*.com, March 30, 2006.
61. David Freddoso, "Democrats Threaten Funding for Visa-Tracking System," *Human Events,* February 3, 2003.
62. Ibid.
63. *Fox News,* May 23, 2007.
64. *FoxNews.com,* "Reid: Someone Tell Bush the War in Iraq is Lost," April 19, 2007.
65. *FoxNews.com,* Transcript: "Hillary Clinton on FOX News Sunday," February 3, 2008.

Chapter Two: Politically Calculated Amnesia

1. Arthur Herman, "Why Iraq Was Inevitable," *Commentary,* July-August 2008.
2. Clinton signed the Iraq Liberation Act on October 31, 1998 (H.R. 4655).
3. Arthur Herman, "Why Iraq Was Inevitable," *Commentary,* July–August 2008.
4. Ibid.
5. Ibid.
6. Ibid.
7. Ibid.
8. Ibid.
9. Ibid.
10. Ibid.
11. Ibid.
12. Ibid.
13. Senator Charles Schumer, Statement on the Senate Floor, Congressional Record, October 10, 2002.
14. Senator Hillary Clinton, Statement on the Senate Floor, Congressional Record, October 10, 2002.
15. Senator John Rockefeller, Statement on the Senate Floor, October 10, 2002.
16. Senator Joseph Biden, Statement on the Senate Floor, October 10, 2002.
17. Arthur Herman, "Why Iraq Was Inevitable," *Commentary,* July-August 2008.

18. David Horowitz, Ben Johnson, *Party of Defeat, How Democrats and Radicals Undermined America's War on Terror, Before and After 9/11* (Dallas: Spence Publishing Company 2008), pp 5, 164.
19. Ibid., pp 7, 102.
20. Ibid., p.12.
21. Ibid., p.13.
22. Jessica Smith, "No Candidate Wins Majority in MoveOn.Org PAC First-Ever Democratic Online 'Primary'," Common Dreams, June 27, 2003.
23. Jeffrey Goldberg, "The Starting Gate, Foreign Policy Divides The Democrats," *The New Yorker,* January 17, 2007.

Chapter Three: Lies, Spies and Yellowcake

1. Commission on The Intelligence Capabilities of the United States Regarding Weapons of Mass Destruction, April 2005 (www.gpoaccess.gov/wmd/index.html)
2. Senate Select Committee on Intelligence, "Report on the U.S. Intelligence Community's Pre-War Intelligence Assessments on Iraq," July 9, 2004.
3. David Horowitz, Ben Johnson, *Party of Defeat, How Democrats and Radicals Undermined America's War on Terror Before and After 9/11* (Dallas: Spence Publishing Company 2008), pp. 96,97.
4. *CNN.com,* "Bush's State of the Union Speech," January 29, 2003.
5. David Horowitz, Ben Johnson, *Party of Defeat,* p. 97.
6. Ibid., p. 98.
7. Norman Podhoretz, "Who Is Lying About Iraq?," *The Wall Street Journal,* November 14, 2005.
8. Kenneth R. Timmerman, *Shadow Warriors, The Untold Story of Traitors, Saboteurs and The Party of Surrender* (New York: Crown Forum 2007), pp. 111,112.
9. Ibid., p. 97.
10. David Horowitz, Ben Johnson, *Party of Defeat,* p. 97.
11. Senate Select Committee on Intelligence, U.S. Senate, July 2004, pp. 43-74.
12. David Horowitz, Ben Johnson, *Party of Defeat,* p. 98.
13. Ibid., p. 99.
14. Kenneth R. Timmerman, *Shadow Warriors,* p. 104.
15. David Horowitz, Ben Johnson, *Party of Defeat,* p. 102.
16. Kenneth R. Timmerman, *Shadow Warriors,* p. 105.
17. David Horowitz, Ben Johnson, *Party of Defeat,* p. 102.

18. Ibid., p. 128.
19. Kenneth R. Timmerman, *Shadow Warriors*, p. 107.
20. Reynolds Holding, "Why Libby's Sentence Was So Tough," *Time.com* June 5, 2007.
21. *CNN.com*, "Sandy Berger Fined $50,000 For Taking Documents," September 8, 2005.
22. *The Washington Post* editorial, "End of an Affair," September 1, 2006.
23. David Horowitz, Ben Johnson, *Party of Defeat*, p. 129.
24. Ibid., p. 129.
25. Kenneth R. Timmerman, *Shadow Warriors*, pp. 109,110. Go to www.kentimmerman.com/shadow-warriors.htm. to see Plame's e-mail.

Chapter Four: Saddam's WMDs: Fact or Fiction?

1. Kenneth R. Timmerman, *Shadow Warriors, The Untold Story of Traitors, Saboteurs, and the Party of Surrender* (New York: Crown Forum 2007) p. 119.
2. Randall Hoven, "No WMDs? Really?," *American Thinker*, March 7, 2005.
3. *Investor's Business Daily*, "Bush Was Right," February 21, 2006.
4. *Investor's Business Daily*, "Saddam Had WMD," February 27, 2006.
5. Ibid.
6. Federation of American Scientists, "Uranium Production," August 27, 2009.
7. *Investor's Business Daily*, "Saddam had WMD," February 27, 2006.
8. Ibid.
9. *Investor's Business Daily*, "Saddam had WMD (Cont'd)," February 28, 2006.
10. Ibid.
11. Kenneth R. Timmerman, "Ex-Officia Russia Moved Saddam's WMD," *Newsmax*, February 19, 2006.
12. *NewsMax.com*, "Did Dems Mislead on Saddam's WMD Threat?," October 13, 2003.
13. *Associated Press*, "U.S. Removes Yellowcake from Iraq. Last Major Stockpile from Saddam's Nuclear Efforts Arrives in Canada," July 5, 2008.
14. Ibid.

Chapter Five: Saddam's Real Connections to Al-Qaeda

1. *The Weekly Standard,* "Inadvertent Truths," May 14, 2007.
2. Ibid
3. *Investor's Business Daily,* "Global War on Terror," May 1, 2007.
4. *Investor's Business Daily,* "Intelligence Failure in the Senate," September 12, 2006.
5. Ibid.
6. Ibid.
7. Stephen Hayes, "Saddam's Dangerous Friends, What a Pentagon Review of 600,000 Iraqi Documents Tells Us," *The Weekly Standard,* March 24, 2008.
8. *Investor's Business Daily,* "Intelligence Failure in the Senate," September 12, 2006.
9. Ibid.

Chapter Six: Everyone Thinks Republicans Caused the Mortgage Crisis...

1. Wikipedia.com, Community Reinvestment Act.
2. Terry Jones, "How a Clinton-Era Rule Rewrite made Subprime Crisis Inevitable," *Investor's Business Daily,* September 24, 2008.
3. Ibid.
4. *Investor's Business Daily,* "CRA Defenses Sound More Like CYA," December 9, 2008.
5. Matthew Vadum, "Rico Probe of ACORN Needed Now," *Human Events,* May 25, 2009.
6. Terry Jones, "How a Clinton-Era Rule Rewrite Made Subprime Crisis Inevitable," *Investor's Business Daily,* September 24, 2008.
7. *Investor's Business Daily,* "Stop Covering Up and Kill the CRA," November 28, 2008.
8. Ibid.
9. Ibid.
10. Ibid.
11. Stanley Kurtz, "Spreading the Virus," *New York Post,* October 13, 2008.
12. Ibid.
13. Ibid.
14. *Investor's Business Daily,* "CRA Defenses Sound More Like CYA," December 9, 2008.
15. Ibid.
16. Terry Jones, "Congress Lies Low to Avoid Bailout Blame," *Investor's Business Daily*, September 18, 2008.

17. Peter J. Wallison, "The True Origins of the Financial Crisis, As Opposed to a Desperate Liberal Legend," *The American Spectator,* February 2009.

18. Ibid.

19. Ibid

20. Ibid.

21. John Perazzo, "Fannie, Freddie and the Left," *FrontPageMagazine.com*, October 13, 2008.

22. Ibid.

23. Ibid.

24. Ibid.

25. Ibid.

26. Brian Ross and Rhonda Schwartz, "Emanuel Was Director of Freddie Mac During Scandal," *abcnews,* November 7, 2008.

27. John Perazzo, "Fannie, Freddie and the Left," *FrontPageMagazine.com,* October 13, 2008.

28. Ibid.

29. *Investor's Business Daily*, "Don't Blame Bush for Subprime Mess," December 1, 2008.

30. M. Jay Wells, "Why the Mortgage Crisis Happened," *American Thinker,* October 26, 2008.

31. Stephen Labaton, "New Agency Proposed to Oversee Freddie Mac and Fannie Mae," *The New York Times,* September 11, 2003.

32. M. Jay Wells, "Why the Mortgage Crisis Happened," *American Thinker*, October 26, 2008.

33. Ibid.

34. Kevin Hassett, "How the Democrats Created the Financial Crisis," *Bloomberg.com,* September 22, 2008.

35. Ibid.

36. M. Jay Wells, "Why the Mortgage Crisis Happened," *American Thinker,* October 26, 2008.

37. *Associated Press,* "Bush Administration Ignored Clear Warnings, Under Pressure From Banking Industry, U.S. Government Eased Lending Rules," December 1, 2008.

38. Terry Jones, "Saddest Thing About This Mess: Congress had a Chance to Stop It," *Investor's Business Daily*, September 26, 2008.

39. *The Wall Street Journal*, "Barney The Underwriter," June 25, 2009.

Chapter Seven: Republican Deregulation — Or Democrat Disinformation?

1. James L. Gattuso, "Meltdowns and Myths: Did Deregulation Cause the Financial Crisis," The Heritage Foundation, October 22, 2008.

2. Laura Litvan and Brian Faler, "Congress Pushes For Bigger Role in Resolving Financial Crisis," *Bloomberg.com,* September 16, 2008.

3. *CNN Politics.com*, "Transcript of Second McCain, Obama Debate," October 21, 2008.

4. Peter J. Wallison, "Obama Voted Present on Mortgage Reform," *The Wall Street Journal,* October 15, 2008.

5. *Investor's Business Daily,* "Dispelling the 'Deregulation' Myth," September 19, 2008.

6. Ibid.

7. James L. Gattuso, "Meltdowns and Myths: Did Deregulation Cause the Financial Crisis," The Heritage Foundation, October 22, 2008.

8. Charles W. Calomiris, "Most Pundits Are Wrong About the Bubble," *The Wall Street Journal,* October 18, 2008.

9. James Freeman, "Spitzer and Sarbox Were Deregulation?," *The Wall Street Journal,* October 31, 2008.

10. Ibid.

11. Ramesh Ponnuru, "Getting Our Phil: Smearing Phil Gramm," *National Review,* June 30, 2008.

12. *The Wall Street Journal,* "Barack Wrote a Letter…," October 29, 2008.

13. Ibid.

14. *The Wall Street Journal,* "Another Deregulation Myth," October 18–19, 2008.

15. Ibid.

16. Ibid.

17. Ibid.

18. Ibid.

19. Ibid.

Chapter Eight: Easy Money Leads To Hard Times

1. Alan Reynolds, "A Recession's Import, The Economic Troubles Were Not Made in America," *National Review*, May 4, 2009. Mr. Reynolds is a Senior Fellow at the Cato Institute.

2. Ibid.

3. David Roche, "Eastern Europe and the Financial Crisis," *The Wall Street Journal*, March 28, 2009.

4. John B. Taylor, *Getting Off Track, How Government Actions and Interventions Caused, Prolonged and Worsened the Financial Crisis* (Stanford: Hoover Institution Press 2009), pp. 8, 9.

5. Ibid., p. 8.

6. Ibid., p, 8.
7. Marc Faber, "Synchronized Boom, Synchronized Bust," *The Wall Street Journal,* February 18, 2009.
8. *Charlie Rose Show*, Public Broadcasting System, May 6, 2009.
9. John Taylor, *Getting Off Track*, Epilogue.
10. John Taylor, *Getting Off Track,* pp. 22, 23, 24.
11. Alan Reynolds, "A Recession's Import," *National Review*, May 4, 2009.
12. Ibid.

Chapter Nine: Less Taxes, More Revenue

1. National Taxpayers Union, www.ntu.org
2. Kevin A. Hassett, "The Rich, Soaked," *National Review,* September 15, 2008 (source: IRS Statistics-of-Income Division).
3. Brian M. Riedl, "The Myth of Spending Cuts for the Poor, Tax Cuts for the Rich," The Heritage Foundation, February 14, 2006.
4. National Taxpayers Union, www.ntu.org.
5. The Tax Foundation, "Comparing Income Taxes under Bill Clinton and George Bush," February 19, 2009 (www.taxfoundation.org/publications/show/23003.html).
6. Brian M. Riedl, "The Myth of Spending Cuts for the Poor, Tax Cuts for the Rich," The Heritage Foundation, January 29, 2007.
7. *The Wall Street Journal,* "The Spending Explosion," September 10, 2008.
8. Brian M. Riedl, "Ten Myths about the Bush Tax Cuts," The Heritage Foundation, January 29, 2007.
9. Ibid.
10. Ibid.
11. *Investor's Business Daily,* "A Record Tax Hike," June 4, 2008.
12. John F. Kennedy, President's News Conference, November 20, 1962 (viewed on Yahoo.com)
13. www.house.gov/jec/growth/longterm/longterm.htm.

Chapter Ten: Who's the Party of Wall Street and Big Money?

1. Center for Responsive Politics (www.opensecrets.org). The figures are based on contributions from PACs and individuals giving $200 or more to federal candidates and parties as reported to the Federal Election Commission. All the numbers are for the 2008 election cycle and are based on data released by the FEC on March 2, 2009.
2. Ibid.
3. Timothy P. Carney, "Obama's Hidden Bailout of General Electric," *The Washington Examiner,* March 4, 2009.
4. Kevin D. Williamson, "Losing Gordon Gekko, Wall Street Has Gone Over to the Democrats, Should Conservatives Miss It?," *National Review,* March 9, 2009.
5. Ibid.
6. Julianna Goldman, "Obama's Volcker-Led Board Includes Ferguson, Immelt (Update1), *Bloomberg.com,* February 6, 2009.
7. *The Washington Times,* "How to Get Back the AIG Bonuses," March 23, 2009.
8. *CNN.com,* "Dodd: Administration Pushed for Language Protecting Bonuses," March 19, 2009.

Chapter Eleven: Coddling Clinton

1. Allan H. Ryskind, "How GOP Principles Saved Clintonomics," *Human Events,* September 22, 2008.
2. Ibid.
3. Office of Management and Budget, *Budget of the United States Government, FY 2010, Historical Tables,* Table 1.1 at *http://www.whitehouse.gov/omb/budget/Historicals* July 15, 2009).
4. Allan H. Ryskind, "How GOP Principles Saved Clintonomics," *Human Events,* September 22, 2008.
5. Ibid.
6. Peter Jennings, *ABC Radio,* November 14, 1994.
7. Allan H. Ryskind, "How GOP Principles Saved Clintonomics."
8. Ibid.
9. Ibid.
10. John H. Makin, "The Myth of Clintonomics," American Enterprise Institute, December 1, 1999.
11. *Investor's Business Daily,* "The Myth of Clintonomics," November 14, 2008.

12. John H. Makin, "The Myth of Clintonomics," American Enterprise Institute, December 1999.

13. Daniel J. Mitchell Ph.D., "Ten Deceptive Myths About Social Security, The Budget and The Economy," The Heritage Foundation, August 23, 2001.

14. *Investor's Business Daily*, "The Myth of Clintonomics," November 14, 2008.

15. Ibid.

16. Robert W. Hahn, "Why the Microsoft Case Matters," *The Baltimore Sun*, September 22, 1999.

17. Allan H. Ryskin, How GOP Principles Saved Clintonomics," *Human Events*, September 22, 2008.

18. Lt. Col. Robert "Buzz" Patterson, *Reckless Disregard, How Liberal Democrats Undercut our Military, Endanger Our Soldiers and Jeopardize Our Security* (Washington, D.C.: Regnery Publishing Inc. 2004) pps. 114, 115.

19. Ibid, p. 122.

20. *USA Today:* It's Official: 2001 Recession Only Lasted Eight Months," July 17, 2003.

21. Lisa Desjardins, "Calculating National Debt a Number Nerd's Paradise," *CNN.com,* December 21, 2009.

22. U.S. Treasury, Bureau of the Public Debt, "National Debt to the Penny," (www.treasurydirect.gov/NP/BPDLogin?application=np).

23. Ibid.

Chapter Twelve: Bashing Bush

1. Tom Shales, "A Story with a Few Holes," *The Washington Post,* August 18, 2008.

2. Ralph Peters, "Al Qaeda's Market Crash," *New York Post,* July 21, 2008.

3. Ibid.

4. Ibid.

5. Kenneth R. Timmerman, *Shadow Warriors, The Untold Story of Traitors, Saboteurs, and the Party of Surrender* (New York: Crown Forum 2007), p. 7.

6. *National Review.com,* "Stop the Leaks," June 26, 2006.

7. Jay Nordlinger, "Diplomatic Health, On Bush, Our Alliances and Varied Perceptions," *National Review,* December 29, 2008.

8. Stephen Dinan, "Bush AIDS Fight Saved 1.1 M, Study Says," *The Washington Times,* April 7, 2009.

9. Jay Nordlinger, "Diplomatic Health," *National Review,* December 29, 2008.
10. Ibid.
11. Ibid.
12. Ibid.
13. Ibid..
14. *The Wall Street Journal,* "The Bush Economy," January 17-18, 2009.
15. Brian M. Riedl, "Federal Spending by the Numbers 2008," The Heritage Foundation, February 25, 2008. Numbers are based on Office of Management and Budget and Congressional Budget Office historical data.
16. Department of Homeland Security, Release Date February 22, 2006 (www.dhs.gov/xnews/releases/press_release_0865.shtm).
17. Implementing Recommendations of the 9/11 Commission Act of 2007 (www.nctc.gov/docs/ir-of-the-9-11-comm-act-of-2007.pdf).
18. Brian M. Riedl, "Federal Spending by the Numbers 2008," The Heritage Foundation, February 25, 2008.
19. Brit Hume, "Clinton Staffers Trash the White House," *FoxNews.com,* April 22, 2002.
20. Deb Reichmann, "Clintons Return $28,000 Worth of Gifts to White House," *Associated Press,* February 8, 2001.
21. Nile Gardiner, PhD., "George W. Bush: Winning The War on Terror," The Heritage Foundation, December 27, 2008.
22. Joseph W. Smith III, "Harry Truman Book a Trip Down Memory Lane," *Williamsport Sun-Gazette,* December 16, 2009.

Chapter Thirteen: Bamboozling Black America

1. Frances Rice, "Why Martin Luther King was a Republican," *Human Events,* August 16, 2006.
2. Ibid.
3. Deroy Murdock, "Grand Old Party, Blacks might be surprised to compare Republican history with the Democrats', " *National Review,* February 18, 2005.
4. Frances Rice, "Why Martin Luther King was a Republican," *Human Events,* August 16, 2006.
5. Ibid.
6. Deroy Murdock, "Grand Old Party," *National Review.* February 18, 2005.
7. Frances Rice, "Why Martin Luther King was a Republican," *Human Events,* August 16, 2006.
8. Ibid.

9. Ibid.
10. Wayne Perryman, *Unfounded Loyalty, An In-Depth Look into the Blind Love Affair between Blacks And Democrats* (Seattle: Hara Publishing Group 2004), p. 120.
11. Deroy Murdock, "Grand Old Party," *National Review,* February 8, 2005.
12. John Fonte, "After Lott," *National Review,* February 18, 2005.
13. Deroy Murdock, "Grand Old Party," *National Review,* February 8, 2005.
14. Robert Oliver, "Should the Democratic Party Apologize for Supporting Slavery," *Intellectual Conservative,* February 18, 2008.
15. Conservapedia.com, "Barry Goldwater."
16. Dr. Alveda C. King, "A Covenant With Life: Reclaiming MLK's Legacy," *Priests for Life* Fall/Winter 2008 publication
17. Deroy Murdock, "Grand Old Party," *National Review,* February 8, 2005.
18. Office of Management and Budget, Historical Tables, Budget of the United States Government, Fiscal Year 2007 (Washington, D.C.: U.S. Government Printing Office, 2006) pp.55-72. Table 3.2 and pp. 137-142, Table 8.5 at www.whitehouse.gov/omb/budget/fy2007/pdf/hist.pdf. (February 9, 2006).
19. Ibid. Total antipoverty spending consists of housing aid, food aid, other income support and Medicaid and S-CHIP for healthcare.
20. Frances Rice, "Why Martin Luther King was a Republican," *Human Events*, August 16, 2006.
21. Ibid.
22. Duncan Currie, "Family Ties," *The Weekly Standard,* March 27, 2008.
23. The Heritage Foundation, "Out of Wedlock Birthrate Out of Control," March 19, 2009.
24. David Boaz, "BOAZ: We miss you, Bubba," *The Washington Times,* January 11, 2010.
25. *The New York Times,* "Turning Success Into Failure," July 7, 2004.
26. Angela McGlowan, *Bamboozled, How Americans Are Being Exploited by the Lies of the Liberal Agenda* (Nashville:Thomas Nelson 2007), p. 18.
27. Maggie Gallagher, "Welfare Reform at Ten," *Townhall.com*, April 25, 2006.
28. Angela McGlowan, *Bamboozled,* p. 14.
29. Ann Coulter, *Guilty: Liberal "Victims" and their Assault on America* (New York: Crown Forum 2008), pp. 37, 38.
30. Robert Rector and Katherine Bradley, "Stimulus Bill Abolishes Welfare Reform Successes," *Human Events*, February 16, 2009.
31. Center for Responsible Politics (www.opensecrets.org).

Chapter Fourteen: Anatomy of a Scam:
The Science, Politics and Money Behind Global Warming.

1. *Investor's Business Daily,* "The Chill Is On," April 4, 2008.
2. Josiah Ryan, "Senators Debate Global Warming Policy Despite Global Cooling Evidence,"*CNSNews.com,* March 4, 2009.
3. Deroy Murdock, "How Global Cooling Arrived," *Human Events,* January 5, 2009.
4. Alan Carlin, "Comments on Draft Technical Support for Endangerment Analysis for Greenhouse Gas Emissions Under the Clean Air Act," March 16, 2009 (found at Competitive Enterprise Institute website).
5. Kimberley A. Strassel, "The EPA Silences A Climate Skeptic," *The Wall Street Journal,* July 3-5, 2009.
6. Mark Tapscott, "Suppressed EPA scientist breaks silence, speaks on Fox News," *The Examiner,* June 30, 2009.
7. Deroy Murdock, "Has Global Cooling Arrived," *Human Events,* January 5, 2009.
8. The National Academy of Sciences, "Surface Temperature Reconstructions for the Last 2,000 Years," 2006.
9. Fred Singer, ed., "Nature, Not Human Activity Rules the Climate: Summary for Policymakers of the Report of the Nongovernmental International Panel on Climate Change, Chicago, IL.:The Heartland Institute, 2008.
10. *Newsweek,* "The Cooling World," April 28, 1975.
11. *The New York Times,* May 21, 1975.
12. *Science News,* March 1, 1975 and *Science Magazine* December 10, 1976.
13. Senator James Inhofe (R-Okla.), "A Challenge to Journalists Who Cover Global Warming,"(from his speech on the U.S. Senate floor on September 25, 2006. Mr. Inhofe is the Chairman of the Environment and Public Works Committee). http://www.epw.senate.gov/speechitem.cfm?party=rep&id=263759.
14. From Senator Inhofe's speech on the Senate floor September 25, 2006.
15. www.cbsnews.com/blogs/2006/03/22/publiceye/entry1431768.shtml.
16. From Senator Inhofe's speech on the Senate floor September 25, 2006. Find Johannessen's study at http://www.co2science.org/scripts CO2 scienceB2C/articles/V8/N44/ci.jsp.
17. From Senator Inhofe's speech on the Senate floor September 25, 2006.
18. *CNN.com* interview aired on October 19, 2007.
19. From Senator's Inhofe's speech on the Senate floor on September 25, 2006.
20. www.globalwarmingheartland.org for a complete list of scientists or www.oism.org.

21. CFIF.org, "31,000 Scientists Shatter the Myth of a 'Scientific Consensus' on Global Warming," May 2008.

22. Full page ad displayed in *National Review*, May 4, 2009.

23. Ibid.

24. Deroy Murdock, "Has Global Cooling Arrived," *Human Events*, January 5, 2009.

25. George Will, "Real Calamity Makes Climate Fears Fade," Washington Post Writers Group, published in *Ft. Lauderdale Sun-Sentinel*, February 18, 2009.

26. Bill Steigerwald, "Cool News About Global Warming," *FrontPageMagazine.com* March 3, 2008.

27. S. Fred Singer, ed., "Nature, Not Human Activity, Rules the Climate: Summary for Policymakers of the Report of the of the Nongovernmental International Panel on Climate Change," Chicago, IL: The Heartland Institute, 2008.

28. Ibid

29. Ibid.

30. Ibid.

31. Ibid.

32. Ibid.

33. Ibid.

34. Ibid.

35. Ibid.

36. Henry Lamb, "Global Warming Hypocrisy," February 5, 2007, found at www.canadafreepress.com/2007/lamb020507.htm.

37. S. Fred Singer, ed., "Nature."

38. Ibid.

39. The National Academy of Sciences, "Surface Temperature Reconstructions for the Last 2,000 Years," 2006.

40. Ibid.

41. S. Fred Singer, ed., "Nature."

42. Ibid.

43. Ibid.

44. Alan Carlin, "Comments," March 16, 2009.

45. S. Fred Singer, ed., "Nature."

46. Ibid.

47. Ibid.

48. Ibid.

49. *The Wall Street Journal,* "A Glacier Meltdown," January 23-24, 2010.

50. *Investor's Business Daily*, "Seeing Chuckchi," May 29, 2009.

51. Peter C. Glover, "Media Credibility, Not Ice Caps, In Meltdown," *American Thinker,* February 3, 2010.

52. Tom Harris and Dr. Ian Clark, "Ask Questions of Global Warming," *Ft. Lauderdale Sun-Sentinel,* October 7, 2007. (Tom Harris is an Ottawa-based engineer and Executive Director of the Natural Resources Stewardship Project (www.nrsp.com). Dr. Ian Clark, a science advisor to NRSP, is a Professor of Earth Sciences at the University of Ottawa, focusing on Paleoclimatology and Isotope Hydrogeology.

53. Ibid.

54. Ibid.

55. Sally Peck, "Al Gore's 'nine Inconvenient Untruths," *Telegraph.co.uk,* November 10, 2008.

56. Senator James Inhofe speech September 25, 2006.

57. *The Washington Times,* The Education of Al Gore," March 25, 2000.

58. S. Fred Singer, ed. "Nature."

59. Sergei Golubchikov, "Global Warming: Horror Fiction or Real Challenge," *Russian News and Information Agency,* August 11, 2007.

60. Christopher C. Horner, *The Politically Incorrect Guide to Global Warming and Environmentalism* (Washington, D.C.: Regnery Publishing, Inc. 2007), p. 40.

61. S. Fred Singer, ed. "Nature."

62. Christopher C. Horner, *The Politically Incorrect Guide,* p. 301.

63. John Heilprin, "UN: Poorest Countries Most Vulnerable to Climate Change, Need Help from the Rich," *Associated Press,* November 27, 2007.

64. Joanne Nova, "Climate Money," Science and Public Policy Institute, July 21, 2009.

65. Ibid

66. Fred Lucas, "Gore Financially Invested in Climate Cause," *CNSNews.com,* May 14, 2008.

67. Ibid.

68. Steve Milloy, "Al Gore Invests Millions to Make Billions in Cap and Trade Software,"*Canadafreepress.com,* June 3, 2009.

69. Fred Lucas, "Gore Financially Invested in Climate Cause," *CNSNews.com,* May 14, 2008.

70. Christopher C. Horner, *Red Hot Lies, How Global Warming Alarmists Use Threats, Fraud, and Deception to Keep You Misinformed* (Washington, D.C.: Regnery Publishing, Inc. 2008), p.223.

71. Joanne Nova, "Climate Money," Science and Public Policy Institute, July 21, 2009.

72. Ibid.

73. Bill Steigerwald, "Cool News About Global Warming," *FrontPageMagazine.com,* March 3, 2008.

74. Joanne Nova, "Climate Money."

75. Ibid.

76. Ibid.
77. Ibid.
78. Noel Sheppard, "Czech President Calls Man-Made Global Warming a Myth, Questions Al Gore's Sanity," *NewsBusters,* February 12, 2007.
79. Phil Valentine, "Al Gore is Like Jim Jones, and We're Drinking His Kool-Aid," *Tennessean.com,* November 18, 2007.

Chapter Fifteen: An Energy Policy — For Less Energy

1. Robert Samuelson, "Drilling For Oil Still Makes Sense, But, Sadly, Politics Gets In The Way," *Investor's Business Daily,* May 1, 2009.
2. Ibid.
3. Energy Information Administration, U.S. Department of Energy, ANNUAL ENERGY REVIEW, 2007, Report No. DOE/EIA — 0384 (2007), posted June 23, 2008.
4. Fred Barnes, "No Energy From This Executive," *The Weekly Standard,* June 15, 2009.
5. Ibid.
6. Ibid.
7. Ibid.
8. Ibid.
9. Robert J. Samuelson, "The Bias Against Oil and Gas," *The Washington Post,* May 4, 2009.
10. *Investor's Business Daily,* "Seeing Chukchi," May 29, 2009.
11. Robert J. Samuelson, "The Bias Against Oil and Gas," The *Washington Post,* May 4, 2009.
12. Rep. Tim Walberg, "Democrats Blocking Vote on Energy Production Bill,"*Human Events,* June 20, 2008.
13. Fred Barnes, "No Energy From This Executive," *The Weekly Standard,* June 15, 2009.
14. Carla Marinucci, "Palin Suggests Chronicle Withheld Obama Remarks," *San Francisco Chronicle,* November 3, 2008.
15. Alex Alexiev, "Green Bubbles Bursting, The Delusions of Renewables and the Realities of Nuclear Power," *National Review,* April 20, 2009. (Mr. Alexiev is an adjunct fellow at the Hudson Institute in Washington, D.C.).
16. Ibid.
17. *Associated Press,* "Official: No Nuke Waste at Yucca Mountain, Energy Secretary Stephen Chu says site is not an option, despite $13.5 billion spent," March 5, 2009, found at *cbsnews.com.*
18. Ibid.

19. Ibid.
20. Ibid.
21. Ibid.
22. Ibid.
23. Ibid.
24. *The Wall Street Journal*, "Obama to Propose More Oil Drilling in Gulf," March 30, 2010.
25. Ibid.
26. Senator James Inhofe, "Beware President Obama's Offshore Drilling Scam," *Human Events*, April 12, 2010.
27. *The Wall Street Journal*, "An Energy Head Fake," March 11, 2010.
28. Senator James Inhofe, "Beware President Obama's Offshore Drilling Scam," *Human Events*, April 12, 2010.

Chapter Sixteen: The Answer, My Friends, Ain't Blowin' In The Wind

1. *The New York Times*, Transcript of Barack Obama's Inaugural Address, January 20, 2009.
2. Andrew P. Morriss, William T. Bogart, Andrew Dorchak, Roger E. Meiners, "Green Jobs Myths,"University of Illinois Law and Economics Research Paper Series No.LE09-001.
3. Jack Spencer and Nick Loris, "Critics of Nuclear Power's Costs Miss the Point," The Heritage Foundation, June 18, 2008.
4. William Tucker "Tilting We Will Go? Windmills Are Not An Energy Policy," *National Review*, August 18, 2008.
5. Eric Rosenbaum, "A Problem With Wind," featured in *At Issue: What Energy Sources Should be Pursued, (*Greenhouse Press 2005*)* and *Opposing Viewpoints: Global Resources* (Gale 2007).
6. William Tucker, "Lo, a Smart Grid!," *National Review*, March 9, 2009.
7. Ibid.
8. Ibid.
9. Ibid.
10. William Tucker, "His Winter of Discontent," *American Spectator*, January 29, 2009.
11. Ibid.
12. William Tucker, "Lo, a Smart Grid!," *National Review*, March 9, 2009.
13. Andrew P. Morriss, William T. Bogart, Andrew Dorchak, Roger E. Meiners, "Green Jobs Myths," University of Illinois Law and Economics Research Paper Series No.LE09-001.
14. William Tucker, "The Solar and Renewable Utopia," *National Review*, March 23, 2009.

Chapter Seventeen: Democrats' Nuclear Nuttiness

1. Reuters, "UPDATE 1 – Obama criticizes McCain's nuclear power plan," June 24, 2008

2. Ibid.

3. William Tucker, "There Is No Such Thing As Nuclear Waste," *The Wall Street Journal,* March 13, 2009.

4. Iain Murray, "Nuclear Power?," *National Review,* June 16, 2008.

5. William Tucker, "There Is No Such Thing As Nuclear Waste," *The Wall Street Journal,* March 13, 2009.

6. Iain Murray, "Nuclear Power?," *National Review,* June 16, 2008.

7. Ibid.

8. Max Schulz, "If Not Yucca For Waste, Then Where?," *Investor's Business Daily,* March 30, 2009.

9. Jack Spencer, "The American Energy Act Puts Nuclear on the Fast Track," The Heritage Foundation, June 10, 2009.

10. Max Schulz, "Will Harry Reid's Dream Come True," *The Weekly Standard,* March 9, 2009. (Mr. Schultz is a Senior Fellow at the Manhattan Institute).

11. Ibid.

12. Ibid.

13. U.S. Department of Energy, Oak Ridge Office, "About Radiation," October 29, 2007.

14. Ibid.

15. Iain Murray, "Nuclear Power?," *National Review,* June 16, 2008.

16. Ibid.

17. Max Schulz, "Will Harry Reid's Dream Come True," *The Weekly Standard,* March 9, 2009.

18. William Tucker, "Going Nuclear," *National Review,* October 15, 2008.

19. *Associated Press,* Official: No Nuke Waste at Yucca Mountain, Energy Secretary Stephen Chu Says Site is Not An Option, Despite $13.5 B Spent," March 5, 2009, found at cbsnews.com.

20. Max Schulz, "Will Harry Reid's Dream Come True," *The Weekly Standard,* March 9, 2009.

21. Senator Lamar Alexander, "Needed: 100 New Nuclear Power Plants in 20 Years," *Human Events,* June 15, 2009.

22. The Heritage Foundation, "Facts, Safety and Three Mile Island," February 25, 2008.

23. Senator Lamar Alexander, "Needed: 100 New Nuclear Power Plants in 20 Years," *Human Events,* June 15, 2009.

24. Ibid.

25. Iain Murray, "Nuclear Power?," *National Review,* June 16, 2008.

26. Senator Lamar Alexander, "Needed: 100 New Nuclear Power Plants in 20 Years," *Human Events,* June 15, 2009.

27 Iain Murray, "Nuclear Power?".

28 World Nuclear Association, "Transport of Radioactive Material," October 2003.

29. Jack Spencer and Nicolas Loris, "Dispelling Myths About Nuclear Energy," The Heritage Foundation, December 3, 2007.

30. William Tucker, *Terrestrial Energy, How Nuclear Power Will Lead the Green Revolution and End America's Energy Odyssey* (Savage, Md.: Bartleby Press 2008), p. 303.

31. Energy Policy Act of 2005: Summary and Analysis of Enacted Provisions (found at ncseonline.org/NLE/CRSreports/06/Apr/RL33302.pdf).

32. Rebecca Smith, "U.S. Chooses Four Utilities to Revive Nuclear Industry," *The Wall Street Journal,* June 17, 2009.

33. Max Schutz, "Will Harry Reid's Dream Come True," *The Weekly Standard,* March 9, 2009.

34. Jack Spencer and Nicolas D. Loris, "Five Free Market Priorities For a Nuclear Energy Renaissance," The Heritage Foundation June 9, 2009.

35. H. Josef Hebert, "Pro-nuclear loan program dropped from stimulus," *Associated Press,* February 12, 2009, found at *FoxNews.com.*.

Chapter Eighteen: Obamanomics: A Roadmap to Fiscal Ruin

1. Jeb Hensarling and Paul Ryan, "Why No One Expects a Strong Recovery," *The Wall Street Journal,* November 20, 2009.

2. Ibid.

3. Karl Rove, "Voter Anger Is Building Over Deficits," *The Wall Street Journal,* November 26, 2009.

4. *Investor's Business Daily,* "Runaway Debt Must Be Stopped Now," December 15, 2009.

5. Ibid.

6. Martin Crutsinger, "Federal Deficit Hits Record $1.42 Trillion," *The Associated Press,* October 17, 2009.

7. Office of Management and Budget, *Budget of the United States Government, FY 2010, Historical Tables,* Table 1.1 at http://www.whitehouse.gov/omb/budget/Historicals (July 15, 2009).

8. Daniel Foster, "Obama's $3.8 Trillion Budget," *National Review.com,* February 1, 2010.

9. Lawrence Kadish, "Taking The National Debt Seriously," *The Wall Street Journal,* October 12, 2009.

10. Corey Boles, "Senate Approves Amendment To Raise Debt Ceiling by $1.9 Trillion," *The Wall Street Journal,* January 29, 2010.

11. *Investment Business Daily,* "Runaway Debt Must Be Stopped Now," December 15, 2009.

12. Ibid.

13. Ibid.

14. Ibid.

15. Lawrence Kadish, "Taking The National Debt Seriously," *The Wall Street Journal,* October 12, 2009.

16. Michael J. Boskin, "An Alternative Stimulus Plan," *The Wall Street Journal,* November 18, 2009.

17. Kim Geiger, "What the bill would mean for you," *Tribune Newspapers,* March 21, 2010.

18. *The Wall Street Journal,* "ObamaCare's Worst Tax Hike," March 17, 2010.

19. David Reilly, Ellen E. Schultz and Ron Winslow, "AT&T Joins in Health Charges," *The Wall Street Journal,* March 27-28, 2010.

20. David W. Kreutzer, Ph.D., "Heritage Analysis of Waxman-Markey Hits Where Others Miss," The Heritage Foundation, August 6, 2009.

21. Steven F. Haywood, "The EPA's Power Grab," *The Weekly Standard,* December 28, 2009.

22. *The Wall Street Journal,*" Zero to 35 in 24 Hours," December 10, 2009.

23. Matthew J. Slaughter, "How to Destroy American Jobs," *The Wall Street Journal,* February 3, 2010.

24. Martin Feldstein, "Tax Increases Could Kill The Recovery," *The Wall Street Journal,* November 26, 2009.

25. *Investor's Business Daily,* "The Green Wind of Destruction," May 12, 2009.

26. Ibid.

27. *The Wall Street Journal,* "Zero to 35 in 24 Hours," December 10, 2009.

28. Carl Schramm, Robert Litan and Dane Stangler, "New Business, Not Small Business is What Creates Jobs," *The Wall Street Journal,* November 6, 2009.

29. *The Wall Street Journal,* "Washington vs. Silicon Valley," August 7, 2009.

30. Matthew J. Slaughter, "How to Destroy American Jobs," *The Wall Street Journal,* February 3, 2010.

31. Mark Steyn, "Prime Minister Obama, Will European Statism Supplant the American Way?," *National Review,* March 23, 2009.

32. *The Wall Street Journal,* "The Young and the Jobless," October 3-4, 2009.

33. Ibid.

34. James Sherk and Rea S. Hederman Jr., "Heritage Employment Report: Thanks for the November Jobs Report?," The Heritage Foundation, December 4, 2009.

35. Ibid.
36. Daniella Markheim, "Energy Cap and Trade Threatens American Prosperity," The Heritage Foundation, June 16, 2009.
37. Reuters, "FACTBOX: Buy American Provision in U.S. Stimulus Bill," February 13, 2009.
38. *The Wall Street Journal,* "Mexico Retaliates," March 19, 2009.
39. *The Wall Street Journal,* "A Protectionist President," September 15, 2009.
40. *The Wall Street Journal,* "Trading Barbs With China," February 10, 2010.
41. Jeb Hensarling and Paul Ryan, "Why No One Expects a Strong Recovery," *The Wall Street Journal,* November 20, 2009.
42. Ibid.
43. Elaine L. Chao, "Two Steps Back on Labor Rights," *The Wall Street Journal,* March 19, 2009.
44. Ibid.
45. Ibid.
46. Ibid.
47. Ibid,
48. *Investor's Business Daily,* "Same Old New Deal," March 3, 2009.
49. George L. Priest, "The Justice Department's Antitrust Bomb," *The Wall Street Journal,* June 2, 2009.
50. Ibid.
51. Ibid.
52. Bret Stephens, "Obama and the Underpants Gnomes," *The Wall Street Journal,* May 26, 2009.
53. Patrice Hill, "Bailouts No Longer Money in the Bank," *The Washington Times,* June 15, 2009.
54. Fred Barnes, "The Triumph of Crony Capitalism," *The Weekly Standard,* July 13, 2009.
55. Phyllis Schlafly, "Obama Pursuing Socialist Agenda for America," *Human Events*, June 8, 2009.
56. Elaine L. Chao, "Two Steps Back on Labor Rights," *The Wall Street Journal,* March 19, 2009.

Chapter Nineteen: Keynesian Kraziness

1. James K. Glassman, "Stimulus: A History of Folly," *Commentary,* March 2009.
2. Ibid.
3. Ibid.
4. Ibid.

5. Thomas E. Woods Jr., *Meltdown, A Free-Market Look at Why the Stock Market Collapsed, the Economy Tanked, and Government Bailouts Will Make Things Worse* (Washington, D.C.: Regnery Publishing Inc. 2009), p. 149.

6. Alan Reynolds, "Faith-Based Economics, Keynes makes a comeback, but his ideas are still wrong," *National Review*, February 9, 2009.

7. James K. Glassman, "Stimulus: A History of Folly," *Commentary*, March 2009.

8. Ibid.

9. Thomas E. Woods Jr., *Meltdown*, p. 82.

10. *The Wall Street Journal*, "Barack Obama-san," December 16, 2008.

11. Ibid.

12. Ibid.

13. Thomas E. Woods Jr., *Meltdown*, p. 94.

14. Ibid., pp. 94, 95.

15. Ibid., p. 95.

16. Donald Lambro, "Many Economic Unconnected Dots," *The Washington Times*, February, 16, 2009.

17. Cato Institute full page advertisement as seen in *National Review*, February 23, 2009, p. 5.

18. Ibid.

19. Brian Riedl, "Why the Stimulus Failed, Fiscal policy cannot exnihilate new demand,"*National Review*, September 7, 2009.

20. Ibid.

21. Walter E. Williams, "There Is No Santa," *Townhall.com*, January 20, 2009.

Chapter Twenty: Six Fatal Flaws of the Stimulus Bill

1. *The Wall Street Journal*, "A 40-Year Wish List, You Won't Believe What's in That Stimulus Bill," January 28, 2009.

2. Ibid.

3. Fred Barnes, "The Obama Agenda Bogs Down," *The Wall Street Journal*, July 20, 2009.

4. Ibid.

5. Ibid.

6. Thomas Lifson, "Obama delays signing 'urgent' stimulus for Chicago fun," *American Thinker*, February, 15, 2009.

7. Phil Kerpen, "NY's Tax-Funded Ex-Terrorist," *New York Post*, September 9, 2009.

8. Ibid.
9. John Perazzo, "The Marxist Revolutionary and Obama's Environmental Policies," *FrontPageMag.com,* September 17, 2009.
10. Phil Kerpen, "NY's Tax-Funded Ex-Terrorist," *New York Post,* September 9, 2009.
11. Patrick McCrory, "The Lessons of the 'Stimulus' Bill," *The Wall Street Journal,* August 13, 2009.
12. Brett J. Blackledge and Matt Apuzzo, "Bridges Lose to Paving in Stimulus Aid Projects," *Associated Press,* July 31, 2009.
13. Ibid.
14. Patrick McCrory, "The Lessons of the 'Stimulus' Bill," *The Wall Street Journal,* August 13, 2009.
15. *The Wall Street Journal,* "Governors v. Congress," February 23, 2009.
16. Ibid.
17. Ibid.
18. Ibid.
19. Ibid.
20. Ibid.
21. Karl Rove, "The President Moves the Economic Goalposts," July 16, 2009.
22. Ibid.
23. The Heritage Foundation, "True Cost of Stimulus: $3.27 Trillion," February 12, 2009.
24. www.recovery.gov
25. Matt Cover, "Only 23 Percent of Stimulus Will Be Spent This Fiscal Year, Congressional Budget Office Finds," *CNSNews.com*, February 18, 2009.
26. Ibid.
27. Ibid.
28. Ibid.
29. Vincent Gioia, "What is the Stimulus Bill All About?," www.rightsidenews.com, February 28, 2009.
30. Matthew Continetti, "The Right Stimulus," *The Weekly Standard,* February 9, 2009.
31. *Investor's Business Daily,* "Waste, Fraud, Abuse," June 16, 2009.
32. *Glen Beck Show,* December 11, 2009.
33. David Goldman, "Why Stimulus Jobs Aren't Built to Last," *CNNMoney.com,* November 2, 2009.
34. Peter Morici, "Economic Predictions: Modest Recovery, Soaring Market," *Ft. Lauderdale Sun-Sentinel,* August 2, 2009.
35. Fred Barnes, "The Obama Agenda Bogs Down," *The Wall Street Journal,* July 20, 2009.
36. *Human Events,* "When Will The Stimulus Package Start Working?," July 27, 2009.

37. Ibid.
38. Stephan Dinan, "CBO: Obama Stimulus Harmful Over Long Haul," *The Washington Times*, February 4, 2009.
39. Karl Rove, "The President Moves the Economic Goalposts," *The Wall Street Journal*, July 16, 2009.

Chapter Twenty One: Democrats and Their Unholy Alliances

1. Jim DeMint, *Saving Freedom, We Can Stop America's Slide Into Socialism* (Nashville: Fidelis Books 2009), p.45.
2. OpenSecrets.org, Top Industries Giving to Members of Congress 2009-2010 cycle.
3. OpenSecrets.org, Top Industries Giving to Members of Congress 2004 cycle.
4. Jim DeMint, *Saving Freedom*, p.50.
5. Center for Responsive Politics, OpenSecrets.org, Labor: Long Term Contribution Trends.
6. Jim DeMint, *Saving Freedom*, p.46.
7. The Heritage Foundation, "Employee 'No' Choice Act, Increasing the Federal Government's Role, Again," March 10, 2009.
8. *The Wall Street Journal*, "The New Old 'Card Check," July 20, 2009.
9. Govtrack.us, H.R. 800: Employee Free Choice Act of 2007.
10. *The Wall Street Journal*, "Mexico Retaliates," March 19, 2009.
11. Ibid.
12. *The Wall Street Journal*, "The Denver Democrats," August 25, 2008.
13. *The Wall Street Journal*, "Europe Thumps U.S., Again," July 20, 2009.
14. Ibid.
15. David Pierson, "China Files Complaint On Tire Tariffs By U.S.," *Tribune Newspapers*, September 15, 2009.
16. *The Wall Street Journal*, "Obama's Trade Test," August 4, 2009.
17. Edmund L. Andrews, "U.S. Adds Tariffs on Chinese Tires," *The New York Times*, September 11, 2009.
18. David Pierson, "China Files Complaint On Tire Tariffs By U.S.," *Tribune Newspapers*, September 15, 2009.
19. *The Wall Street Journal*, "Obama's Trade Test," August 4, 2009.
20. Ibid.
21. Ibid.
22. Tony Pugh, "Non-Union Workers May Miss Stimulus Jobs," *McClatchy Newspapers*, March 29, 2009.
23. James Sherk, "Davis-Bacon Wage Provisions Depress The Economy," The Heritage Foundation. January 28, 2009.

24. Todd J. Zywicki, "Chrysler and the Rule of Law," *The Wall Street Journal,* May 13, 2009.

25. Newt Gingrich, "Auto Bailout a Payback to UAW," *Human Events,* June 15, 2009.

26. Ibid.

27. Ibid.

28. Ibid.

29. Ibid.

30. *The Wall Street Journal,* "The UAW's Defined Benefactor," July 25-26, 2009.

31. Center for Responsive Politics, OpenSecrets.org, Teachers Unions: Long-Term Contribution Trends.

32. *The Wall Street Journal,* "Obama's School Choice," February 26, 2009.

33. Ibid.

34. Center for Responsive Politics, OpenSecrets.org, Lawyers/Law Firms: Long-Term Contribution Trends.

35. Jim DeMint, *Saving Freedom*, p. 47.

36. Center for Responsive Politics, OpenSecrets.org, Environment: Long-Term Contribution Trends.

37. Fred Barnes, "No Energy From This Executive," *The Weekly Standard,* June 15, 2009.

38. Jack Spencer and Nicolas D. Loris, "Five Free Market Priorities For a Nuclear Energy Renaissance," The Heritage Foundation, June 9, 2009.

39. Fred Barnes, "No Energy From This Executive," *The Weekly Standard,* June 15, 2009.

40. *The Wall Street Journal,* "California's Man-Made Drought," September 2, 2009.

41. Ibid.

42. Ibid.

43. Bill Jennings, "Another Bullet Dodged in Corporate Agriculture's War on Fish and People, Compared to Pearl Harbor," San Francisco Bay Area Independent Media Center, September 25, 2009.

44. Ibid.

45. Matthew Vadum, "Rico Probe of ACORN Needed Now," *Human Events,* May 25, 2009.

46. John Fund, "More ACORN Voter Fraud Comes to Light," *The Wall Street Journal,* May 9-10, 2009.

47. John Fund, "An ACORN Whistleblower Testifies in Court," *The Wall Street Journal,* October 30, 2008.

48. John Fund, "More ACORN Voter Fraud Comes to Light," *The Wall Street Journal,* May 9-10, 2009.

49. Ibid.

50. Matthew Vadum, "Rico Probe of Acorn Needed Now," *Human Events,* May 25, 2009.

51. John Fund, "More ACORN Voter Fraud Comes to Light," *The Wall Street Journal,* May 9-10, 2009.

52. Jim DeMint, *Saving Freedom,* p.48.

Chapter Twenty Two: The Green Jobs Fairy Tale

1. Max Schulz, "Don't Count on 'Countless' Green Jobs," *The Wall Street Journal,* February, 20, 2009.

2. Gabriel Calzada Alvarez PhD., "Study of The Effects on Employment of Public Aid to Renewable Energy Sources," King Juan Carlos University, Madrid, Spain, March 2009.

3. Ibid.

4. Ibid.

5. Ibid.

6. Andrew P. Morriss, William T. Bogart, Andrew Dorchak, and Roger E. Meiners, "Green Jobs Myths," University of Illinois Law and Economics Research Paper Series NO. LE09-001.

7. Robert Michaels and Robert P. Murphy, "Green Jobs: Fact or Fiction?," Institute for Energy Research, January 2009.

8. Max Schulz, "Don't Count on 'Countless' Green Jobs," *The Wall Street Journal,* February, 20, 2009.

9. Ibid.

10. Ibid.

11. Ibid.

12. Gabriel Calzada Alvarez PhD., "Study of the Effects on Employment of Public Aid to Renewable Energy Sources," King Juan Carlos University, Madrid, Spain, March 2009.

13. Ibid

14. *The Wall Street Journal,* "King Canute at the G-8," July 10, 2009.

15. *Investor's Business Daily,* "The Green Wind of Destruction," May 12, 2009.

16. Andrew P. Morriss, William T. Bogart, Andrew Dorchak and Roger E. Meiners, "Green Jobs Myths."

17. Ibid.

Chapter Twenty Three: Cap and Trade: Handi-"Capping"
America's Economic Future

1. David W. Kreutzer, Ph.D., "Heritage Analysis of Waxman-Markey Hits Where Others Miss," The Heritage Foundation, August 6, 2009.
2. Jeremy Lott and William Yeatman, "Aces Up Her Sleeve," *The American Spectator,* June 29, 2009.
3. Kerry Picket, "Obama: Energy Prices Will Skyrocket Under My Cap and Trade Plan," *Newsbusters.org.* November 3, 2008.
4. Peter Ferrara, "Cap and Trade Dementia," *The American Spectator*, July 1, 2009.
5. *Investors.com*, "Climate of Control," July 14, 2009.
6. Ibid.
7. John Griffing, "Cap and Trade: The Big Con," *American Thinker,* July 3, 2009.
8. Myron Ebell, "House Energy Committee Passes Biggest Tax Increase in World History," *Human Events*, June 8, 2009.
9. Stephen Spruiell and Kevin Williamson, "A Garden of Piggish Delights," *National Review*.com, July 2, 2009.
10. *The Wall Street Journal,* "The Carbonated Congress," July 3, 2009.
11. Stephen Spruiell and Kevin Williamson, "A Garden of Piggish Delights," *National Review*.com, July 2, 2009.
12. Stephen Spruiell "What's Wrong With Cap-and-Trade? Everything," *National Review,* August 10, 2009.
13. Stephen Spruiell and Kevin Williamson, "A Garden of Piggish Delights," *National Review*.com, July 2, 2009.
14. *The Wall Street Journal,* "The Cap and Tax Fiction," June 25, 2009.
15. Ibid.
16. Howard Richman, Raymond Richman and Jesse Richman, "Capping and Trading Away Our Jobs," *American Thinker,* July 3, 2009.
17. Ibid.
18. Amanda De Bard, "Energy Job Losers Could Get Windfall," *The Washington Times,* July 3, 2009.
19. Ibid.
20. Howard Richman, Raymond Richman and Jesse Richman, "Capping and Trading Away Our Jobs," *American Thinker,* July 3, 2009.
21. *Investor's Business Daily,* The Green Wind of Destruction," May 12, 2009.
22. Ibid.
23. Stephen Spruiell, "What's Wrong With CAP-AND-TRADE? Everything," *National Review,* August 10, 2009.
24. Daniella Markheim, "Energy Cap and Trade Threatens American Prosperity," The Heritage Foundation, June 16, 2009.

25. Stephen Spruiell and Kevin Williamson, "A Garden of Piggish Delights," *National Review*.com, July 2, 2009.

26. Ibid.

27. Ibid.

28. *The Wall Street Journal,* "The Cap and Tax Fiction," June 25, 2009.

29. David W. Kreutzer Ph.D., "Heritage Analysis of Waxman-Markey Hits Where Others Miss," The Heritage Foundation, August 6, 2009.

30. *The Wall Street Journal,* "The Cap and Tax Fiction," June 25, 2009.

31. Jeremy Lott and William Yeatman, "Aces Up Her Sleeve," *The American Spectator*, June 29, 2009.

32. Ibid.

33. Myron Ebell, "House Energy Committee Passes Biggest Tax Increase in World History," *Human Events,* June 8, 2009.

34. Ibid.

Chapter Twenty Four: Obama's Foreign Policy: All You Need is Love

1. Charles Krauthammer, "Decline is a Choice, The New Liberalism and the End of American Ascendancy," *The Weekly Standard,* October 19, 2009.

2. Ibid.

3. Ibid.

4. Jeffrey T. Kuhner, "The Obama Doctrine," *The Washington Times,* July 25, 2009.

5. Ibid.

6. David Feith and Bari Weiss, "Denying the Green Revolution," *The Wall Street Journal,* October 24-25, 2009.

7. Ibid.

8. Ibid.

9. *The Wall Street Journal,* "The Honduras Mess," September 23, 2009.

10. Elliott Abrams, "Détente and the Bunker, How to Oppose a President's Disastrous Foreign Policy," *The Weekly Standard,* October 12, 2009.

11. *The Wall Street Journal* "Obama's Missile Offense," September 23, 2009.

12. Ibid.

13. Ibid.

14. *The Washington Times,* "Worst Foreign Policy Ever," September 28, 2009.

15. Ibid.

16. Marc Champion and Jay Solomon, "Russia Says No to Iran Nuclear Sanctions," *The Wall Street Journal,* September 11, 2009.

17. *The Washington Times,* "Worst Foreign Policy Ever," September 28, 2009

18. Philip Sherwell, "Detroit bomber 'singing like a canary' before arrest," *Telegraph.co.uk,* January 9, 2010.
19. Reuters, "U.S. drops Guantanamo charges per Obama order," February 6, 2009.
20. Debra Burlingame, "Obama and the 9/11 Families," *The Wall Street Journal,* May 8, 2009.
21. Charles Krauthammer, "Uncertain Trumpet," Townhall.com, December 4, 2009.
22. Tom Baldwin, "President Obama's first call was to President Abbas," *Timesonline.co.uk,* January 22, 2009.
23. *abcnews.com,* "President Obama Does First Formal Interview As President with Al-Arabiya," January 26, 2009.
24. *CNNPolitics.com,* "Obama signs order to close Guantanamo Bay facility," January 22, 2009.
25. Peter Finn, "Obama Seeks Halt to Legal Proceedings at Guantanamo," *The Washington Post,* January 21, 2009.
26. Reuters, "Obama orders Guantanamo's closure within a year," January 22, 2009.
27. *The Washington Times,* "Worst Foreign Policy Ever," September 28, 2009.
28. Warner Todd Huston, *newsbusters.org,* February 15, 2009.

Chapter Twenty Five: America Exposed

1. *Washington Times,* "Aloha, Star Wars," June 29, 2009.
2. Ibid.
3. Ibid.
4. *The Wall Street Journal,* "Target: Hawaii," June 29, 2009.
5. *Washington Times,* "Aloha, Star Wars," June 29, 2009.
6. Dr. John Foster, Jr. et al., "Report of the Commission to Assess the Threat to the United States from Electromagnetic Pulse (EMP) Attack: Volume 1: Executive Report," report to Congress, 2004.
7. Brian T. Kennedy, "What a Single Nuclear Warhead Could Do," *The Wall Street Journal,* November 24, 2008.
8. *Investor's Business Daily,* "Death to America?," July 10, 2008.
9. Brian T. Kennedy, "What a Single Nuclear Warhead Could Do," *The Wall Street Journal,* November 24, 2008.
10. *Investor's Business Daily,* "Death to America?," July 10, 2008.
11. Joseph Farah, "Iran Plans to Knock Out U.S. with 1 Nuclear Bomb," *WorldNetDaily,* April 25, 2005.
12. Jack Spencer, "The Electromagnetic Pulse Commission Warns of an Old

Threat With a New Face," The Heritage Foundation, August 3, 2004.

13. Joseph Farah, "Iran Plans to Knock Out U.S. with 1 Nuclear Bomb," *WorldNetDaily*, April 25, 2005.

14. Jack Spencer, "The Electromagnetic Pulse Commission Warns of an Old Threat with a New Face," The Heritage Foundation, August 3, 2004.

15. Ibid.

16. Mario Loyola, "Budget Defense, President Obama proposes to spend dangerously little on the military," *National Review*, May 4, 2009.

17. *Investor's Business Daily*, "Missile Defense Takes Off," December 3, 2008.

18. *Investor's Business Daily*, "Shooting Down Missile Defense," April 7, 2009.

19. Mario Loyola, "Budget Defense," *National Review*, May 4, 2009.

20. *Investor's Business Daily*, "Missile Defense Takes Off," December 3, 2008.

21. *The Wall Street Journal*, "A Laser Defense Hit," August 15-16, 2009.

22. Ibid.

23. *Washington Times*, "Aloha, Star Wars," June 29, 2009.

24. Mario Loyola, "Budget Defense," *National Review*, May 4, 2009.

25. *Investor's Business Daily*, "A Disarmingly Low Priority," February 26, 2009.

26. *Investor's Business Daily*, "And Now, President Strangelove," April 28, 2008.

27. *Investor's Business Daily*, "Attacking Our Patriots," August 28, 2008.

28. Mario Loyola, "Budget Defense," *National Review*, May 4, 2009.

29. *Investor's Business Daily*, "Missile Defense Takes Off," December 3, 2009.

30. Charles Krauthammer, "Options Down to Deterrence, Missile Defense," *Investor's Business Daily*, April 17, 2008.

31. Ibid.

Chapter Twenty Six: Democrats Wage War— Against the War on Terror

1.   Peter Hoekstra, "Congress Knew about Interrogations," *The Wall Street Journal*, April 23, 2009. Mr. Hoeskstra is the ranking Republican on the House Permanent Select Committee on Intelligence.

2.   Richard B. Cheney, Speech to the American Enterprise Institute on May 21, 2009.

3.   Bobby Ghosh, "Why the CIA Turned Down Dick Cheney," *Time.com* May 14, 2009.

4.   Andrew McCarthy, "Torture is a State of Mind," *National Review*, May 25, 2009.

5.   Jennifer Rubin, "Eric Holder's Anti-CIA Witch Hunt," *The Weekly Standard*, September 7, 2009.

6. Stephen F. Hayes and William Kristol, "More Partisan Hackery," *The Weekly Standard*, July 27, 2009.

7. Ibid.

8. Ibid.

9. Ibid.

10. Peter J. Goss, "Security Before Politics," *The Washington Post*, April 25, 2009.

11. *The Wall Street Journal*, "Pelosi v. CIA," July 9, 2009.

12. Stephen F. Hayes and William Kristol, "More Partisan Hackery," *The Weekly Standard*, July 27, 2009.

13. *The Washington Times*, "Countering Intelligence," July 20, 2009.

14. Julian E. Barnes, "Congress May Probe Secret CIA Program," *Tribune Newspapers*, July 13, 2009.

15. Ibid.

16. Stephen F. Hayes and William Kristol, "More Partisan Hackery," *The Weekly Standard*, July 27, 2009.

17. Ibid.

18. *The Washington Times*, "Countering Intelligence," July 20, 2009.

19. Ibid.

20. *The Wall Street Journal*, "Pelosi v. CIA," July 9, 2009.

21. Andrew C. McCarthy, "The Myth of Bush's Torture Regime," *National Review*, December 2008.

22. Michael Hayden and Michael B. Mukasey, "The President Ties His Own Hands on Terror," *The Wall Street Journal*, April 17, 2009.

23. Ibid.

24. Jed Babbin, "Obama Continues Stonewalling on Waterboarding Documents," *Human Events*, June 15, 2009.

25. Richard B. Cheney, Speech to the American Enterprise Institute on May 21, 2009.

26. Peter Hoekstra, "Congress Knew about Interrogations," *The Wall Street Journal*, April 23, 2009.

27. Richard Saccone, "Shame on the Press, " *Pittsburgh Post-Gazette*, May 24, 2009.

28. Stephen F. Hayes, "Miranda Rights for Terrorists," *The Weekly Standard*, June 10, 2009.

29. *FoxNews.com*, "Combat or Criminal? Reading Miranda Rights to Detainees Draws Criticism," June 11, 2009.

30. Arthur Herman, "The Gitmo Myth and the Torture Canard," *Commentary*, June 2009.

31. Ibid.

32. Ibid.

33. Ibid.

34. Ibid.

35. Ibid.
36. Ibid.
37. Ibid.
38. Ibid.
39. *The Washington Times*, "EXCLUSIVE: Panetta Faces Rendition Queries," January 15, 2009.
40. Arthur Herman, "The Gitmo Myth and the Torture Canard," *Commentary*, June 2009.
41. *The Wall Street Journal*, "Bush's Gitmo Vindication," May 25, 2009.
42. Ibid.
43. Ibid.
44. *The Wall Street Journal*, "Obama Channels Cheney, Obama adopts Bush view on the powers of the presidency," March 7, 2009.

Chapter Twenty Seven: A Rogue's Gallery of Radicals

1. *Investor's Business Daily*, "Barack Obama's Stealth Socialism," July 28, 2008.
2. Cliff Kincaid, "Obama's Communist Mentor," Accuracy in Media, February 18, 2008.
3. Joshua Muravchik, "Obama's Leftism," *Commentary*, October 2008.
4. *Investor's Business Daily*, "Barack Obama's Stealth Socialism," July 28, 2008.
5. Ibid.
6. *Investor's Business Daily*, "Community Organizer in Chief ," September 16, 2008.
7. Joshua Muravchik, "Obama's Leftism," *Commentary*, October 2008.
8. Stanley Kurtz, "Context, You Say? A Guide to the Radical Theology of the Rev. Jeremiah Wright, " *National Review*, May 19, 2008.
9. Ibid.
10. Ibid.
11. Ibid.
12. Fred Lucas, "Despite Campaign Claim, Obama Told Paper He Attended Trinity Church 'Every Week,' *CNSNews.com*, November 13, 2008.
13. *The Weekly Standard* editorial, "Right About Obama," May 12, 2008.
14. *Investor's Business Daily*, "Revisiting Obama's Church," March 7, 2008.
15. Joshua Muravchik, "Obama's Leftism," *Commentary*, October 2008.
16. Ibid.
17. Ibid.
18. Sol Stern, "Ayers is No Education Reformer," *The Wall Street Journal*, October 16, 2008.

19. Ibid.
20. Ibid.
21. Ibid.
22. *Investor's Business Daily,* "Annenberg Papers: Putting on Ayers?,"
    August 27, 2008.
23. Joshua Muravchik, "Obama's Leftism," *Commentary,* October 2008.
24. Stephen Spruiell, "By His Friends Ye Shall Know Him," *National Review,*
    May 5, 2008.
25. Aaron Klein, "Ex-Obama adviser's pro-Hamas views 'well known,'
    Robert Malley quit after media reported his contacts with terror groups,"
    World NetDaily, May 11, 2008.
26. *Investor's Business Daily,* "No End of Bile From Obama's Bully Pulpits,"
    May 30, 2008.
27. Michael Burnham, "Author-activist tapped as White House 'green' jobs
    adviser," *The New York Times,* March 10, 2009.
28. Phil Kerpen, "NY's Tax-Funded Ex-Terrorist," *New York Post,* September
    9, 2009.
29. John Perazzo, "The Marxist Revolutionary and Obama's Environmental
    Policies," *FrontPageMag.com,* September 17, 2009.
30. Eliza Strickland, "The New Face of Environmentalism," *East Bay Express,*
    November 2, 2005.
31. Ibid.
32. *NYDailyNews.com,* "Obama's 9/11 Problem: Advisor Van Jones
    Signed Creepy Conspiracy Petition," September 4, 2009.
33. *FoxNews.com,* "Raw Data: Van Jones in His Own Words," September
    3, 2009.
34. Michael Elliott, "Heroes of the Environment 2008, *Time.*
35. *Washington Post,* "Senate Confirms Harvard Professor to Oversee
    Regulatory Affairs," September 10, 2009.
36. Cass Sunstein, *The Second Bill of Rights: FDR's Unfinished Revolution
    and Why We Need It More Than Ever* (New York: Basic Books 2004), p. 1.
37. Cass Sunstein, *Republic.com 2.0* (Princeton University Press 2007), p.137.
38. Kyle Smith, "Gag The Internet," *New York Post,* July 11, 2009.
39. Ed Lasky, "Cass Sunstein's Despicable Ideas on Regulating the Internet,"
    American Thinker, July, 12, 2009.
40. Ibid.
41. Cass Sunstein and Martha Nussbaum, *Animal Rights: Current Debates
    and New Directions* (Oxford University Press, USA 2004), introduction.
42. *MSNBC.com,* "Obama's science adviser starts job," March 24, 2009.
43. Ben Johnson, "Obama's Biggest Radical," *FrontPageMag.com,* February 27,
    2009.
44. Ibid.
45. Ibid.

46. http://zombietime.com/john_holdren/
47. Ibid.
48. Ben Johnson, "Obama's Biggest Radical," *FrontPageMag.com,* February 27, 2009.
49. Ibid.
50. Ibid.
51. Ibid.
52. S. Fred Singer, ed., "Nature, Not Human Activity, Rules the Climate: Summary for Policymakers of the Report of the Nongovernmental International Panel on Climate Change," Chicago, IL: The Heartland Institute, 2008.
53. Cliff Kincaid, "Obama Czar Favors Planetary Regime," Accuracy in Media, August 17, 2009. (www.aim.org/aim-report/print/obama-czar-favors-planetary-regime/)
54. Ibid.
55. FCC Press Release, July 29, 2009.
56. Media Research Center, "Obama's FCC Diversity Officer Plans to Cripple Conservative Talk Radio," October 2009.
57. Jillian Bandes, "The Fairness Doctrine is Dead, But Here Comes the Chief Diversity Officer," *Townhall.com* August 12, 2009.
58. Seton Motley, "FCC 'Diversity' Czar on Chavez's Venezuela: 'Incredible…Democratic Revolution'," *Newsbusters.org,* August 28, 2009.
59. Media Research Center, "Obama's FCC Diversity Officer Plans to Cripple Conservative Talk Radio," October 2009.
60. Ibid.
61. Ibid.
62. Wikipedia.com, "Carol Browner."
63. Stephen Dinan, "Obama Climate Czar Has Socialist Ties," *The Washington Times,* January 12, 2009.
64. Steven Milloy, "Browner: Redder Than Obama Knows," *FoxNews.com,* January 15, 2009.
65. Ibid.
66. Myron Ebell, "House Energy Committee Passes Biggest Tax Increase in World History," *Human Events,* June 8, 2009.
67. WhiteHouse.gov, March 23, 2009.
68. Andrew C. McCarthy, "Global Kohordinates, Meet the Radical Transnationalist Preparing to Take Up Residency at State," *National Review,* May 4, 2009.
69. Ibid.
70. Ibid.
71. Meghan Clyne, "Obama's Most Perilous Legal Pick," *New York Post* April 4, 2009.
72. Troy Silva, "Kevin Jennings' Twisted Terminology," *American Thinker,*

October 8, 2009.

73. Ibid.

74. Tony Perkins, "Kevin Jennings – Unsafe for America's Schools," *Human Events,* June 29, 2009.

75. John Fund, "From Mao to Obama, Mao Tse Tung is One of White House Communications Director Anita Dunn's Favorite Philosophers," *The Wall Street Journal,* October 21, 2009.

76. *FoxNews.Com,* "Top White House Official Says Obama Team 'Controlled' Media Coverage During Campaign," October 19, 2009.

77. *Washington Post.com,* "Obama Expands Car Czar's Duties," September 8, 2009

78. breitbart.tv/obama-czar-agrees-with-mao-too-and-thinks-free-market-is-nonsense/

Chapter Twenty Eight: The Demise of Dissent and Democracy

1. The Heritage Foundation, "Morning Bell: The Durbin Doctrine's Assault on Free Speech," March 16, 2009 (posted on heritage.org)

2. Reuters, "O'Leary Report: FCC Chairman Copps and Diversity Committee Chairman Rivera Talk…," May 8, 2009.

3. Drew Zahn, "31 horsemen of talk radio's apocalypse? FCC anoints diversity panel with 'Fairness Doctrine' mission," *WorldNetDaily,* May 2, 2009.

4. The Heritage Foundation, "Morning Bell: The Durbin Doctrine's Assault on Free Speech," March 16, 2009.

5. Jim Boulet Jr., "Obama Declares War on Conservative Talk Radio," *American Thinker,* November 17, 2008.

6. The Heritage Foundation, "Morning Bell: The Durbin Doctrine's Assault on Free Speech," March 16, 2009.

7. Adam Thierer, "Why the Fairness Doctrine is Anything But Fair," The Heritage Foundation, October 29, 1993.

8. Christopher Ruddy, "Obama's Diversity Offensive Against Talk Radio," *Newsmax.com,* August 30, 2009.

9. Ibid.

10. Michelle Oddis, "UPDATED: Obama Official Linked to Racially Charged Boycott of Glenn Beck," *Human Events.com,* August 13, 2009.

11. *FoxNews.com,* "White House Urges Other Networks to Disregard Fox News," October 19, 2009.

12. Glenn Beck, "Freedom of Speech is Under Attack," *FoxNews.com,* October 21, 2009.

13. Michael Barone, "Obama's M.O.: Government By Thugocracy,"

Investor's Business Daily, October 10, 2009.

14. Don Feder, "Being Shouted Down," *FrontPageMag.com*, March 30, 2009.
15. *FoxNews.com,* "GOP Sounds Alarm Over Obama Decision to Move Census to White House," February 9, 2009.
16. *CNN.com*, Transcripts, September 15, 2009.
17. John Fund, "An ACORN Whistleblower Testifies in Court," *The Wall Street Journal,* May 9-10, 2009.
18. Wikipedia, National Voter Registration Act of 1993.
19. Tom Hoffman, "The End of Fair Elections?," *American Thinker,* April 9, 2009.
20. Cato Institute, "The Motor Voter Act and Voter Fraud," March 14, 2001.
21. Hans A. von Spakovsky, "Holder Winks at Voter Intimidation," *The Wall Street Journal*, June 9, 2009.
22. Ibid.
23. Tom Curry, "What Role for Democratic 'Super-Delegates'?," *MSNBC.com,* April 26, 2007.
24. David Horowitz, "The Left's Campaign to Destroy Glenn Beck," newsrealblog.com, September 17, 2009.

Chapter Twenty Nine: The Community Organizer's Community Organizer

1. www.youtube.com, October 31, 2008.
2. John Perazzo, "Democrats' Platform for Revolution," *FrontPageMag.com*, May 5, 2008.
3. *Investor's Business Daily,* "Obama's Radical Roots and Rules," August 14, 2008.
4. Ibid.
5. Ibid.
6. John Perazzo, "Democrats' Platform for Revolution," *FrontPageMag.com*, May 5, 2008.
7. L. David Alinsky, "Son Sees Father's Handiwork in Convention," *The Boston Globe,* August 31, 2009.
8. John Perazzo, "Democrats' Platform for Revolution," *FrontPageMag.com,* May 5, 2008.
9. Saul Alinsky, *Rules for Radicals* (New York: Vintage Books 1971), p. xxii.
10. John Perazzo, "Democrats' Platform for Revolution," *FrontPageMag.com*, May 5, 2008.
11. David Horowitz, *Barack Obama's Rules for Revolution, The Alinsky Model* (David Horowitz Freedom Center 2009), pp. 23, 26, 29.
12. Eliza Strickland, "The New Face of Environmentalism," *East Bay Express,*

November 2, 2005.

13. Sanford D. Horwitt, *Let Them Call Me Rebel. Saul Alinsky, His Life and Legacy* (New York: Random House 1992) pp. xv –xvi.

14. Saul Alinsky, *Rules for Radicals* (New York: Vintage Books 1971), p. 117.

15. John Perazzo, "A Democrats' Platform for Revolution," *FrontPageMag.com,* May 5, 2008.

16. Saul Alinsky, *Rules for Radicals*, p. 130.

17. Byron York, "The Organizer, What Did Barack Obama Really Do in Chicago," *National Review,* June 30, 2008.

18. John Perazzo, "A Democrats' Platform for Revolution," *FrontPageMag.com,* May 5, 2008.

19. Van Jones in his own words on the *Glenn Beck Show, FoxNews,* September 2, 2009.

20. *Investor's Business Daily,* "Obama's Radical Roots and Rules," August 14, 2008.

21. Saul Alinsky, *Rules for Radicals*, p. 18.

22. Ibid., p.3.

Chapter Thirty One: ObamaCare: Prescription for an Unhealthy America

1. Sally C. Pipes, *The Top Ten Myths of American Health Care* (San Francisco: Pacific Research Institute 2008), p.89.

2. Jason D. Fodeman, MD., and Robert A. Book, Ph.D., "Bending the Curve: What Really Drives Health Care Spending," The Heritage Foundation, February 17, 2010.

3. Ibid.

4. Sally C. Pipes, *The Top Ten Myths of American Health Care,* p. 74.

5. Jason D. Fodeman, MD., and Robert A. Book, Ph.D., "Bending the Curve: What Really Drives Health Care Spending," The Heritage Foundation, February 17, 2010.

6. Sally C. Pipes, *The Top Ten Myths of American Health Care,* p. 74.

7. Jason D. Fodeman, MD., and Robert A. Book, Ph.D., "Bending the Curve: What Really Drives Health Care Spending," The Heritage Foundation, February 17, 2010.

8. Sally C. Pipes, *The Top Ten Myths of American Health Care,* p. 100.

9. Ibid., p. 146.

10. Jason D. Fodeman, MD., and Robert A. Book, Ph.D., "Bending the Curve: What Really Drives Health Care Spending," The Heritage Foundation, February 17, 2010.

11. Ibid. The 12.6 percent figure comes from Fred Barnes, "An Unnecessary Operation," *The Weekly Standard,* September 21, 2009.

12. Jason D. Fodeman, MD., and Robert A. Book, Ph.D., "Bending the Curve: What Really Drives Health Care Spending," The Heritage Foundation, February 17, 2010.
13. Sally C. Pipes, *The Top Ten Myths of American Health Care,* pp. 74, 75.
14. Ibid., p. 76.
15. Ibid., pp. 74, 75.
16. Ibid., p. 142.
17. Sally C. Pipes, *The Top Ten Myths of American Health Care,* p. 76.
18. Ibid.
19. Ibid.
20. Andrew G. Biggs, "Entitlement Apocalypse," *National Review,* March 22, 2010.
21. Robert Lowes, "Will Healthcare Reform Increase Medicaid Pay as Well as Enrollment?," Medscape Medical News, March 23, 2010.
22. Grace-Marie Turner and Joseph R. Antos, "Medicare Is No Model for Health Reform," *The Wall Street Journal,* September 11, 2009.
23. Michael D. Tanner, "The Grass Is Not Always Greener: A look at National Health Care Systems Around the World," CATO Institute, March 18, 2008.
24. Ibid.
25. Ibid.
26. Fred Barnes, "An Unnecessary Operation," *The Weekly Standard,* September 21, 2009.
27. Ibid.
28. Michael D. Tanner, "The Grass Is Not Always Greener: A look at National Health Care Systems Around the World," CATO Institute, March 18, 2008.
29. Fred Barnes, "An Unnecessary Operation," *The Weekly Standard,* September 21, 2009.
30. Ibid.
31. Peter Robinson, "Basically An Optimist — Still," *The Wall Street Journal,* March 27–28, 2010.
32. Fred Barnes, "An Unnecessary Operation," *The Weekly Standard,* September 21, 2009.
33. Ibid.
34. Scott W. Atlas, "Here's a Second Opinion," Hoover Digest, August 8, 2009.
35. Ibid.
36. Ibid.
37. Fred Barnes, "An Unnecessary Operation," *The Weekly Standard,* September 21, 2009.
38. Scott W. Atlas, "Here's a Second Opinion," Hoover Digest, August 8, 2009.

39. Compiled by the Staff of Senator Jim DeMint, as reported in
    Human Events, July 27, 2009.
40. www.johnshadegg.house.gov/News/DocumentsSingle.aspx?
41. Greg D'Angelo and Robert E. Moffit, Ph.D., "Health Care Reform:
    Rational Alternatives to the Congressional Leadership Bills,"
    The Heritage Foundation, October 28, 2009.
42. Connie Hair, "ObamaCare: What you Don't Know Will Really Make you
    Sick," *Human Events,* September 21, 2009.
43. Greg D'Angelo and Robert E. Moffit, Ph.D., "Health Care Reform:
    Rational Alternatives to the Congressional Leadership Bills,"
    The Heritage Foundation, October 28, 2009.
44. Phillip Klein, "The Matter With Myths," *The American Spectator,*
    July 2009 — August 2009.
45. Ibid.
46. Ibid.
47. Sean Higgins, "Uninsured Figures Overhype The Lack of Health
    Coverage," *Investor's Business Daily,* June 29, 2009.
48. Phillip Klein, "The Matter With Myths," *The American Spectator,*
    July 2009 - August 2009.
49. Ibid.
50. Ibid.
51. Wikipedia.org, Emergency Medical Treatment and Active Labor Act.
52. Ramesh Ponnuru, "Media Malpractice," *National Review,* November 2,
    2009.
53. Philip Klein, "The Matter With Myths," *The American Spectator,* July
    2009-August 2009.
54. Ibid.
55. Carl Bialik, "Ill - Conceived Ranking Makes for Unhealthy Debate,"
    The Wall Street Journal, October 21, 2009.
56. Michael D. Tanner, "The Grass Is Not Always Greener: A Look at
    National Health Care Systems Around the World," CATO Institute,
    March 18, 2008.
57. Carl Bialik, "Ill - Conceived Ranking Makes for Unhealthy Debate,"
    The Wall Street Journal, October 21, 2009.
58. Mark B. Constantian, "Where U.S. Health Care Ranks Number One,"
    The Wall Street Journal, January 7, 2010.
59. Fred Barnes, "An Unnecessary Operation," *The Weekly Standard,*
    September 21, 2009.
60. Connie Hair, "ObamaCare: What you Don't Know Will Really
    Make you Sick," *Human Events,* September 21, 2009.
61. Fred Barnes, "An Unnecessary Operation," *The Weekly Standard,*
    September 21, 2009.
62. Connie Hair, "ObamaCare: What you Don't Know Will Really Make you

Sick," *Human Events,* September 21, 2009.

63. *Ft. Lauderdale Sun-Sentinel,* "Study probes infant mortality," November 4, 2009.
64. Ibid.
65. Thomas W. Hazlett, "We're Number Two?,"*Commentary,* December 2009.
66. Ibid.
67. Phillip Klein, "The Matter With Myths," *The American Spectator,* July 2009- August 2009.
68. Ibid.
69. Mark B. Constantian, "Where U.S. Health Care Ranks Number One," *The Wall Street Journal,* January 8, 2010
70. Ibid.
71. *USA Today,* "U.S. life expectancy lags behind 41 nations," August 11, 2007.
72. Fred Barnes, "An Unnecessary Operation," *The Weekly Standard,* September 21, 2009.
73. Connie Hair, "ObamaCare: What You Don't Know Will Really Make you Sick," *Human Events,* September 21, 2009.
74. Fred Barnes, "An Unnecessary Operation," *The Weekly Standard,* September 21, 2009.
75. Ramesh Ponnuru, "The Cost of Audacity," *National Review,* May 4, 2009.
76. *The Wall Street Journal,* "Health Reform and Competitiveness," June 17, 2009.
77. Ibid.
78. Ibid.
79. George Newman, "Parsing the Health Reform Arguments," *The Wall Street Journal* July 1, 2009.
80. Manta.com, "Health Insurance Carriers in the United States," March 13, 2010.
81. Ibid.
82. Brett J. Skinner, "The Medical Bankruptcy Myth," The American, The Journal of the American Enterprise Institute, August 19, 2009.
83. Ibid.
84. Ibid.
85. Ibid.
86. Ibid.
87. Ibid.
88. *The Wall Street Journal,* "Paul Ryan v. the President," March 4, 2009.
89. Noam N. Levey and Janet Hook, "Final Stretch for Health Bill," *Tribune Newspapers,* March 19, 2010.
90. James C. Capretta, "The President's Health Reform Proposal: More Like $2.5 Trillion," The Heritage Foundation, February 24, 2010.
91. Paul Ryan, "Dissecting the Real Cost of ObamaCare," *The Wall Street*

Journal, March 4, 2010 (From the health care summit held on February 25, 2010).

92. Ibid.

93. James C. Capretta, "The President's Health Reform Proposal: More Like $2.5 Trillion," The Heritage Foundation, February 24, 2010.

94. Paul Ryan, "Dissecting the Real Cost of ObamaCare," *The Wall Street Journal,* March 4, 2010 (From the health care summit held on February 25, 2010).

95. Ibid.

96. James C. Capretta, "The President's Health Reform Proposal: More Like $2.5 Trillion," The Heritage Foundation, February 24, 2010.

97. Ibid.

98. Ibid.

99. Ibid.

100. *The Wall Street Journal,* "Health Costs and History," October 20, 2009.

101. Ibid.

102. Ibid.

103. *The Wall Street Journal,* "The Cost-Control Illusion," March 13-14, 2010.

104. Brian Blase, " Obama's Proposed Medicaid Expansion: Lessons from TennCare," The Heritage Foundation, March 3, 2010.

105. Fred Barnes, "There's No Free Health Care," *The Weekly Standard.* September 28, 2009.

106. Brian Blase, " Obama's Proposed Medicaid Expansion: Lessons from TennCare," The Heritage Foundation, March 3, 2010.

107. Fred Barnes, "There's No Free Health Care," *The Weekly Standard.* September 28, 2009.

108. Ibid.

109. Ibid.

110. Ibid.

111. Ibid.

112. James Oliphant and Kim Geiger, "Massachusetts health bill is a model, warning," *Tribune Newspapers,* October 19, 2009.

113. *The Wall Street Journal,* "Back to the ObamaCare Future," March 1, 2010.

114. John F. Cogan, R. Glenn Hubbard, and Daniel Kessler, "Doubling Down on a Flawed Insurance Model," *The Wall Street Journal,* September 15, 2009.

115. Ibid.

116. Grace-Marie Turner, "The Failure of RomneyCare," *The Wall Street Journal,* March 17, 2010.

117. Christopher Neefus, "Nearly One-Third of Doctors Could Leave Medicine if Health Care Reform Bill Passes, According to Survey Reported in New England Journal of Medicine," *CNSNews.com,*

March 16, 2010.

118. Scott Gottlieb, "What Doctors and Patients Have to Lose Under ObamaCare," *The Wall Street Journal,* December 24, 2009.

119. Ibid.

120. Josh Hafenbrack, "Florida warns of extra $1 billion tab for Medicaid," *Ft. Lauderdale Sun-Sentinel,* March 24, 2010.

121. OpenCongress.org, Health Care Reconciliation Bill Summary, March 18, 2010.

122. Josh Hafenbrack, "Florida warns of extra $1 billion tab for Medicaid," *Ft. Lauderdale Sun-Sentinel,* March 24,2010.

123. David Reilly, Ellen E. Schultz and Ron Winslow, "AT&T Joins in Health Charges," *The Wall Street Journal,* March 27-28, 2010.

124. *The Wall Street Journal* "ObamaCare Day One," March 25, 2010.

125. *The Wall Street Journal,* "The ObamaCare Writedowns," March 27-28, 2010.

126. Bob Tita, "Caterpillar Income Hit by Health Bill Provision," *The Wall Street Journal,* March 25, 2010.

127. Kim Keiger, "What the bill would mean for you," *Tribune Newspapers,* March 21, 2010.

128. Ibid.

129. Ibid.

130. Ibid.

131. Ibid.

132. *The Wall Street Journal,* "The ObamaCare Writedowns," March 21, 2010.

133. The Center for Health Policy Studies and Center for Data Analysis, The Heritage Foundation, " An Analysis of the Senate Democrats' Health Care Bill," December 18, 2009.

134. Rea S. Hederman, Jr. and Paul L. Winfree, "How Health Care Reform Will Affect Young Adults," Center for Data Analysis at the Heritage Foundation, January 27, 2010.

135. Ibid.

136. *The Wall Street Journal,* "The Truth About Health Insurance," August 12, 2009.

137. Ibid.

138. Ibid.

139. Rea S. Hederman, Jr. and Paul L. Winfree, "How Health Care Reform Will Affect Young Adults," Center for Data Analysis at the Heritage Foundation, January 27, 2010.

140. Shirley Wang, "Winners and Losers in the Affected Industries," *The Wall Street Journal,* March 22, 2010.

141. *The Wall Street Journal,* "Change Nobody Believes In," December 21, 2009.

142. Kim Keiger, "What the bill would mean for you," *Tribune Newspapers,* March 21, 2010.
143. Rea S. Hederman, Jr. and Paul L. Winfree, "How Health Care Reform Will Affect Young Adults," Center for Data Analysis at the Heritage Foundation, January 27, 2010.
144. Ibid.
145. Kim Keiger, "What the bill would mean for you," *Tribune Newspapers,* March 21, 2010.
146. Ibid.
147. *CNSNews.com,* "ObamaCare: 12 Taxes Violate Obama's Pledge Not to Increase Taxes on Households Earning...," March 28, 2010.
148. *MoneyNews.com,* "ObamaCare Would Boost Taxes on Wages, Investment," March 19, 2010.
149. *The Wall Street Journal,* "ObamaCare's Worst Tax Hike," March 17, 2010.
150. Ibid.
151. Fred Barnes, "Caving to Trial Lawyers," *The Weekly Standard,* September 7, 2001.
152. Ibid.
153. *The Wall Street Journal,* "...And a Buried Tort Bomb," November 12, 2009.
154. Sally C. Pipes, *The Top Ten Myths of American Health Care,* p. 146.
155. Charles Krauthammer, "A Health Plan That's Radical *And* Sensible," The Washington Post Writers Group, August 7, 2009.
156. Sally C. Pipes, *The Top Ten Myths of American Health Care,* p. 146.
157. Charles Krauthammer, "A Health Plan That's Radical *And* Sensible," The Washington Post Writers Group, August 7, 2009.
158. Sally C. Pipes, *The Top Ten Myths of American Health Care,* p. 141.
159. Ibid., p. 141.
160. Charles Krauthammer, "A Health Plan That's Radical *And* Sensible," The Washington Post Writers Group, August 7, 2009.
161. Sally C. Pipes, *The Top Ten Myths of American Health Care,* p. 141.
162. Ibid.
163. John Shadegg, "The No-Cost Path to Cheaper Health Care," *The Wall Street Journal,* November 6, 2009.
164. Sally C. Pipes, *The Top Ten Myths of American Health Care,* p. 142.
165. Ibid., pp. 143,144.
166. Ibid., p. 144.
167. John Fund, "Health Reform's Hidden Victims," *The Wall Street Journal,* July 24, 2009.
168. Sheila Guilloton, "IRS announces 2010 contribution limits for Health Savings Accounts," *Examiner.com,* June 10, 2009.
169. Sally C. Pipes, *The Top Ten Myths of American Health Care,* p. 144.

170. Ibid., p. 145.
171. Ibid.
172. Ibid.
173. *The Wall Street Journal,* "The Truth About Health Insurance," August 12, 2009.
174. Sally C. Pipes, *The Top Ten Myths of American Health Care,* p. 139.
175. Ibid., p. 139.
176. Ibid., p. 140.
177. *The Wall Street Journal,* "Confessions of an ObamaCare Backer," November 10, 2009.
178. Victor Davis Hanson as reported in *The Wall Street Journal* in Notable and Quotable, excerpted from his article in Pajamasmedia.com, March 23, 2010.
179. Byron York, "Pelosi: 'Once we kick through this door,' more reform will follow," *Washingtonexaminer.com,* March 16, 2010.
180. Rasmussen Reports, "Health Care Reform," March 21, 2010.